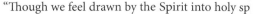

D0836627

"Though we feel drawn by the Spirit into holy sp we call worship too often reflects merely our own needs and desires. Yet how we worship God must be linked with why we worship him, the central Storyteller of all creation. A wise and deep researcher, Robbie Castleman showcases how story-shaped liturgical patterns form the seasons of the Christian year."

Luci Shaw, writer-in-residence, Regent College

"Robbie Castleman has written a book that brings sanity to the worship wars. The sweep of her engagement with biblical and theological material is very impressive, and her conclusions are rightly challenging to all sides. The clarity of writing and the straightforward treatment make this a book that is accessible to anyone who wants to worship in ways that please God. This book deserves to be on ministers' must-read lists, on adult Sunday school curriculum and well thumbed by congregational worship committees."

Andrew Purves, Pittsburgh Theological Seminary

"In *Story-Shaped Worship* Robbie Castleman carefully explores the biblical basis for worship, not as something that pleases us, the worshiper, but as something meant to be pleasing to God. She then puts this in historical and practical contexts in a way that is both winsome and wise. This book is a wonderful, carefully written guide that will be helpful for worship leaders, pastors or anyone who cares about worshiping well. I'm already looking forward to working through the excellent discussion questions at the end of each chapter with other worship leaders in my church. What a great resource!"

Robert J. Keeley, Calvin College

"Robbie Castleman's *Story-Shaped Worship* skillfully places the biblical teachings on worship within the larger narrative of salvation history. It represents a valuable contribution to the resurgent evangelical interest in the theology and practice of worship. I heartily commend it to all pastors and seminarians who want to take worship to the next level of excellence."

John Jefferson Davis, Gordon-Conwell Theological Seminary

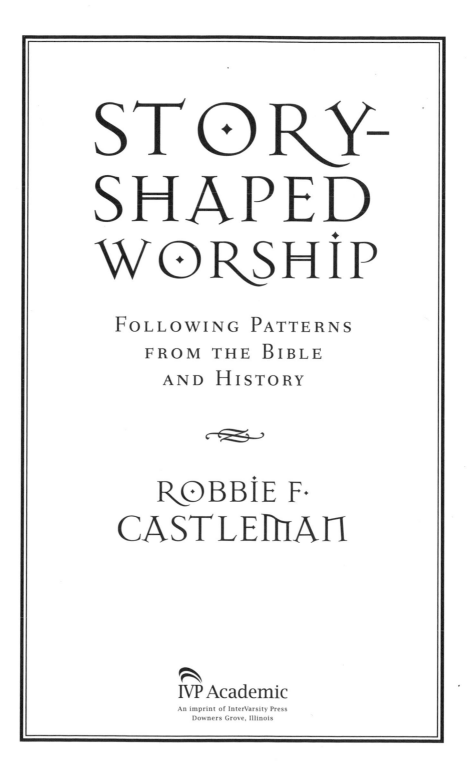

STORY-SHAPED WORSHIP

FOLLOWING PATTERNS FROM THE BIBLE AND HISTORY

ROBBIE F. CASTLEMAN

IVP Academic

An imprint of InterVarsity Press
Downers Grove, Illinois

InterVarsity Press
P.O. Box 1400, Downers Grove, IL 60515-1426
World Wide Web: www.ivpress.com
E-mail: email@ivpress.com

©2013 by Robbie F. Castleman

All rights reserved. No part of this book may be reproduced in any form without written permission from InterVarsity Press.

InterVarsity Press® is the book-publishing division of InterVarsity Christian Fellowship/USA®, a movement of students and faculty active on campus at hundreds of universities, colleges and schools of nursing in the United States of America, and a member movement of the International Fellowship of Evangelical Students. For information about local and regional activities, write Public Relations Dept., InterVarsity Christian Fellowship/USA, 6400 Schroeder Rd., P.O. Box 7895, Madison, WI 53707-7895, or visit the IVCF website at <www.intervarsity.org>.

Scripture quotations, unless otherwise noted, are from the New Revised Standard Version of the Bible, copyright 1989 by the Division of Christian Education of the National Council of the Churches of Christ in the USA. Used by permission. All rights reserved.

While all stories in this book are true, some names and identifying information in this book have been changed to protect the privacy of the individuals involved.

Cover design: Cindy Kiple
Images: © Linda Steward/iStockphoto
Interior design: Beth Hagenberg

ISBN 978-0-8308-3964-3

Printed in the United States of America ∞

green press INITIATIVE *InterVarsity Press is committed to protecting the environment and to the responsible InterVarsity Press is committed to protecting the environment and to the responsible use of natural resources. As a member of Green Press Initiative we use recycled paper whenever possible. To learn more about the Green Press Initiative, visit <www.greenpressinitiative.org>.*

Library of Congress Cataloging-in-Publication Data

Castleman, Robbie, 1949-
 Story-shaped worship : following patterns from the Bible and history / Robbie F. Castleman.
   pages cm
 Includes bibliographical references and index.
 ISBN 978-0-8308-3964-3 (pbk. : alk. paper)
 1. Worship in the Bible. 2. Worship—Biblical teaching. 3. Worship—History. I. Title.
 BS680.W78C37 2013
 264--dc23

                                                                                    2012051730

| P | 21 | 20 | 19 | 18 | 17 | 16 | 15 | 14 | 13 | 12 | 11 | 10 | 9 | 8 | 7 | 6 | 5 | 4 | 3 | 2 | 1 |
| Y | 31 | 30 | 29 | 28 | 27 | 26 | 25 | 24 | 23 | 22 | 21 | 20 | 19 | 18 | 17 | 16 | 15 | 14 | 13 |

For Breck

Romans 15:5-6

CONTENTS

Acknowledgments 9

Introduction 13

PART ONE: BIBLICAL PATTERNS
STORY-SHAPED LITURGY

1 GENESIS AND THE GOSPEL 27
The Beginning of Worship
Workshop 38

2 WORSHIP AND IDENTITY 42
Yahweh and Sabbath in the Torah, Prophets and Gospels
Workshop 59

3 WORSHIP AND SACRED SPACE 62
The Grace of Invitation, the Holiness of Boundaries
Workshop 75

4 THE SHAPE OF BIBLICAL WORSHIP 77
Workshop 92

5 WORSHIP BY THE BOOK 95
Workshop 108

6 WORSHIP AND HOLINESS 111
Workshop 126

7 WORSHIP IN EXILE, SYNAGOGUES
AND THE EARLY CHURCH 128
Workshop 139
Excursus: History and Development of the Synagogue 140

PART TWO: HISTORICAL PATTERNS
THE INTERPRETATIONS OF WORSHIP

8 EARLY PATTERNS FOR CHRISTIAN WORSHIP. 147
  Clarifying the Faith
  Workshop 164
  Excursus: The *Didache* 166

9 REFORMATION PATTERNS FOR CHRISTIAN WORSHIP. 168
  Recovering the Faith
  Workshop. 184

10 CONTEMPORARY PATTERNS FOR CHRISTIAN WORSHIP 186
  Keeping the Faith
  Workshop. 204

Glossary 207

For Further Reading 215

Subject Index 220

Scripture Index 222

ACKNOWLEDGMENTS

This book was written during the years I occupied the McGee Chair for Biblical Studies at John Brown University. The course release time and research stipend that are a part of this award are deeply appreciated. I would especially like to acknowledge the support of the Bible division chair, David Brisben, who has supported my contributions in teaching and research with great interest and respect. Several of my colleagues at JBU have offered guidance, made suggestions and answered my questions with an expertise that is only exceeded by their grace. Thanks to Jim Blankenship and Dave Vila for their help concerning my work with Hebrew texts and a myriad of issues concerning the murky waters of synagogue development. And thanks to Holly Catterton Allen and Jason Lanker, whose work with children, family and youth ministry helped shape the discussion of intergenerational dynamics for congregational worship. I am also grateful for a Shipp's Summer Grant and the resources from the faculty development committee at John Brown University that provided funding for books and trips and time to think and research before the actual book writing began.

I would also like to acknowledge the students I have the privilege to teach at John Brown University, especially the students in "Theology of Worship" who took the time to offer valuable feedback and ideas for the present book. Their enthusiasm for this study was only exceeded by their relish for finding typos in a preliminary draft. The shape of what was needed took place in conversations with these students through the questions they asked, the ideas they really had a hard time accepting, and the liturgies they studied and learned to appreciate. It is my hope that God's story will always shape their service of worship.

To Bill Dyrness who led a seminar on worship at Schloss Mittersill as part of an International Fellowship of Evangelical Students program, I offer my thanks. You were the one, in conversation about this book and my academic life, who said most loudly, "You can do this!" Thanks for opening more than a few doors for me. I am also grateful for the encouragement I received for this book and my work in liturgical studies from a young scholar, Michael Farley. Reading Michael's methodology for a canonical framework in liturgical studies helped me find my voice and define my own method.

To my work-study student, Joey Morningstar, who helped me with indexes and kept my teaching responsibilities afloat in a variety of helpful ways, I owe not only my thanks, but several dinners and lunches and coffee breaks. Joey and I are both grateful for David Instone-Brewer of Tyndale House in Cambridge for developing the technological tools that make research, referencing and the making of indexes easier to do and more accurate in the end. Great thanks is also due Diane Swysgood, the administrator of the Bible division at John Brown, who graciously deals with the details of my faculty life and, in doing so, makes the work of teaching and writing doable at all.

Allison Hamm is a graduate of John Brown University and served as my first reader for this book. Her excellence as a writer and the clarity of her thinking have helped make this book more readable and better organized. Allison not only understands my approach to worship, she anticipates my cumbersome moments with the English language. Everyone who likes this book should thank Allison for making it easier to read.

To Andy Le Peau of InterVarsity Press I owe thanks for my first book on worship, *Parenting in the Pew*. Years later, it was Andy who believed I had a "grown-up" book in me and helped shepherd this text to completion. To my editors, Gary Deddo and David Congdon, I am grateful for such kindred spirits in the faith and on the journey. Gary's keen and honest appraisal (and that of two anonymous readers!) helped me actually communicate what I wanted to with better discipline and focus. Heartfelt thanks!

Finally, I owe my deepest thanks to my family. We have answered God's call to worship together. To our sons, Robert Dayton Castleman and Scott Breckinridge Castleman, thanks for such grace in being parented in the pew. As my original guinea pigs, you received my best and my worst. And you have grown into men who love God, serve the kingdom and in your own vocations remind others of God's call to worship. Thanks for being such good thinkers as Christian disciples. Your conversational exchange

I've included in this book will challenge readers to think creatively and biblically about worship, symbol and sacramental faith. You are, indeed, stone-husher sons, and I am grateful for your contribution to *Story-Shaped Worship*.

And, to Breck, my husband, pastor, friend, lover, disciple-maker and Pop-pops to this Nona: Yes, I would do it all over again. You gave me Europe, children and all your love. You also opened the church door for me and showed me what it means to love the body of Christ in sickness and in health, whether richer or poorer, for better or for worse. On our wedding day, you selected Psalm 103 for our Scripture reading. Little did we know that this psalm would become our life's song for our journey together. This book, my darling, is a bit of our life in print.

Soli Deo Gloria
Advent 2012

INTRODUCTION

Bless the LORD, O my soul,
and all that is within me,
bless his holy name.

PSALM 103:1

The first verse of Psalm 103 is familiar to many people and in many congregations is often sung to a memorable tune by Andraé Crouch. The verse is simple to memorize, easy to sing and very difficult to actually hear. This difficulty is especially notable in the attitudes of many regarding their expectations of corporate worship. The words may be right on the lips of worshipers, but too often the heart is singing a different lyric:

Bless my soul, O Lord,
And all that is within you,
Bless me and those who share my name.

This lyric is the one that can reflect why people really go to a service of worship—to be blessed, to be refueled spiritually for the week ahead, to feel better about life in general and get help in living a less hypocritical life. Worship leaders and pastors, of course, are well aware of congregational needs and do their best to design a service of worship that feeds the flock, soothes troubled souls, and rallies enthusiasm for congregational witness, mission and church programs. None of these are bad things, but they are neither the sole focal point nor ultimate purpose of worship as designed by God throughout the story of Scripture.

The purpose of this text is to help evangelicals, especially those in historically independent communities of faith, rediscover in the great story of God's salvation related in the Bible, God's design for worship that is focused on God's pleasure. It is this story that, from beginning to end, gives biblical shape to services of worship. And it is God's story of salvation that keeps as the focal point of worship the triune God of grace revealed in the Scripture. God's story is a great story, and it is God's story that puts our individual stories in their proper place and in appropriate perspective. When corporate worship takes the shape of God's great salvation story, the hearts of worshipers will join their voices to sing Psalm 103 with integrity, holiness and rightly focused hope. This is what it means to worship "in spirit and in truth" and to present God with a "living sacrifice" and to engage in worship that is "holy and acceptable."

Story-shaped liturgy is outlined in Scripture, enacted in Israel, refocused in the New Testament community of the early church, regulated and guarded by the apostolic fathers, recovered in the Reformation and still shapes the liturgy of many congregations today. A worshiper does not have to return to Rome or Westminster to engage in story-shaped worship. Story-shaped liturgies aren't just found in the Post–Tridentine Mass, the *Book of Common Prayer* or a variety of worship guides for the Reformed faith. Any worship leader or team of worship leaders can create story-shaped worship that has blessing God as its primary focus.

This book is mainly addressed to Christians with whom I share a broad evangelical identity. I teach at John Brown University, a fine liberal arts university in the very northwest corner of Arkansas less than two miles from the Oklahoma border. John Brown University is an unaffiliated, nonsectarian and interdenominational comprehensive liberal arts institution. John Brown is therefore "evangelical" and carries within its short history (JBU was founded in 1919) both an independence and an inclusiveness that is typical of evangelicals and their institutions. There are basically three major hallmarks of what constitutes evangelicalism: a high view of the unique nature of biblical authority, an affirmation of the importance of a conversion experience by God's grace through faith alone, and the absolute sufficiency of the work of Christ Jesus for salvation.

Evangelicals can be described as a subset of other historically linked and defined communities of faith. For instance, there are evangelical Presbyterians, evangelical Lutherans, evangelical Anglicans, and even evangelical Roman Catholics. And, of course, there are a myriad of evangelical "independent" congregations that claim no particular historical connection to the family tree of the Christian faith. Some of these faith communities claim their identity, first and last, in the "church of the New Testament." However, the problem with this claim is that even within the pages of the New Testament congregations tended to branch out into "denominational" bodies usually identified by a particular founder or evangelist. Paul laments this reality when he writes, "What I mean is that each of you says, 'I belong to Paul,' or 'I belong to Apollos,' or 'I belong to Cephas,' or 'I belong to Christ'" (1 Corinthians 1:12). Of course Paul, in many of his letters, affirms the unity of all believers in the body of Christ under the headship of the Lord Jesus,[1] but in many of those same letters he also describes, corrects and regulates a variety of worship practices of congregational communities.

Because Paul and all New Testament writers, with the possible exception of Luke, assumed their readers were familiar with the worship practices of Israel, the foundation of God's people upon which Christian congregations were built, there is very little description in the New Testament of corporate worship. When descriptions do emerge in the earliest documents of the Christian church, it is not surprising that they reflect the influence of Jewish patterns for the worship of God. In addition, Luke, whose first readers were predominantly Gentile, often includes details concerning Jewish customs to aid early non-Jewish Christians in understanding the Jewish foundation for the faith and practice of the church. And this is as it should be. God has, in fact, given his people in the context of his story of salvation, the shape of worship designed for God's own pleasure and blessing. It is this great story that God employs as the basic shape for worship that is, indeed, biblical. This book is written to contribute to the recovery of that biblical shape and the reenactment of God's story of salvation in Christian worship for a variety of evangelical congregations.

This recovery and practice of reenactment will help evangelical believers engage in worship that is biblically shaped and more conscious of God's own mediation of worship that is well-focused on God's own pleasure.

---

[1]Throughout the book, I use the terms *church* and *congregation* in particular ways for specific purposes. I only use *church* to indicate the panhistorical, pancultural reality of the body of Christ under the lordship of Jesus, the Head. In this I recognize Paul's affirmation "one Lord, one faith, one baptism" (Ephesians 4:5). I use *congregation* to indicate local communities of Christians who gather together for worship, witness, mission and fellowship. Congregations participate as members of the one holy, catholic and apostolic church.

Story-shaped worship has a particular pattern, but within this pattern there is still plenty of room for creativity and the inclusion of the congregation's spiritual gifts. There is a shape to story-based worship, but within this basic biblical shape, a great variety of styles can be accommodated. Services of worship can be "traditional" (hymnbooks, organs, robes, choirs and a set pattern), "contemporary" (overhead projection, praise songs and choruses, no robes, a worship team, praise band) or "blended" (various ways of combining the first two "styles"). However, it is vital to keep in mind that it is God's story that is central to worship, and this keeps the focus on God's presence, mediation and blessing and not the style preferences of or a self-generated experience for the congregation. Unfortunately, congregational worship wars are usually waged over style, and this is an indication that the most important point of worship has been overlooked.

In order to get at the heart of story-shaped worship, however, there are significant challenges to recognize at the very outset.

THE CHALLENGE OF DISCERNING EARLY LITURGICAL PATTERNS

There are some practical guidelines to be considered when dealing with practices of any kind in antiquity that are helpful for determining how much or how little Christian worship was rooted in Jewish patterns of worship in the temple or synagogue. First, it is helpful to keep in mind that it was and is typical for writers in any age to not mention what they presume their readers already know. This rule is easily discernible in the writings of the New Testament. In contrast to Luke's account of Jesus' inaugural teaching in the synagogue of Nazareth, Matthew offers no details of the event for his very Jewish readership. Matthew assumed that the Jews who first read or heard his Gospel did not need descriptions of activities that were very familiar to them. However, Luke's first readers (and hearers) were predominantly Gentile and it was helpful for them to have a bit of a detailed description of what went on in a Galilean Jewish synagogue. Likewise, the writer of the Gospel of John tends to describe sites, especially in Jerusalem, for his original audience more often than the Synoptic Evangelists. Most scholars date the writing of the fourth Gospel during the last decade of the first century, at least twenty years after the destruction of Jerusalem, so the inclusion of descriptive detail was necessary: most readers of John's Gospel had never seen Jerusalem prior to A.D. 70.

The point is, the Synoptic Gospels, particularly Matthew and Mark, are much less descriptive of place and topography because they assumed more firsthand knowledge of their readers. In discerning liturgical connections between Jewish practice and early Christian worship, a lack of description may not mean something wasn't included or practiced, but that the practice or liturgical pattern was assumed and well developed and didn't need explication.

Second, when a mention of a liturgical practice is first made in early church documents or letters, it may not indicate the inauguration of a new practice, but rather an attempt to bring some conformity to the practice of a long-standing element in the liturgy. The absence of explication may indicate an assumed and ongoing pattern in a service of worship and/or that the uniformity of the practice needed no regulation or promotion. The research required for the study of liturgical history should incorporate not only documents but archaeological, artistic and other disciplines that can help make connections as carefully and responsibly as possible.[2]

It is important that discerning the patterns and practice of worship in the early Christian church should not be limited to what scholar Michael A. Farley designates as a "praxis-oriented regulative principle." Farley defines this approach for historical liturgical studies as

> a hermeneutical approach to a biblical theology of worship that defines the norm for Christian worship as the apostolic *practice* of corporate worship in the first-century church. Thus, according to this principle, liturgical practices are biblical only if there are explicit NT commands or normative examples of those particular practices.[3]

The central concern of a praxis-oriented research focus is finding explicit

---

[2]The work of Paul F. Bradshaw in liturgical history informs much of this section of the introduction. Bradshaw's books, *The Search of the Origins of Christian Worship* (2002) and *Early Christian Worship* (1996), are considered two of the finest works in the field of liturgical history. Both these texts are published by Oxford University Press. Although I have a different approach to liturgical study, Bradshaw's careful historical connections and cautious guidance concerning making liturgical assumptions too hastily or too dogmatically have created helpful parameters for my own work.

[3]Michael Farley, "What Is 'Biblical' Worship? Biblical Hermeneutics and Evangelical Theologies of Worship," *Journal of the Evangelical Theological Society* 51, no. 3 (September 2008): 591-613.

biblical warrant for worship practice, but the inherent limitations of this approach tend to neglect the riches of liturgical patterns embodied in the development of Israel's worship in the Old Testament. Michael Farley notes this regrettable truncation of biblical liturgical possibilities in some post-Reformation worship tendencies and Puritan publications, as well as in contemporary promotions of de-institutionalizing, delocalizing and deritualizing Christian worship by some scholars and popular clergy. With its narrow use of Scripture, as well as its dismissal of any practice not explicitly mentioned in the New Testament, praxis-oriented research neglects a wealth of biblical patterns and theological richness that can shape and inform Christian liturgical practice and the communities engaged in worship.

Because there is actually very little praxis-oriented description that can be clearly discerned in the writings of the New Testament, praxis-oriented conclusions can end up neglecting some important aspect of worship that the New Testament writers assumed but did not explicate for a variety of reasons. In addition, the worship practices that are clear are not uniformly presented across the geographical, cultural or temporal span of the New Testament. When a Christian congregation claims to "worship like the early church in the New Testament" one must ask two questions: Which one? and How do you know?

Farley designates a second approach to historical liturgical study as a "theologically oriented regulative principle," which does not limit biblical patterns for Christian worship to practices explicit in New Testament texts, but

> broadens the locus of liturgical norms in Scripture to include general theological principles in addition to explicit descriptions of liturgical practice . . . [and] derives its norms for Christian worship by evaluating the way that particular liturgical practices communicate biblical truths in ritual and symbol. . . . [Thus] liturgical forms or rituals are biblical insofar as they embody truths taught in the Bible, and not merely because the apostolic church actually practiced the forms or rituals in question.

One value of the theologically oriented regulative approach in liturgical studies is recognizing patterns of worship in the early church that build on the summary affirmations of faith in the early church and not just the glimpses of the church's explicit practices. The emergence of the church calendar is an example Farley uses to illustrate how this approach recognizes worship practices that helpfully emerge not out of explicit command or teaching or illustration in the New Testament, but from Christian theology established from meditation on the birth, life, suffering, death, resurrection and ascension of the Lord Jesus. However, some proponents of a theologically oriented regulative principle often focus exclusively on New Testament texts and practices during the patristic period of liturgical development, something Farley terms the "patristic-ecumenical model." When the theologically oriented regulative principle is limited to the New Testament and the patristic period, it can neglect the sturdier foundation of a more thorough and fully canonical approach.

The limitations of these models used in the work of liturgical theology can be addressed by discerning the biblical patterns of Christian worship using what I term the canonical-theological approach, the model incorporated for this book. Using the illustration of the church calendar above, the canonical-theological model recognizes that the chronological rhythm of Christian worship has older and deeper roots than the richness of the patristic patterns or even the unique authority of the New Testament. The church calendar is grounded in the rhythm of creation itself. Also, the worship life of Israel unfolded in the Old Testament is richly explicit in its theological patterns manifest in the sacrificial rites and festivals of God's people. Both explicit narrative models and canonical theology should help inform and shape the church calendar and Christian worship.

THE CANONICAL-THEOLOGICAL MODEL FOR LITURGICAL STUDIES

The canonical-theological model for liturgical studies presented in this text is very similar to Michael Farley's "biblical-typological model." One value of the canonical-theological model is that it challenges the rather common contemporary neglect of ecclesiology in general. This neglect not only contributes to the epidemic of worship wars within faith communities but is a major reason why many services of worship today have a pronounced tendency to devolve into entertainment for the flock, becoming merely functional evangelistic meetings for the seeker or the well-intentioned but self-guided effort of a congregation to prompt an engagement with God.

The Scripture of the Old *and* New Testaments reveals God's heart and

God's guidance concerning worship. The transition from the praxis of synagogue to the patterns of early house churches, the patristic teaching and councils of the church, and the refocusing of pastor-scholars on worship, preaching and sacraments in the Reformation and the Counter-Reformation have much to offer for instructing God's people how to offer God worship that is right "in spirit and in truth." But reaching farther back and further in to the unique revelation of God in the whole of the biblical canon provides a robust and uniquely authoritative foundation for such worship.

There is no question that the often historically anemic ecclesiology of some Christian congregations has often resulted in Sunday morning programs that are focused on the subjective experience of the individual rather than true worship that is mediated by and focused on the blessing of the triune God of grace. The necessity of worship as a service mediated by the Spirit, through the Son and for the Father is often lost in the pragmatism of the commodified liturgies of many services of worship. Sunday mornings too often have become storefront windows designed to attract and keep shoppers in the store in order to buy into congregational programs. The grace of Word and Sacrament has been sacrificed on the altar of a subtle self-help theology that actually seeks to control the divine encounter with the ultimate intention of feeling at least a bit better about oneself and life circumstances. Story-shaped worship can help contribute to a service that is more biblically theological and less personally therapeutic. Farley points to a disconnect between what Christians affirm about the faith and their practice of worship when he writes,

> To accept the creeds, on the one hand, and reject the liturgies by inattention that often expresses itself in disdain, on the other, is contradictory and unwise. For orthodoxy was primarily given shape in the liturgy, and the creeds were originally part of the larger liturgical witness.[4]

In his book *Liturgical Theology*, Simon Chan writes, "It is rather ironic that the evangelicalism that claims to be the heir of the opponents of Protestant liberalism in the nineteenth century should find itself unwittingly concurring with the father of liberalism, Friedrich Schleiermacher, who understood the source of religion to be found precisely in human subjec-

---

[4]Farley, "What Is 'Biblical' Worship?" p. 601.

tivity." However, Chan's insightful summary in *Liturgical Theology* actually reflects how compromised worship may become if theological and ecclesiological concerns are not included in liturgical studies. Patterns of biblical worship must be discerned from the whole canon and its theological integration of belief as well as practice.[5]

An illustration of what can result from the neglect of these patterns discerned through the canonical-theological model can often be seen in evangelical sacramental theology (or its absence). Many Christians are well-entrenched in a new kind of disembodied "only the spirit matters" practice in worship. This can be seen when a congregation sings songs or hymns that generalize the love of God in terms limited to a feeling of divine affection for needy people without the particularity of how God has demonstrated this through Christ Jesus and by the Spirit in time and space. God has "so loved the world" in the particularity of the incarnation. Christian worship needs to reflect this story, this particularity. The appreciation for both divine and human embodiment in worship practice is vital for distinguishing Christian worship as a unique reenactment of the gospel, the good news of God's salvation of his people through the incarnation, life, suffering, death, resurrection and ascension of Jesus of Nazareth, God's only begotten Son.

The canonical-theological model for liturgical studies certainly looks to New Testament practice, as well as early church documents, catechisms and teaching, but it also draws on biblical texts that attend more directly with the corporate worship mandates and patterns in the Old Testament. The Mosaic framework for the sequence of sacrificial offerings, sacred space and ritual outlines, the liturgies embedded in the records of divine encounters in the Hebrew Scripture, and the language of worship used in Psalms and the teaching of the prophets all shape the worship of Israel. And the worship of Israel in homes, synagogues and temple provided the rich patterns that were the foundations of Christian worship in its earliest days. The full spectrum of canonical-theological resources should still inform and shape the worship of the church.

---

[5]Simon Chan, *Liturgical Theology: The Church as Worshiping Community* (Downers Grove, Ill.: InterVarsity Press, 2006).

The Shape of This Text for Students and Teachers

There are two primary sections in this text. The first consists of seven chapters that explore in depth the biblical patterns for Christian worship found within the canon of Scripture. First I look at texts of origins, Genesis 1–4, and examine the character of God, the creation of humankind, the corruption of the fall and the beginning of the first "worship wars." The first important idea for any worshiper to consider is who is worshiped and how that "who" has desired to be worshiped. The basic rhythm and pattern of biblical worship has been designed by God from the very beginning.

The second chapter is an overview of how God's people have been identified by their exclusive relationship with God throughout the canon. This theme is expanded specifically in the consideration of sabbath holiness and the importance of sacred space. Chapter three builds on that overview and considers specifically the exclusive nature of worship that dethrones all other potential gods. The issue of worship leadership and the nature of sacred space and holiness are explored more fully. The fourth chapter brings together the pattern of divine liturgy that reflects the story of God's salvation and gives shape to biblical worship.

Chapter five examines the danger of ambiguity of intentions that can render worship unworthy of God. Using worship as a direct means to ends other than the blessing of God erodes the true fear of the Lord that reminds all worshipers of their humble status that needs God's initiative and depends on God's grace alone. It is the fear of the Lord that lends needed wisdom to worship leaders to lead the congregation through a service that both blesses God and recognizes the necessity of God's mediation for that very intention.

Chapter six considers the issue of holiness, righteousness and justice for those called to worship the God whose character reflects all those attributes. Chapter seven concludes the first section of the book that looks at the canonical sources for the design of biblical worship by considering the transition between the worship of Israel in the Hebrew Scriptures during the exile, intertestamental period, the development of synagogues and the worship of the early church reflected in New Testament texts.

The second part of the book considers how the biblical pattern for

Christian worship has been kept, corrupted, reformed, reclaimed and challenged throughout church history. Chapter eight focuses on the patristic centuries that in many ways made a noble effort to clarify the faith through the worship practices of the church. Chapter nine considers medieval Christendom and the challenges of faithfulness to story-shaped worship in an age of powerful clergy and the marginalization of laity. This chapter goes on to discuss the efforts of the early reformers to recover both story-shaped worship as well as the priesthood of all believers. Chapter ten concludes this section with a survey of post-Reformation challenges to story-shaped worship that particularly concern the rise of individualism during the Enlightenment. The chapter addresses issues concerning the potential corruption of worship when God's story of salvation is eclipsed by an individual's or congregation's experience of that salvation.

There is a brief "workshop" section after each chapter in the book that offers a variety of ways to specifically think through and respond to ideas and challenges from the preceding chapter. There are suggestions on how to consider the content of the chapter in the light of particular congregational liturgies, particular worship space and historical patterns, and many other variables for specific situations. Teachers and students can select all or some of the ideas for assignments, research, writing projects, or individual and group praxis sessions. Right now, write a one-sentence definition of worship for your first "workshop."

At the end of the book there is a short glossary as well as a bibliography for further reading and study. This is followed by a topical index and Scripture index.

As You Begin

The central objective of this book is to help students, teachers, worship leaders and congregations ask better questions about the intention of worship and the God who is worshiped. The questions one often asks in teaching, designing or engaging in worship are very often centered on our personal satisfaction, pleasure, comfort zones and style preferences. However, it is wiser to ask questions that center first on the character of God, the truth of Scripture, the pattern of worship with the biblical account and what the church has learned (for good or for ill) about what is pleasing and acceptable to God. Too often one's consideration of worship centers on utility and outcome: "Did it work? Did it move the congregation? What did I get out of it? Was the style, my style?" Too often the means are justified by the positive evaluation of our own desired outcome. But means and ends are both important to God. And worship is best shaped by *first* considering the God who is worshiped, not the preferences of significantly flawed people whose "righteousness is a filthy rag"! One way to curtail well-intentioned but self-centered ambition in worship is through the study of Scripture, the consideration of who God is, and what God regards as an offering of worship that is "holy and acceptable" (Rom 12:1). And, within my own limitations, that's what this book is all about!

It has taken me a lifetime to write this book. Although Paul assures me that I have been known by God "before the foundation of the world" (Ephesians 1:4) and that I was "crucified with Christ" (Galatians 2:19) and raised with him and "hidden with Christ in God" (Colossians 3:3), I did not know this God who loved me first (1 John 4:19) until I was a nineteen-year-old college junior. Although I was raised in a loving, affectionate and very functional home, we were a family that occasionally "went to church" but knew nothing of really "going to worship." I began my Christian journey with a new Bible and a few friends who met in Liberty Park to celebrate the Lord's Supper with french fries and Coke. And God began his good work (Philippians 1:6).

I had a lot to learn about God's story revealed in Scripture. I had a lot to learn about worship that is shaped by that story and not the seasons of my own life. I had a lot to learn about the church as the bride of Christ beloved by God and indwelled by the Spirit to be "the fullness of him who fills all in all" (Ephesians 1:23). I am grateful that God loves his work in me and in us. I am grateful that the stories of poor Uzzah, Ananias and Sapphira only happened once. We'd all be dead. I am grateful that God still calls his people to worship and that God helps us learn through word and Spirit in the company of his people to answer that call in a way that is holy and acceptable to him. I am grateful that God's love is steadfast and everlasting, because it does take a lifetime to learn well. I wrote this book as a work of thanksgiving for what I've learned so far as a disciple of Jesus in the company of faithful pilgrims on the journey to God's kingdom.

PART ONE

BIBLICAL PATTERNS

STORY-SHAPED LITURGY

GENESIS AND THE GOSPEL

The Beginning of Worship

And the LORD had regard for Abel and his offering.

GENESIS 4:4

Worship, like witness and mission, is part of a "living sacrifice" of one's life to God that must be "holy and acceptable" (Romans 12:1). And God has every right to express what is "good and acceptable and perfect" (Romans 12:2)—what is pleasing to him and what is not. Worship must be focused on the character and the pleasure of the One who is worshiped. To "worship" with no thought of God, who is both the object of and mediator for worship, usually results in a service that merely manifests the effort, gifts or intentions that please worshipers and that they find acceptable. This chapter will highlight foundational principles of biblical worship from the beginning of God's story in the texts of origins through the practices of the patriarchs of God's people prior to the emergence of Israel as a nation under the leadership of Moses.

It's not unusual today for Christian congregations to have two styles of worship, usually designated "traditional" and "contemporary"— and often meeting in two different settings. Often the decision to develop these two styles is based on congregational interest in attracting different kinds of worshipers with distinct preferences, especially in music. When worship is designed for congregational taste and preferences, however, God as the mediator and center of the worshiper's intent is easily lost. Services of worship can become storefront windows advertising the attractions of a community instead of an offering of the congregation's gifts intended for God's acceptance and pleasure, centered on God's glory.

Worship that is pleasing and acceptable to God can be offered in many different styles; style itself is not the issue. A liturgy encompassing biblical patterns and focused on God as the only "audience" can please God no matter the style of accompaniment, whether praise band and bongo drums or pipe organ and handbells. A congregation may use either hymnals or overhead projections, but worship itself is evaluated not by the satisfaction of personal preference but by its acceptance by God as pleasing and honoring to him.

THE FIRST "WORSHIP WAR"

Today's "worship wars" are often waged around issues, such as "style," that are not of ultimate concern. A congregation may split into two communities, usually designed to offer what each group wants. People with the praise band in the gym, a short sermon with a shirt-sleeved pastor propped on a stool, assume the people in the sanctuary with no overhead projection—just hymnbooks, a choir, a robed pastor and a pulpit—really need to loosen up. And the sanctuary pew people assume the gymnasium people in their folding chairs need to get serious. But those who attend the traditional service and those who attend the contemporary service can *both* fail at worship that pleases God because they are more concerned with what pleases them!

"Worship wars" can be pretty serious. The first murder in the Bible happened as the result of a worship war! Genesis 4 is an account of two brothers who each brought an offering from their chosen work to the LORD as an act of worship. Both brothers were engaged in work that God had mandated (Genesis 1:29-30; 2:15). The elder brother, Cain, was a farmer who tilled the land, and his younger brother Abel engaged in animal husbandry as a shepherd. Genesis summarizes God's response to each offering: "the LORD had regard for Abel and his offering, but for Cain and his offering he had no regard" (Genesis 4:4-5). In the Hebrew text the word rendered "regard" literally conveys the idea that God "looked" at Abel's offering and God "did not look" at Cain's offering.

Biblical scholars often affirm the ancient opinion that Abel's offering was consumed by fire as a sign that God accepted the offering of the younger sibling, but that Cain's offering was essentially ignored, as no fire fell on it. Regardless of this ancient interpretive assumption, it is also common for scholars, as well as pastors and Bible students, to note the subtle distinction of quality in the offerings themselves. Abel offered "the firstlings of his flock, their fat portions" (4:4); Abel offered the first and best of the flock's increase. However, Cain's offering is an apparent contrast in quality, as he brought the LORD, without any superlatives noted in the Hebrew text, "an offering of the fruit of the ground" (4:3). From this it might be surmised that God is pleased with an offering of the "best," not just the ordinary. However, this may or may not be helpful in discerning biblical patterns of Christian worship. Aren't all believers called to "sing to the LORD a new song," not just the choir-worthy or those with great voices fit for the worship team? One must look carefully at the text to rightly discern what pleased or failed to please God in the offering of worship given by these two brothers.

The most significant indicator of what may have pleased or not pleased the LORD in this biblical account is Cain's reaction to God's disregard of his gift. Cain got angry and "his countenance fell" (4:5). The repetition of Cain's reaction in the following verse (4:6) is one way that Hebrew writing reflects what is important and is to be remembered in the text. The repetition may reflect the long oral history of the story. The storyteller is saying, "Now listen and remember this point." The point in this text is that Cain's anger and resulting emotional frown betrays his thorough preoccupation with himself. In fact, Cain is so angry about the LORD's regard for Abel's offering that he kills his brother! God's pleasure in Abel's gift and how he might make a pleasing offering was the farthest thing from Cain's mind.

Furthermore, this self-centeredness is underscored in the text by Cain's protest of the LORD's discipline and banishment. Genesis 4:13-14 recounts Cain's biggest concerns about how the situation affects him, his punishment and his estrangement from all he had known. And this reveals the heart of what was wrong with Cain's worship. It was all about Cain himself from beginning to end.

The LORD's attempt to refocus Cain's attitude toward worship is reflected in God's last question, "If you do well, will you not be accepted?"(4:7). The LORD knows that Cain's true self is reflected in his offer of the fruit of his labors as worship. How one "serves" the LORD is indicative of how one "worships" the LORD. What one does and how one does it really is indicative of who one is and what one truly believes. Cain's heart, life, being was centered on what *he* wanted, even in his worship.

Genesis 4:1-16, for the most part, centers on Cain's dilemma and serves as a cautionary picture about the fulminating nature of sin, and the divine willingness to reach out to this wayward son even as the Lord God had sought his parents (Genesis 3:9; 4:6-7, 9). However, one must ask, what was it about Abel's sacrifice that caught God's eye in his divine regard? While acknowledging the limits of what the texts of origins in Genesis reveal, one must also consider the whole of Scripture's story, which affirms that "without the shedding of blood there is no forgiveness of sins" (Hebrews 9:22); it may be that Abel reenacted the story of salvation that he had learned through his family's experience with Yahweh. Yahweh himself, in "making garments of skins," had sacrificed an animal as a foreshadowing work of atonement to cover the sin of his parents (Genesis 3:21). Abel had discerned by grace that worship was all about God and his saving work on behalf of humankind. Abel symbolically reenacted that story of salvation—and this is the heart of worship that God still regards as acceptable and perfect. God regarded (took notice of) Abel's sacrifice because God saw himself reflected in this act of worship.

Lex orandi, lex credendi is an ancient Latin phrase coined by the early church fathers. It translates as "The law of prayer is the law of belief." The phrase highlights the reality that how people pray and how much people truly depend on prayer reflects not just what people say they believe, but what they actually do believe. How people worship, what they say and sing in worship, how they listen, respond, and act during worship (disregarding for the moment the possibility of physical constraints or situational factors) does reflect what they truly believe about the God they worship.

IN THE BEGINNING

Who is the God of the Bible? What does Scripture reveal about this God who is to be worshiped? The beginning texts of Genesis reflect a God who is a Creator radically distinct from what he creates. God creates all that is *ex nihilo*, out of nothing. The affirmation of this idea is foundational to biblical faith. Faith as defined in the New Testament book of Hebrews is "the assurance of things hoped for, the conviction of things not seen" (Hebrews 11:1-2). To illustrate examples of such a faith for God's people, Hebrews 11:3 begins a long litany of the faithful with a declaration of divine creation *ex nihilo*: "By faith we understand that the worlds were prepared by the word of God, so that what is seen was made from things that are not visible." Hebrews' first "Hall of Faith" inductee is Abel, who "offered to God a more acceptable sacrifice than Cain's. Through this he received approval as righteous, God himself giving approval to his gifts" (Hebrews 11:4).

The first three chapters of Genesis are commonly referred to as "texts of origins" and are a foundational introduction to the story of God's revelation to and history with his people in time and space. These opening chapters give us a brief yet vital glimpse of something no one living has ever experienced: life before the fall of humankind into sin and rebellion. It's important to consider these texts, even in a limited way, because they offer an idea of what has been on God's heart and what was God's ultimate desire and design for his people and his creation. The texts of origins echo throughout the biblical canon. For example, the description of the garden, its orientation toward the east, and its rivers and trees are re-created symbolically in the design and décor of the tabernacle and the temple. In garden and in sanctuary, God calls his people to meet with him. The terms used for work given to humankind in the pre-fall chapters of Genesis are echoed in the description of the priestly labors in the tabernacle.

Allen Ross, in his book *Recalling the Hope of Glory*, makes the point that "the worship of God, the Creator, is therefore also the worship of God, the Redeemer, for what God did in creation set the pattern not only for redemption but also for the worship of the redeemed."[1] Over the course of several chapters Ross underscores the importance of the relationship between the details of the garden in the texts of origins and the unfolding of God's revelation of his redemptive work which culminates in the gospel of Jesus and his headship over the body of Christ.

It is significant to note that the texts of origins were important to Jesus in his dealing with the contemporary ideas and questions of his audience in

---

[1] Allen P. Ross, *Recalling the Hope of Glory: Biblical Worship from the Garden to the New Creation* (Grand Rapids: Kregel, 2006), p. 82.

the first century. For instance, when the Pharisees asked Jesus about the issue of divorce and appealed to the Mosaic law and its allowances, Jesus appealed to the texts of origins, making the point that at "the beginning it [divorce] was not so" (Matthew 19:8). Jesus asserts that the Mosaic law provided for the terms of divorce only because of the Israelites' hardness of heart, not because it was ever part of God's design or desire. (See Matthew 19:4-8 and its parallel in Mark 10:3-9 to note how Jesus uses the texts of origins as the basis of his reply.) Texts of origins are important to consider when dealing with questions of who God is and what God desires. Texts of origins are significant when trying to understand what pleases God in worship, work and human relationships.

From the opening chapter of Genesis, the Creator God made the cosmos by the divine word in an orderly, sequential fashion. The breath of God hovered over the primordial chaos and then spoke all that is into being. God mitigates chaos by preparing, planning and ordering the work of creation. By extension, one might anticipate that the worship of such a God should reflect God's character in how it is prepared, planned and ordered. Worship liturgies and even the sacred space in which one worships this God should reflect a God who brings order out of chaos, light out of darkness.[2]

Many medieval European cathedrals portray this idea visually. The back of the nave, whether having a vaulted Gothic ceiling or a Romanesque flattened ceiling, is usually darker as the worshiper enters. The area might be barely lit by small windows, but the eye is quickly drawn to the front of the sanctuary which is made brighter in a variety of ways: by windows, art, candles and lamps. As worshipers enter this kind of sacred space, they move from darkness toward the light. Even in less ornate worship settings, sanctuaries are often designed with a large stained-glass window or graced with bright artwork on the wall that will face the congregation as they enter the place designated for worship.

The opening chapters of Genesis also reflect a God who is creative as the "maker of heaven and earth." It doesn't seem like God creates everything the same way. Rather, the first chapter of Genesis relates that God

---

[2]For a brief but fine treatment of the historical development of sacred space see James F. White, "The Language of Space," in *Introduction to Christian Worship*, 3rd ed. (Nashville: Abingdon Press, 2008).

created in a variety of ways. God's creative activity is reflected in the variety of Hebrew verbs used in the biblical record. God "separated," "gathered," "brought forth," "set" and "created" in a deliberate and multifaceted way that honored God's own character. So the God who is the object of biblical worship is a God who enjoys variety within the rhythmic orderliness of creation.

One of the ways that worship can reflect both variety and ordered rhythm is the design of worship throughout the liturgical year. Within biblical patterns for worship, the regular order of worship elements for a liturgy helps worshipers enter into the divine rhythm, not just for the service but for all of life. Within this liturgical rhythm there can be a variety of expressions to help keep the rhythm fresh and vibrant. God's design in creation itself displays a "liturgy" that helps people know what to expect next, like the phases of the moon, the rising and setting times of the sun. And, the myriad of things within the cosmic order—fruit, birds, flowers and the like—reflect God's affection for variety and help us experience creation's rhythm in a new way.

Early twentieth-century writer G. K. Chesterton, in his book *Orthodoxy*, catches a bit of God's affection for order as well as surprise when he reflects with his typical humorous edge:

> Now, to put the matter [the idea that repetition inherently leads to boredom] in a popular phrase, it might be true that the sun rises regularly because he never gets tired of rising. His routine might be due, not to a lifelessness, but to a rush of life. The thing I mean can be seen, for instance, in children, when they find some game or joke that they specially enjoy. A child kicks his legs rhythmically through excess, not absence, of life. Because children have abounding vitality, because they are in spirit fierce and free, therefore they want things repeated and unchanged.
>
> They always say, "Do it again"; and the grown-up person does it again until he is nearly dead. For grown-up people are not strong enough to exult in monotony. But perhaps God is strong enough to exult in monotony.
>
> It is possible that God says every morning, "Do it again" to the sun; and every evening, "Do it again" to the moon. It may not be automatic necessity that makes all daisies alike; it may be that God makes every daisy separately, but has never got tired of making them. It may be that He has the eternal ap-

petite of infancy; for we have sinned and grown old, and our Father is younger than we. The repetition in Nature may not be a mere recurrence; it may be a theatrical *encore*.[3]

This rather fanciful reflection celebrates both the rhythm and the variety embedded in creation itself. To worship the Creator of the cosmos in a way that reflects the divine character would display a repetitive rhythm as well as variations in expression. This is a significant bedrock aspect of liturgical development.

ORDER, RHYTHM AND CREATIVE VARIETY IN WORSHIP

The word "liturgy" comes from the Greek language and originally meant "the public work or service to their god(s)." The use of the word "liturgy" therefore focuses on how a particular group of people go about worshiping God. So a "liturgy" essentially is an order of worship. Worship is work. Worship is how God's people serve the maker of heaven and earth. Liturgy is the rhythm and design of this work through which all worshipers join together to please God. Biblical liturgies, whether they reflect an historically full or only partially developed pattern, all have a rhythm that helps the worshiper anticipate what comes next in a congregation's service to God. Regrettably, the use of the word "liturgy" is sometimes misused as a shorthand for a particular style of worship. Liturgy is often attached only to services with an atmosphere of formality, such as services that incorporate written prayers, set refrains used as congregational responses, three hymns and a benediction. However, all orders of worship use a liturgy, all congregational worship is liturgical.

It is not uncommon in certain communities to hear someone say, "We don't have a liturgy. We come in and sing for about a half an hour and then we have a teaching. Then we end with a prayer and another set of songs." That is still a liturgy. That sequence, which rarely varies, is how people in that community of faith go about serving God through worship. A similar point was made earlier regarding "style," whether the congregation meets week after week in the gymnasium for a "contemporary" service or in the

---

[3]G. K. Chesterton, *Orthodoxy: The Romance of Faith* (New York: Doubleday, 1959), p. 60. Originally published in 1908, Chesterton's classic is a creative autobiography that relates the spiritual awakening and journey that led to his conversion to the Christian faith.

sanctuary for the "traditional" service. In light of this, it is honoring to God and helpful for the congregation if the ordering of worship elements is repetitive even if variations are evident within a set liturgical rhythm.

What a congregation does sequentially in the liturgy not only reflects a particular understanding of who God is as Creator (and Redeemer) but, in the long run, will shape congregations and individual believers as disciples. For example, for nearly two thousand years Christian worship has incorporated another source for a biblical pattern of worship, that of the birth, life, suffering, death, resurrection and ascension of Jesus. Throughout the course of a year, songs and sermons, readings, creeds, testimonies, and sometimes the color of pastoral vestments, choir stoles, and even the colors of coverings for tables, altars, lecterns and pulpits mark the sequence of the Christian year. The liturgical season may influence what parts of Scripture are read and preached, what songs, hymns, and choir anthems are sung, what creed or congregational prayers are included.

Using the incarnation, public ministry life, and Jesus' death, resurrection and ascension as a rhythm for worship year after year helps to school the congregation's theological balance and helps counter an overemphasis on only part of the story that may lead to a truncation of the whole gospel for all of life. Congregations usually begin to mark the liturgical year during Advent, the season of several weeks prior to Christmas. This is followed by a conscious reflective period during Lent, the time from Ash Wednesday to Easter Sunday. Holy Week, the week before Easter, is an exercise in slow motion that contemplates Jesus' suffering and celebrates the triumph of God's Son over sin and death in his own death and resurrection. The time closely following Easter Sunday marks the ascension of the Lord and the sending of the Spirit. The ascension and Pentecost are highly significant events in the Christian story and should be incorporated thoughtfully into Christian worship.

The central significance of marking the liturgical year is to help shape the christocentric reality of the church. Jesus' story is the Christian story, the foundational story that shapes, tests, and vindicates Christian life and faith. This is the rhythm of the Christian faith: the anticipation of God's visitation, the narrative of Jesus' birth, life, suffering, death, resurrection and ascension, the Spirit's empowerment of the church's witness and mission, and the anticipation of the consummation of God's eternal kingdom. Christian worship reflects this rhythm, this story, through the order of worship and its great cycle throughout the Christian liturgical year.

However, the church's liturgical year and its profoundly helpful christocentric focus finds its roots "in the beginning" of God's story of creation and the covenant of God's faithfulness to Israel. God's truth is inseparable from God's story. It is the story itself that is the context of God's revelation of himself, the identity of his people, the anticipation and accomplishment of salvation and the design of worship that is glorifying to him. God began to teach his people the pattern of worship practice from the very beginning of the biblical story.

A SUMMARY OF PATRIARCHAL WORSHIP PATTERNS BEFORE THE LAW

After the texts of origins and during the time of Israel's earliest patriarchs, the book of Genesis contains a few key ideas regarding the emerging patterns of biblical worship. The first is the practice of people who began to "invoke the name of the LORD" (Genesis 4:26; 13:4) and the second is that of building altars to the Lord (Genesis 8:20; 12:7-8; 13:18; 22:9; 26:25; 33:18-20; 35:1, 3, 7). The limited record of prayer addressing God, invoking God's name or giving God thanks seems to be part of how God heightened the awareness of his unique supremacy before the covenant with Abraham that set apart a particular people to embody his story of salvation. During this period there is a growing sense of the exclusive nature of allegiance to the one God who made heaven and earth. In the future this exclusive allegiance will be forged into a major component of Israel's identity, a people who worship only one God.

The recognition of one God who made all heaven and earth lends itself to the idea that Israel's deity is not restricted to a certain territory like the gods of others. During the time of the patriarchs, altar building happens as a commemorative habit whenever the patriarchs are confronted or comforted by God, regardless of circumstances and place. Noah builds an altar after the flood waters recede (8:20). Abram builds altars to mark God's faithfulness as he enters Canaan and it marks a place in the land promised to him to which he returns (12:7-8; 13:3). Abram builds yet another altar in Hebron (13:18) and one in Moriah (22:9). Abraham's son Isaac builds an altar in what will become Beersheba (26:23-25). Isaac's son Jacob builds an altar as he flees his homeland (28:16-22) and another in Shechem upon his return (33:18-20).

Most Old Testament scholars acknowledge that these were altars compiled of rocks upon which an animal would be sacrificed in a way similar to that of neighboring Canaanites. However, what is noteworthy and counter to the surrounding culture is that many patriarchal altars were erected not to evoke a divine encounter but to commemorate such an encounter when God had met someone in a surprising way. The importance of this distinction cannot be overstated. These altars were not erected to get a god's attention or to try to gain a god's favor but to mark the site of an encounter with the God who had revealed himself to humans. To serve or to worship[4] this God who proved himself faithful is a foundational idea for the practices of God's people. Christians do not worship or serve God to either merit or encourage divine faithfulness. Worship, mission, witness and all Christian service is a *response* to the God who has demonstrated his faithfulness already. The basic pattern of biblical worship evident in these texts is that it is God who initiates the encounter, not the worshiper. This leads to a foundational pattern for biblical worship in which a "call to worship" using God's Word signals that it is God, not the worship leader, who invites his people to worship. Worship is a response to the call of God. Worship happens at the initiative of God's grace and is only made possible by his mediating presence on the worshiper's behalf. Throughout Scripture, biblical worship is increasingly marked by the need for God to provide the efficacious grace that makes worship acceptable and pleasing to him.

The episode of Abraham's near-sacrifice of Isaac is of particular interest as a way the God of the patriarchs worked to differentiate the worship of his people from those of the surrounding Canaanite people who initiated worship practices to gain the attention and favor of their gods. The episode recounted in Genesis 22 is a rather complicated story that comes to its climax when God substitutes a ram as the sacrifice in place of Abraham's son Issac. God initiates this encounter to get Abraham's attention and display his favor. The substitutionary sacrifice of the ram for Abraham's son anticipates both the nature and intention of the Mosaic law concerning the

---

[4]In Hebrew the word translated either "to worship" or "to serve" is a single word: ʿābad.

sacrificial rite of Israel as well as its prohibition of human sacrifice. In this story of Abraham and Issac, and in the law which follows under the ministry of Moses, God himself provides the means to bridge the gap between divine holiness and human need. All biblical worship is necessarily mediated by God himself to bridge the gap between fallen humanity and that which is holy and acceptable to God.

The foreshadowing of the Gospel story has not been lost on artists as "the ram caught in the thicket" is often a side panel or a background picture in paintings or windows where the cross of Christ Jesus is central. Jesus has gone before his people into the presence of God the Father. He leads the way to worship. And the Spirit is sent not only to empower God's people for mission and witness in the world but to make worship a vital part of a living sacrifice that is holy and acceptable to God.

The worship of sinful and fallen people necessitates divine mediation if the sacrifice is to be good, perfect and acceptable to God. The pagan worship that surrounded the patriarchs was often a work of appeasement, a work initiated by people seeking to win divine favor. Biblical worship emerges in the Hebrew and Christian Scripture as that which is initiated by God, mediated by God, and is a response of the people of God to the grace and favor of God they have already experienced. The reality of worship-as-response to the grace of God through the substitutionary sacrifice of Christ Jesus on our behalf and the sanctifying work and presence of the Holy Spirit indicates how God is actively engaged in the mediation of worship from the beginning of God's story until its neverending culmination in the heavenly tabernacle. This pattern will become more apparent as it is further developed in the Pentateuch beginning with God's call to Moses and the inauguration of the Mosaic law.

WORKSHOP FOR CHAPTER ONE

1. Summarize what style of a service of worship you prefer.

   - What are your reasons for this preference?

   - What makes this preference important to you?

   - What is the relationship of this preference to your experience (or lack of experience) in a Christian congregation as a child?

2. Read Genesis 4:1-16 and consider some of the ancient and contemporary challenges of worship present in this text (style, preference, what God regards as worthy, the focus on God's pleasure, etc.).

   • How much of worship planning and participation is intended to meet personal needs?

   • "I got a lot out of it" is a common expression of satisfaction with a service of worship. Evaluate this familiar sentiment in the light of the first "worship war" in Genesis 4.

   • What might you do and what might your congregation do to help end the worship wars?

3. Consider how the design of worship space might help or hinder a person's understanding of the God who is worshiped. Ask yourself what a young child might assume about God's character upon entering the sacred space where you worship most regularly.

4. Take a moment to think about the "order of worship" in which you participate most often.

   • What does the ordering and content of the service say about how the congregation understands God?

   • What does the liturgy reflect about how the congregation understands its relationship to God?

   • In your reflection, consider what is not regularly included (or consistently absent) from this liturgy, like a confession of sin or the Lord's Supper.

   • If you note things that are not regularly included in the service, or even included rarely, what may be the reasoning behind these liturgical exclusions or changes in the liturgy that are regular but different from week to week or even month to month?

   • What seems to be central to the service you are most familiar with regardless of its occasional variations?

   • Is the focus of your congregational liturgy the Lord's Supper, the sermon, the music or another liturgical element?

5. Christ the King Sunday was introduced in the Roman Catholic Church

calendar on December 11, 1925. It's interesting to note how this liturgical focus on Christ and his kingdom began in the difficult days after World War I in Europe, which ended the German empire (1871–1918). The European continent was beleaguered by war and needed hope for a better future. The church recognized that people were anxious, as the leadership of nations was uncertain. Christ the King Sunday was partly an effort to remind Roman Catholics, especially European Catholics, of God's victory and the security of God's reign over world affairs.

- For Catholics the addition of Christ the King Sunday was a poignant reminder of God's sovereign and benevolent reign after the indescribable destruction of WWI, especially in Europe. Germany was particularly humiliated as a nation from both the terms and restrictions of the postwar treaty and severe economic depression. How might both the inclusion of this Sunday and the attention of worshipers to its central truth have helped their faithfulness to God during this time?

- Christ the King Sunday was first celebrated in December 1925. On January 30, 1933, less than eight years later, Adolf Hitler was inaugurated as the chancellor of Germany. How might attention to the the liturgical rhythm of the church year make a difference in the lives of God's people then and now?

6. How does your congregation celebrate the highlights of the Christian year?

- What traditions are practiced in the community of faith that help worhipers focus on the gospel story?

- What traditions are reflections of the congregation's (or denomination's) history?

7. The Hebrew word ʿābad can be translated either "to serve" or "to worship." Considering the dual nature of ʿābad, respond to the following questions:

- How is the LORD served well by the worship of his people?

- How do you or your faith community discern the regard or the pleasure of the LORD in what is offered to God in worship?

- If God were to disregard, or not be pleased with, the worship of your congregation, how might you respond?

- What would worship look like if it was centered on the LORD's regard and pleasure rather than on one's own gifts, tastes or preferred style?

- How is the gospel story rehearsed in the liturgical rhythm of your congregation's year?

- How does the service of worship that you participate in acknowledge God's grace in initiating the call to worship?

- How might both personal and corporate worship include the idea of "altar building," ways of marking times and places God has encountered you in surprising ways?

8. After participating in corporate worship in the coming week, think reflectively about what in the service may have pleased the Lord.

   - Think critically about the content of the service and how it reflected or failed to reflect what you understand about God from the Scriptures, such as God as triune, holy, all-knowing, all good, all powerful, etc.

   - Ask if there was anything in the service designed more for the pleasure of the congregation than for God's pleasure. These are not necessarily mutually exclusive, but note distinctions in the dynamics of the service of worship.

   - Consider how you bring an offering to corporate worship that reflects the goodness of your work, witness, life and faith.

   - In the course of a year, what traditions of faith are particularly meaningful to you and your congregation?

WORSHIP AND IDENTITY

Yahweh and Sabbath in the Torah, Prophets and Gospels

I will be with you; and this shall be the sign for you that it is I who sent you:
when you have brought the people out of Egypt, you shall worship
God on this mountain.

Exodus 3:12

After Genesis, worship is particularized and greatly shaped through the Mosaic law. In fact, the identity of Israel centers on the practice of worship faithfully offered only to the Lord God who delivered them. From the time Israel is brought out of Egypt and eventually into the land God had promised Abraham, the people of God are distinguished from all others by the unique characteristics of their worship. The people of God are a people called to the exclusive worship of the God who has saved them and made them a people for himself. This chapter will summarize the major tenants of the patterns of worship indicated through the Mosaic law concerning both the sacrificial system and the temporal calendar of Israel's year through annual festivals and the weekly rhythm of sabbath observance. Connections will then be drawn between these patterns and the practices of first-century Palestinian Jews seen in Jesus' life and his ministry with the disciples.

Israel's essential identity as a people delivered from bondage in Egypt was to be manifest in Israel's worship of the one true God. This God, who spoke to Moses on the mountain through the theophany of the bush that burned but was not consumed, promised to go with Moses in order to deliver his people. To return to this sacred place and worship would be the sign that Yahweh had kept his promise to Moses (Exodus 3:12).

In the Pentateuch God's people are identified by how they ʿābad (serve/worship) God through their exclusive allegiance to the One who delivered them and will establish them in the land God promised to Abraham's descendants. Patterns in the Mosaic texts reflect the development of Israel's worship as serving God through the practice of reenactment. Worship for Israel centered on remembering how the LORD God had delivered them and reenacting this deliverance, often through poetic recitation of the story either in song or word. This emphasis on worship-through-reenactment began with Israel at Sinai and continued throughout Israel's history as a nation. Worship-through-reenactment was a pattern sustained in hearing God's word in early synagogue gatherings. Most scholars date the emergence of synagogues during Judah's exilic period. Reenactment through keeping Passover was commanded in the Mosaic law and was a unifying event after the exile under the leadership of Ezra.

At the beginning of Moses' story it was important to the patriarch to know the name and, therefore, the identity of the God who called him into such challenging service. Moses needed assurance that this God who called him was a God whose actions would prove to be an extension of divine character. The God who claims the self-identity of "I AM" was a challenge for the early weakness of Moses' faith when this shepherd was more interested in a God of "I do"!

In his struggle to obey, Moses wanted to know *how* God would accomplish something. Moses wanted to know how God could possibly overrule powerful Pharaoh, deliver a small nation of people from a powerful kingdom, or even equip himself, a reluctant, ungifted fugitive, for such an undertaking. "Who am I that I should go to Pharaoh?" Moses asked (Exodus 3:11), and Yahweh first responded to Moses' concern by promising his divine presence and making the prophet another promise: "I will be with you; and this shall be the sign for you that it is I who sent you: when you have brought the people out of Egypt, you shall worship God on this mountain" (Exodus 3:12). Essentially, Yahweh's relationship to Moses was all that ultimately mattered (Exodus 3:14).

So he could more fully understand the promise of this God to deliver Israel from Pharaoh's bondage, Moses needed to know the name of the God he was being called to serve (Exodus 3:1-15). The divine name, *Yahweh*, is usually translated in English as "LORD God," but is often rendered YHWH, which can be translated "I am who I am" or "I will be what I will be." The perfect suitability of this name for identifying Israel's God actually reveals the complete and perfect integrity between who God is and what God does. Yahweh does what he does because of who he is. This was the God Moses was asked to trust, obey and worship. The important idea here regarding worship is that Moses was called to worship (and obey) because of who God is. The divine character would be affirmed by what God did, and he would bring his people out of Egypt to worship on the "holy ground" (Exodus 3:5) of Horeb, the mountain of God (3:1). The sign of Yahweh's covenant-keeping triumph would be celebrated by Moses and the people gathering to commemorate and worship the God who had delivered them (Exodus 3:12).

Yahweh promised to bring the whole company of his people back to "this mountain" to worship him with praise and thanks. Israel would come to know Yahweh through his faithfulness to them. God kept his promise, and Moses and the people assembled at the mountain of God to worship as a "priestly kingdom and a holy nation" (Exodus 19:6). And in this place, as Yahweh promised, Israel received the Decalogue (Ten Commandments) and the Law that were the definitive texts for the worship and life of Israel.

It is important to note that the first four of the Ten Commandments focus on how Israel was to worship the God who had delivered them (Exodus 20:1-7). The following six show how this worship would be manifest in Israel's conduct in every aspect of life (Exodus 20:8-17). The first four commandments of the Decalogue still provide the foundation for biblical patterns of worship. First, the worship of God's people is exclusively for Yahweh alone (Exodus 20:2-3). Second, the worship of Israel's God is to be free from the use of idols, any representation of Yahweh that is like anything in creation. Third, the worship of God's people is to shape the integrity of those who are called by God's name. They are to bear the divine name carefully and reverently use the divine name only in ways that honor Yahweh (Exodus 20:7). And fourth, holiness is grounded in how God's people "remember the sabbath day, and keep it holy." To work six days and "cease" (the literal meaning of the Hebrew word for sabbath) working on every seventh day was meant to help Israel reenact the very rhythm of God's work and celebrate a "holiday," a holy day, in the ordering of creation itself (Exodus 20:8-11). Trusting God with time to work and time to rest is foundational to the pattern of holiness that his people were to make evident.

WORSHIP PATTERNS IN THE PENTATEUCH

From the bullet points of the Decalogue, the law develops and details how Yahweh's people are to worship, work and live. In all of this, the law was to enhance Israel's distinctive identity in contrast to surrounding cultures. The distinctive marks of Israel's worship were paramount to this endeavor. In his book *The Religion of Ancient Israel*, Old Testament professor Patrick D. Miller outlines six significant markers for the orthodox worship of Yahweh. First, those faithful to Yahweh were to offer worship exclusively to Yahweh and without any appeal to or mediation of images. Yahweh's worship was to be aniconic, worship without idols. Aniconic worship lent itself to a deepening sense of the biblical understanding of faith as the "conviction of things not seen" (Hebrews 11:1).

Second, Yahweh conveyed the divine will by means of a prophetic word or dream, an oracle inquiry (casting lots within the sacred assembly), or a vision. The law forbade divination, soothsaying or communicating with the dead. The distinction between what was permitted and what was forbidden lies in the fact that those means permitted in the Scripture are God-given, God-directed gifts of divine grace. The latter are humanly initiated attempts to find the will of the gods.

Third, sanctuaries or altars were erected in a variety of places that commemorated events initiated by Yahweh and were used for sacrifices and as gathering places for festival meals, prayer and thanksgiving offerings. Again, certain things associated with the worship of other gods were prohibited for the worship of Israel, such as the fertility rites that involved sacred pillars, poles, cultic prostitutes, images or human sacrifice of any kind.

Fourth, the law set certain times for gathering whole families or the whole community to remember and reenact Yahweh's great acts of deliverance and redemption (see Exodus 23:14-19 and Leviticus 23 for specific examples). Fifth, for the people faithful to Yahweh and set apart for the worship of Yahweh, it was expected that this holiness would extend into every moral and ethical area of life (Exodus 20:12-17). Finally, the leadership of Israel, especially that of the priests and prophets, was expected to address the concerns of the spiritual, social, personal and communal dynamics of everyday life in the holy service of Yahweh and Yahweh's people.[1]

All of these particular traits are incorporated into the rhythm of weekly sabbath-keeping and the attendance of God's people at yearly festivals which constituted the "church year" for Israel. The annual festivals were the reenactment of Passover as the Feast of Unleavened Bread, second, the Festival of Harvest with the offering of "first fruits" and, lastly, the Festival of Ingathering at the end of the harvest. All of these festivals were designed to underscore Israel's dependence on Yahweh as deliverer and provider.

Another practice in the Pentateuch not covered in the Exodus account at Sinai is the Day of Atonement (Leviticus 16:30-34), a yearly event that was distinguished from the festivals by its solemn rituals and its sober focus on the confession of and forgiveness for Israel's sin. The sacrificial offerings designated in the Mosaic law consisted of four kinds of offerings and were a significant part of the festivals that marked the rhythm of God's people. The burnt offering was a component of the peace offering (Leviticus 3:3), the sin offering (Leviticus 4:8-10) and the guilt offering (Leviticus 7:3-5. Some Old Testament scholars, such as Alec Motyer, often refer to the guilt offering as the "satisfaction offering" based on their translation of the Hebrew term for this sacrifice. The burnt offering was completely consumed on the altar and ascended in the smoke, which was an expression of radical commitment before the LORD. Literally nothing was held back from the offering of "atonement, acceptance and consecration."[2]

The peace offering, in contrast, was intended as part of a fellowship meal with only a token amount of the animal offered in the sacrificial rite. Indeed, it was intended to celebrate one's peace with God and the community. The

---

[1]Patrick D. Miller, *The Religion of Ancient Israel* (Louisville: Westminster John Knox, 2000), pp. 48-51. Miller's book is part of the Library of Ancient Israel series published by Westminster John Knox Press and is an exceptionally well-written and well-documented overview of Israel's faith and practice.

[2]Alec Motyer, *The Story of the Old Testament* (Grand Rapids: Baker, 2001), p. 37. The summary of the sacrifices and offerings of Israel in this section is drawn from many sources, but Motyer's work is exceptionally well summarized and illustrated in this primer on the Old Testament.

sin offering, as its name implies, was offered to the LORD as an expression of needed forgiveness for specific offenses. Motyer makes the point that "the sin-offering was a divine provision (Leviticus 17:11) to which was attached a divine promise (of forgiveness); in making his offering the believer rested in faith on that promise."[3] The satisfaction offering (Leviticus 5:14–6:7) was focused on the full covering of all ramifications of sin in human life.

Motyer and others point out that the particular ordering of the sacrifices varied in how the Mosaic law set out the details of festivals and their sacrificial rites.

> In Exodus 29:14,18, 28 and Leviticus 9:8, 11, 18, it is sin-offering, burnt-offering and peace-offering. *This is the order of human need*: from our point of view we are ever aware of sin, and only when sin has been dealt with can we then consecrate ourselves to God and enter into peaceful fellowship.
>
> In Leviticus 6:9, 24; 7:11, it is burnt-offering, sin-offering and peace-offering. *This is the order of priestly duty*: twice daily, burnt offerings must be offered on the LORD's altar where a perpetual fire must be maintained. Constantly sinners needed the priestly ministry of the sin-offering, leading them into peace with God.
>
> In Leviticus 1:3; 3:1; 4:3 it is burnt-offering, peace-offering, sin-offering. *This is the order of divine desire*: the LORD looks for a people wholly yielded to him, and enjoying fellowship with him and with each other. In mercy, he provides a sin-offering to cater for their lapses from that holy obedience which is their great priority.[4]

Through the rhythm of a liturgical year, Israel was to be shaped as a people called into a vibrant and accountable relationship with their God. This relationship was significantly defined by their practice of worship. Yahweh, as deliverer and provider, expected exclusive allegiance, the practice of holiness in every area of life, offerings that fittingly expressed Israel's gratitude, and the rhythmic rehearsal year in and year out that celebrated Israel's dependence upon its God for the gift of life itself. In the practices of early Israel, the sacrifices carried meaning but they were not thought of as symbolic in the sense of prefiguring fulfillment beyond the intention of the practice itself. Only later in Israel's history, most notably in Isaiah,

---

[3]Ibid.
[4]Ibid. Emphasis in the original.

was there the development of a hope for an ultimate fulfillment that was at least a part of messianic expectations.[5]

The weekly and annual rhythms of life and work and worship should mark the communities of God's people today. The particularities of how the elements of worship and community life are carried out may differ between Israel and the church of Jesus Christ, but recognizing the exclusive allegiance God demands is the same—just as God is still the deliverer and provider for his people.

KEEPING THE SABBATH HOLY

The rhythm of sabbath rest was foundational for the identity of Israel and the exclusive nature of Israel's worship. But it is important to remember that the weekly rhythm of the sabbath predates the Mosaic law and is, in fact, grounded in the rhythm of creation itself. The first time the idea of anything being holy is recorded in Scripture is in the hallowing of the seventh day in Genesis 2. From the beginning of creation, holiness is grounded in a particular rhythm of time.

The seventh day of God's creation is inaugurated when

> the heavens and the earth were finished, and all their multitude. And on the seventh day God finished the work that he had done, and he rested on the seventh day from all the work that he had done. So God blessed the seventh day and hallowed it, because on it God rested from all the work that he had done in creation. (Genesis 2:1-3)

It is noteworthy that the refrain for each episode of God's creative initiation ends with "And there was evening and there was morning" (Genesis 1:5, 8, 13, 19, 23 and 31), except for the seventh day. It's as though the sabbath rest of God never comes to an end. God rested, blessed and sanctified a day (a holy day, a holiday) to enjoy what he had made. Later, as the writer of Genesis considers the rest of God in the light of sabbath-keeping reflected in the Mosaic law, he clearly sees its foundation in the character and activity of God himself. In the Mosaic sabbath regulations, God explicitly calls his

---

[5]For another fine treatment of the development of theology in the Old Testament, consider a well-developed volume, William S. La Sor, David A. Hubbard and Frederic W. Bush, eds., *Old Testament Survey: The Message, Form, and Background of the Old Testament* (Grand Rapids: Eerdmans, 1982).

people to cease their work, to rest, and to be blessed and sanctified by God through participating in the divine rhythm of time in keeping sabbath. The invitation to enter into God's rest one day in seven was always an invitation based on divine grace, to join in God's "holiday."

The rhythm of six days for work and the seventh day to rest was expanded in the Mosaic law to a cycle of years for farming (Exodus 23:10-11; Leviticus 25:1-7). The very rhythm of life and work and rest was partly designed to strengthen Israel's faithfulness to Yahweh and faith in Yahweh to provide for his people in a way that could not be accounted for merely by their own own work, their own efforts. The same rhythm dominated Israel's treatment of other people, including slaves, and the legislation of Jubilee (Leviticus 25). The people's relationship to the land as well as to others was deeply rooted in the rhythm commanded by Yahweh through the sabbath law.

It is important, as well as interesting, to note that this rhythm was tied explicitly in the law to the exclusion of idolatry among the people of Israel (Exodus 23:12-13). Old Testament scholar Walter Brueggemann affirms that sabbath-keeping for Israel was meant to foster a deep faith within God's people that "life does not consist in production and acquisition, but in the reception of gifts from YHWH mediated through the community."[6]

The biblical rhythm of work and rest affirms the goodness of creation both before and after the fall. This pattern, of course, comes to its ultimate expression in the life of Christ Jesus, the Lord of the sabbath. Carol Bechtel makes several salient points concerning early Israel, sabbath law in the Pentateuch, and God's grace in the invitation to share God's own rhythm of work and rest as one way of anticipating God's habitation in creation in the incarnation. Bechtel notes that the sabbath law in Exodus 20 is associated with the Genesis account as noted above, but she goes on to consider insightfully why God, who does not need to rest to recover, would set aside a "holy-day" simply to inhabit and enjoy the result of his work.

> God is Alpha and Omega, beginning and end, sovereign over all human time. But by resting on the sabbath, God willingly enters into and becomes subject

---

[6]Walter Brueggemann, *Worship in Ancient Israel* (Nashville: Abingdon Press, 2005), p. 18. Brueggemann's book accents the way Israel's worship was fully dialogical so that both parties knew they were fully present as the relationship of Yahweh with his people was defined over and over again.

to the created framework of human time that God had just created.

This act of divine resting on the sabbath day of creation is the first instance of God's gracious accommodation, God's self-limiting, the first step toward the eventual coming of God in human flesh in the person of Jesus.[7]

Bechtel contrasts God's self-limitation in the incarnation with Jesus' need for sleep and contrasts this with his authority over creation as the Word of God by using an illustration from the Synoptic Gospels. Jesus was asleep on a boat while crossing a lake in Galilee and was awakened by his disciples, who were afraid they might perish during a threatening storm. The man who needed a nap is also the embodiment of the Creator who stills the storm by speaking a word (Matthew 8:23-27; Mark 4:35-41; and Luke 8:22-25). Bechtel concludes,

> The community of Jesus' disciples gathered in a boat was for the early church a common symbol of Christians gathered in community for worship. Even today the inside architecture of many church buildings represents an inverted boat or ship. The image also recalls the story of Noah and the ark, with Noah's family being saved from the raging floods of Genesis 6–9. The Noah narrative is the story of another new creation. This same divine power to create, tame chaos, and begin sabbath rest is evident here in Jesus, who both rests and acts in power to save. Rest, peace, calm—creation's seventh day offers to worshipers a sabbath refuge from the winds, storms, and waves that buffet our workdays and threaten to throw us off balance or even drown us in the waters of chaos.[8]

In the beginning of Israel's practice of sabbath most scholars conclude that "sabbath-keeping" was limited to the rest of people and work animals—it was simply a day of rest. Only later in pre-exilic Judah (Hosea 2:11) and in the post-exilic writings (Chronicles) is there a connection of sabbath rest with the gathering of God's people for corporate worship. The rhythm of life and work and rest was partly designed to strengthen Israel's faithfulness *to* Yahweh; it was also meant to foster faith *in* Yahweh to provide for his people. The law included directions for worship, sacrificial offerings, feast days and other celebrations, all designed to keep Israel focused on her ex-

---

[7]Carol Bechtel, *Touching the Altar: The Old Testament for Christian Worship* (Grand Rapids: Eerdmans, 2008), p. 13.
[8]Ibid., pp. 10-14.

clusive allegiance to Yahweh. Patrick Miller remarks that "as the Sabbath became increasingly a mark of identity for the Jewish people, the holiness of the Sabbath coincided with the holiness of the people as a way of marking them off distinctively from other nations."[9]

In all of this, both orderly sequence and refreshing variety were included in the law given to Moses for the people of God. And, throughout Israel's history, the divine rhythm of work, rest and worship was kept as a central identifying reality of Israel's life. However, as evidenced in the New Testament Gospel accounts, the sabbath practice of Israel was corrupted when sabbath law was divorced from the LORD of the sabbath.

THE LORD OF THE SABBATH

In the narrative texts of the monarchy in the united Israel and after the civil war that divided Israel into northern and southern kingdoms, there is little mention of sabbath law or issues of sabbath-keeping. However, Isaiah and Jeremiah, the pre-exilic prophets of the southern kingdom Judah, denounced the breaking of sabbath law and emphasized how doing so profaned what was holy. Isaiah speaks as the prophetic voice of the LORD, saying,

> If you refrain from trampling the sabbath,
>   from pursuing your own interests on my holy day;
> if you call the sabbath a delight
>   and the holy day of the LORD honorable;
> if you honor it, not going your own ways,
>   serving your own interests, or pursuing your own affairs;
> then you shall take delight in the LORD,
>   and I will make you ride upon the heights of the earth;
> I will feed you with the heritage of your ancestor Jacob,
>   for the mouth of the LORD has spoken. (Isaiah 58:13-14)

---

[9]Miller, *Religion of Ancient Israel,* p. 141. Miller's chapter on the holiness and purity of Israel's religious practice is a fine summary of how the issues surrounding the holiness of the divine cult included space, persons and time in a variety of ways. However, Miller rightly argues how sabbath-keeping was, over time, the supreme identifying mark of those faithful to Yahweh. It should come as no surprise that the distinctive way Jesus and his followers kept the sabbath (or failed to in the eyes of their critics) is highly significant and a central interest in the New Testament Gospels.

It is apparent in this text that Israel's God desired his people to see the day of rest as a delight and not a burden. The sabbath was meant to positively foster the practice and joy of holiness, not negatively fence in God's people for fear of offending the God who invited them into the holy rest of a relationship with him. In the post-exilic period before the New Testament, Israel felt hard pressed to find a way to please God in order to restore the blessing of Yahweh. In the oppressive shadow of a series of pagan conquests and rule, Israel longed to "ride upon the heights of the earth" (Isaiah 58:14) and end their domination by foreign rulers.

Like most people, Israel found that it was easier to control their conduct by the rule of law than the rule of love. A legalistic application of the law was simpler to regulate and more helpful in defining the line between the profane and the holy. Israel wanted to be a people made for the sabbath!

By the time of the New Testament, the relative simplicity of ceasing, resting and celebrating on the seventh day in the Torah had been overwhelmed by "how to" regulations designed to protect the holiness of both the day and the people. This protective wall, intended by Israel's leaders to guard sabbath-keeping, actually created a barrier that impeded the relationship of gift and grace that Yahweh desired with Israel. Sabbath-keeping for Israel regulated every area of life, and by the first century, the rabbinical and scribal traditions that overlay the Mosaic commands had grown into a complex legal industry understood only by the educated elite. However, sabbath law observance was expected of all who wanted to be faithful to Yahweh.

One cannot read the Gospels and fail to realize that, in the light of Jewish practice in the first century, Jesus reinterpreted sabbath law. This reinterpretation led to early and ongoing conflict between Jesus and the Pharisees, the religiopolitical descendents of the Hasmonean dynasty. The Hasmoneans were a priestly family that had prevailed over the Greek Seleucid rulers and had secured for the Jews 103 years (166–63 B.C.) of relatively independent rule that ended with the conquest by the Roman Empire in 63 B.C. One cannot overstate the importance of sabbath-keeping to the average Jew, let alone a Pharisaic Jew, in first-century Palestine. Nevertheless, Jesus, as God's Son who knew the joy, true rest and importance of the sabbath from "the beginning," intentionally engaged with both grace and truth the issues that swirled around the Jewish day of rest.

In the Synoptic Gospels, an inaugural event for Jesus' public ministry was teaching on the sabbath in the synagogue of Capernaum (Mark 1:21-28; Luke 4:31-37). The reaction of those who heard Jesus' teaching is notable: "They were astounded at his teaching, for he taught them as one having authority, and not as the scribes" (Mark 1:22; cf. Luke 4:32). Soon after this, or possibly on the same sabbath day, Jesus healed Peter's mother-in-law of a fever (Mark 1:29-31; Luke 4:38-39). The Gospels continue the story by stating, "That evening, at sunset" (Mark 1:32) and "As the sun was setting" (Luke 4:40), to indicate the time when the inhabitants of Capernaum and the surrounding area came to Peter's house seeking Jesus for healing. Keeping the sabbath rule was so important to the Jews in this seaside Galilean town that they would not come for help until the day ended at sundown. In contrast, it seems that Jesus helped Peter's mother-in-law immediately upon arrival at Peter's home, well before the sabbath sun had set.

This reintroduction of God's grace and goodness as a way of understanding the purpose of the sabbath is repeated in the Gospels when Jesus explicitly defends his practice and those of the disciples when the situation called for it. One notable time in the Synoptic Gospels is the juxtaposition of two stories that center on sabbath law and Jesus' reinterpretation of the sabbath law. These two narrative stories are the episode of Jesus' disciples picking heads of grain while walking through a field on the sabbath and, immediately following, Jesus in a nearby synagogue healing a man with a "withered hand" on the sabbath (Matthew 12:1-8, 9-14; Mark 2:23-28; 3:1-6; Luke 6:1-5, 6-10).[10]

In the first pericope, Jesus defends the freedom of his disciples to have what amounted to a snack, a handful of nuts, on the sabbath. Some regulations within the complexities of sabbath rule would consider plucking grain akin to the full-blown harvesting of a field on the day of rest. Jesus takes this opportunity to remind his critics that "the sabbath was made for humankind, and not humankind for the sabbath" (Mark 2:27). In this way,

---

[10]Only Luke's account clearly states that the two accounts of the disciples eating grain in the field and Jesus healing the man with the withered hand in the synagogue happened on different sabbath days. However, the juxtaposition of the two narrative stories in all three Synoptic Gospel accounts underscores the importance of considering the connection between the two stories and Jesus' teaching in each narrative.

Jesus underscores the intention of Yahweh in giving the rest of the seventh day as a *gift*. The sabbath day is supposed to be good for God's people. However, sinful people find it much easier to work or do something, anything, than to really rest. Human beings have to *learn* how to rest, especially how to enter into the sabbath rest of God. In fact, in Matthew's Gospel, these two pericopes are introduced by Jesus' invitation:

> Come to me, all you that are weary and are carrying heavy burdens, and I will give you rest. Take my yoke upon you, and *learn from me*; for I am gentle and humble in heart, and you will find rest for your souls. For my yoke is easy, and my burden is light. (Matthew 11:28-30; emphasis added)

Jesus underscored one principle of sabbath-keeping: it is a learned discipline meant to be good for God's people. In the pericope that follows, Jesus delineates the boundary of goodness and grace for one's conduct on the sabbath. All three Synoptic Gospels support the notion that the man with the withered hand was in the synagogue as a test to see if Jesus would in fact heal him on the sabbath (Matthew 12:10; Mark 3:2; Luke 6:7). Although different rabbinical traditions set a variety of boundaries for interpreting the sabbath law, the Pharisees, who had the most dominant position in Galilee, taught it was wrong even to pray for healing on the sabbath![11]

It is important to note how carefully Jesus went about healing this man. Jesus began by asking those gathered if it is considered "lawful to do good" on the sabbath. Jesus framed the question by asking the common rabbinical question of whether one would rescue a sheep or an ox from a pit if it were to fall in on the sabbath. Most rabbinical schools, even that of the Pharisees, would have agreed that this was permitted. Notice that Jesus didn't "do" anything but ask the man to step forward and stretch out his hand. As the man did so, his hand "was restored" (Matthew 12:13; Mark 3:5; Luke 6:10).

In this incident, two additional principles of sabbath-keeping are underscored: it is a day appropriate for doing good on behalf of others, and it is a day for attending to the word of God. The New Testament reflects how these principles greatly shaped the sabbath practices of the emerging church

---

[11]One good and easy-to-use resource for cultural background information on the New Testament is Craig Keener's *The IVP Bible Background Commentary: New Testament* (Downers Grove, Ill.: IVP Academic, 1994). Also see Anthony Tomasino, *Judaism Before Jesus: The Events & Ideas That Shaped the New Testament World* (Downers Grove, Ill.: IVP Academic, 2003).

after Pentecost. The freedom of this kind of sabbath observance unfettered the Jewish believers from the matrix of rabbinical *hălākôt*, the interpretations of Torah that derived legal principles from a text. This freedom reoriented God's people around what it means to learn sabbath rest from Jesus, the Lord of the sabbath. As Gentiles flooded into the Christian church, whose foundation was grounded in Judaism, this freedom eventually led to the predominant practice of Christians gathering for worship on the first day of the week, the day of the Lord's resurrection, in distinction from the seventh-day sabbath of Judaism. However, the Christian Sunday retained the central concept of sabbath rest and the principles embedded in what Yahweh intended for Israel in the Mosaic law. Sunday became a day to attend to the word of God and do good for others—indeed, a day that is still a good gift of God's grace for his people.

THE LORD'S DAY RHYTHM IN CHRISTIAN WORSHIP

Because the Christian faith was built on the foundation of Judaism, it is important to remember that the first disciples of Jesus were faithful Jews. Jesus was a good Jew, and even though he reinterpreted sabbath law in distinction to many rabbinical traditions, Jesus and his followers kept the sabbath by doing good to others and attending to the word of God (Mark 1:21; 6:2; Luke 4:16, 31; 13:10). Joseph of Arimathea and the women who followed Jesus and attended to his burial did so within the limits of sabbath observance (Mark 15:42; 16:1-2). These disciples, indeed all the apostles in the early church, including Paul, participated in Jewish festivals, kept vows (Acts 20:16; 21:23-26) and prayed at the times Jewish tradition designated for community prayer (Acts 3:1).

During the early days of the church's post-Pentecost growth in Jerusalem, the temple area was used regularly by the disciples to teach great crowds (see the narratives in Acts 3–5). The fledgling Christian community may have "taken over" Solomon's Portico, a favored teaching place of Jesus (John 10:23), for gathering and teaching (Acts 3:11; 5:12). At least until the end of Paul's third missionary journey and his arrest in the temple court (Acts 21:27-28), Christian Jews had access to the temple as usual. However, Jesus himself warned his followers that they would be put out of the synagogue (John 16:2). In the Synoptic Gospels, Jesus warned of the fracturing of

Jewish homes because of allegiance to him (Matthew 10:34-36; Luke 12:51-53). The expulsion of Jewish Christians from local synagogues began very early (John 9:22) and continued and intensified over time. As Gentiles joined the church in increasing numbers the need grew for both space and time independent from the traditions of Judaism.

In the earliest days of the church, Jewish Christians kept most religious practices on the seventh day. This seems to be the case when Saul of Tarsus was given official permission to arrest and persecute Jewish Christians in Damascus since they could be found in the synagogue on the sabbath (Acts 9:2). The first Jewish Christians functioned in two distinct communities: the Jewish community as a whole and that of Jews who believed in Jesus as Messiah. Therefore it seems that Jewish Christians also began to assemble to pray and hear the teaching of the apostles on the first day of the week, the day after the Jewish sabbath. Jewish believers gathered on "the Lord's Day," the day of Jesus' resurrection, for fellowship, teaching, prayer and worship in the earliest days of the emerging church. While this is particularly notable in the ministry of the apostle Paul, the pattern was also adopted throughout the church as Gentiles joined the Jewish sect of the Nazarene (Acts 24:5).

Paul's earlier writings also reflect that Christian worship on Sunday was assumed. In his first letter to the Corinthians, written around A.D. 55, just a little over twenty years after the crucifixion and resurrection of Jesus, Paul mentions the collection of charitable offerings on "the first day of every week" (1 Corinthians 16:2) as a part of gathering for worship on that day. About a year later, in Troas, the "first day of the week" is mentioned (Acts 20:7) for a gathering of Christians during the evening hours. Meeting on the first day of the week may have been an early pattern in Paul's ministry with Barnabas in Antioch, and its acceptance quickly and easily became widespread. This development makes perfect sense because the earliest Christians were Jews who kept sabbath traditions on the seventh day and yet wanted to gather and worship as believers in Christ too. Worshiping on the first day of the week as a commemoration of Jesus' resurrection was certainly appropriate. Many Jewish Christians may have met early in the morning after the Jewish sabbath was over, not only to mark the time of Jesus' resurrection but to worship the risen Christ before they had to begin their work for the week. Sunday was a regular work day in the Roman Empire. Others may have gathered at the close of Sunday, for similar work-related reasons.[12]

As the second generation of the church emerged in the last third of the first century, the adoption of Sunday worship for the whole church seems well established. The practice of Christian worship on the Lord's Day is clearly delineated in the *Didache* (pronounced did'-ă-kāy), or the "Teaching of the Twelve." The *Didache* was an explanation of "the Way," a moniker for the early church (Acts 19:23; 24:22). Christian worship, the order of baptism and the celebration of the Lord's Supper are mentioned in this ancient writing. Many scholars place the writing of the *Didache* in the last third of the first century. Some date the *Didache* earlier, as it seems to be uninfluenced by the writings of either Paul or John, while others date its writing to the early to mid second century. For the purposes of this chapter, it is sufficient to note that worship on the Lord's Day was a result of the church's early and continuing differentiation of itself from Judaism. However, the content and ordering of Christian worship continued to follow the Jewish patterns of worship forged through the Mosaic law and Israel's historical development.[13]

CONCLUSION

Israel's exclusive faithfulness to Yahweh and the unique aspects of Israel's rhythm of life and worship differentiated Israel from the people who worshiped other gods. From the Hebrew Scripture through the time of the New Testament, this put Israel at odds with the surrounding world. Paul's admo-

---

[12]Laurie Guy, *Introducing Early Christianity* (Downers Grove, Ill.: IVP Academic, 2004), p. 212. Guy makes a point from the admonition in Hebrews 10:25 that "not neglecting to meet together" may imply that not everyone gathered for worship on Sunday. However, Sunday observance would have been a particular challenge for the Christian community for whom the book of Hebrews was written. This first audience for Hebrews was composed of Jewish Christians who struggled with their Jewish identity as the Jewish rejection of Jesus as Messiah accelerated prior to the Jewish War that led to the destruction of the Temple in A.D. 70. It is significant that the writer of the Hebrews underscored the importance of gathering together as Christians for worship and fellowship.

[13]Paul McKechnie has a helpful summary of the *Didache* and its content in his book *The First Christian Centuries: Perspectives on the Early Church* (Downers Grove, Ill.: IVP Academic, 2002), pp. 68-71. The *Didache*'s contribution to understanding the development of Christian worship will be considered more fully in chapter 8 of this book.

nition to the church in Rome to "not be conformed to this world" had been God's admonition to Israel through prophets, priests and the law. Paul's encouragement to "be transformed by the renewing of your mind" had long been God's goal in the rhythms mandated for Israel's life and worship.

Training in holiness has always seemed just as unnatural as it is necessary for the people of God. The sabbath rhythm of Israel which shifted to worship on the Lord's Day in the church is still God's great gift of goodness to his people. It's still true that this weekly rhythm for corporate worship "was made for humankind" as an expression of God's grace (Mark 2:27). Unceasing work and worry, the addiction to controlling our lives, and regulating our own attempts at sanctification show how far God's people have strayed from trusting God for his goodness. It's easier to live by rules than by faith in the Lord who rules. It's good for God's people to enter into the rest of God in this rhythm of grace in order to worship the God who has faithfully kept his promises. God's people are still identified by the God they worship and serve through the biblical rhythm of hallowed time.

Worship-through-reenactment was manifest in the practices of the early church. Jesus' reinterpretation of the Jewish Passover meal in the institution of the "Lord's Supper" clearly reflects the idea of reenactment as a prominent pattern of worship for God's people. Baptism for first-century Jews signaled a commitment to Yahweh as ancient Israel "crossed the Jordan" and for Christians with Jesus' baptism as his identification with human need for God's righteousness through the forgiveness of sin. The pattern of worship-through-reenactment even continued as Christian worship became increasingly distinct from Judaism. The patterns of worship that reenact the unfolding of salvation history are still seen prominently in the liturgies of the Roman Catholic Mass and Orthodox Churches, and in denominations and congregations historically linked to the Reformation.

Patterns of reenactment help shape Christian worship in order to reflect the biblical story that is central to a congregation's identity as God's people. Patterns of reenactment also serve as a corrective to worship which is designed mainly for the contemporary concerns of a congregation. They help worshipers remember that their moment in history is not, in fact, the ultimate moment of salvation history. God's story of salvation is bigger, older and far more comprehensive than our personal part of that story. Corporate worship is a gathering of God's people to serve the God who has saved his people and brought them together to recall, rehearse and enter into the dynamic of God's salvation story. Like Abel who reenacted God's saving grace in the story of his family, like God himself who entered creation to holiday and rest, and like Jesus as the Lord of the sabbath, patterns of reenactment celebrate the character of God and his remptive work in the world.

WORKSHOP FOR CHAPTER TWO

1. Think about the pattern of worship for the congregational service in which you most often participate.

   - What parts of the service are practices of reenactment?

   - How are connections made between the meaning of what is being remembered and the contemporary reenactment of that historical event?

2. Jesus reflects God's identity and perfect integrity when he identifies himself as one who does because of who he is. Jesus said, "I am the resurrection" (John 11:25), not "I do" the resurrection. As God's only begotten Son, Jesus is like Yahweh and bears a seamless integrity between being and doing.

   - How might this dynamic play a part in shaping the dynamic of personal and congregational prayers of praise or intercession?

3. Consider the following questions about sabbath rhythm:

   - How might "ceasing" one day a week foster faith in God's grace to provide for what one needs?

   - How might the divine rhythm of work and rest encourage the growth of holiness in one's life?

   - How might the intentional practice of rest within the community impact one's commitment to corporate worship and investing in God's mission to the world?

4. In the mid second century B.C., the priest Mattathias and his five sons led a successful Jewish revolt against the oppressive rule of the Greek Seleucids. In the early days of the resistance, many Jews from Jerusalem

and Judea fled to the wilderness to escape the onslaught of the ruthlessly brutal Seleucid army.

One confrontation in the wilderness happened on the sabbath, and over one thousand Jewish men, women and children were slaughtered because they refused to take up arms to defend themselves or to even barricade the entrances to the caves in which they were hiding. For these faithful Jews either taking up a sword or moving a rock would have profaned the sabbath.

However, after this the priestly family of Mattathias, the Hasmoneans, held a council and certain regulations for sabbath observance were suspended until the crisis was over. It was determined that the Jews would not initiate any conflict on the sabbath during this time but that they could vigorously defend themselves if attacked.

- Think through how flexibility in resting on the sabbath or the Lord's Day can also help you practice the biblical rhythm of grace. Keep a month-long log of how and when you spend time in prayer, in reading and studying the Scripture, and in worship, both personal and corporate. At the conclusion of the month, note the patterns (or lack of patterns) of time in these pursuits.

5. Consider what changes might be helpful in nurturing a biblical rhythm for work and rest that reflects God's own pattern in creation and God's mandate in the law, "Six days you shall labor and do all your work. But the seventh day is a sabbath to the LORD your God; you shall not do any work" (Exodus 20:9-10). Like most people, Israel found that it was easier to control its conduct by the rule of law instead of the rule of love.

- Consider how the gospel of Jesus Christ can be a corrective to strident legalism that can mark some practices of keeping the sabbath holy. How might the "rule of love" help you truly rest in God's grace?

- Reflect on how you and your faith community "keep the sabbath holy" today.

6. Review the six characteristics of orthodox Yahwism and consider how Christian worship as you've experienced it has kept, modified or eliminated them.

7. The chart below summarizes the major annual festivals of early Israel. How might the intention of these festivals be recognized and celebrated in the yearly calendar of your faith community?

Table 1

NAME	MOSAIC REFERENCES	TIME (based on lunar calendar)	PURPOSE OF FESTIVAL REENACTMENT
Passover	Exodus 12:1-14; Leviticus 23:5; Numbers 9; 28:16	*Abib 14* **March–April**	To recall and celebrate Yahweh's deliverance of Israel from Egypt
Unleavened Bread	Exodus 12:15-20; 13:3-10; 23:15; 34:18; Leviticus 23:6-8	*Abib 15–21* *Abib 16*	To reenact the way Israel left Egypt in haste
First Fruits	Leviticus 23:9-14		To give thanks for Yahweh's provision and bounty in the Promised Land
Festival of Weeks/ Harvest; Pentecost	Exodus 23:16; 34:22; Leviticus 23:15-21; Numbers 28:26-31	*Silvan 6* **May–June**	To offer the first fruits of harvest to thank Yahweh for his favor and faithfulness
Trumpets (now known as Rosh Hashanah/ beginning of Jewish New Year)	Leviticus 23:23-25; Numbers 29:1-6	*Tishri 1* **Sept.–Oct.**	To present Israel before the LORD to acknowledge Yahweh's favor
Yom Kippur (Day of Atonement)	Leviticus 16; 23:26-32; Numbers 29:7-11	*Tishri 10*	To present the burnt offering for the cleansing of priests and people
Tabernacles/Festival of Booths	Exodus 23:16; 34:22; Leviticus 23:33-36, 39-43	*Tishri 15–21*	To reenact Israel's journey in the wilderness and acknowledge Yahweh's faithful presence before arrival in the Promised Land

WORSHIP AND SACRED SPACE

THE GRACE OF INVITATION,
THE HOLINESS OF BOUNDARIES

When . . . you . . . live in their land, take care that you are not snared

into imitating them. . . . Do not inquire concerning their gods, saying,

"How did these nations worship their gods? I also want to do the same."

DEUTERONOMY 12:29-30

The patterns for where, how and why Israel was called to worship are clearly discernible in the Mosaic law and its surrounding narrative, as well as in the book of Joshua as the people enter and settle into the land promised to Abraham. Building on the rhythm of sacred time, this chapter will consider foundational ideas in these biblical texts concerning God's design for sacred space set apart for the worship of Israel's God. Worship as a response to God's gracious invitation is given significantly detailed shape and direction by Yahweh. Israel also learned the hard way about the perils of designing worship shaped by their own ideas, to meet their own needs. Consideration for how the sacred space for Christian worship needs to still reflect the grace of invitation with the boundaries necessitated by God's holiness will conclude the chapter.

HOLY PLACES, SACRED SPACE

Worship that is pleasing to God is offered in places set apart for the purpose of serving[1] God with the fullness of heart, soul, mind and strength. Like Moses, God asks his people to "turn aside" (Exodus 3:3) and focus on a divine encounter as a part of worship. The root meaning of the word "holy" is to be "set apart" for a special purpose. Holy places are those "set apart" for attending to divine service. There is such a thing as "holy ground." Scripture does give guidance for responding to the invitation of God to "turn aside" and reverently and joyfully draw near to be engaged by the God who calls. In terms of sacred space, God still wants a special place to be set apart for one's encounter with the Holy God in corporate worship. Moses was commanded to take off his shoes (Exodus 3:5) and Joshua was told to do the same during his encounter with the divine on "holy ground" (Joshua 5:13-15). In the ancient Near East (ANE), taking off one's sandals was a sign of ridding oneself of impurities in the presence of the holy and was a common practice of priests. In the biblical texts Yahweh commands his servants to remove their shoes as a sign that the Holy One, the God of Israel, has called them to worship and invited them into his presence.[2]

The pattern in biblical worship of divesting oneself of what doesn't belong and investing oneself with what does belong is underscored in the book of Deuteronomy. Deuteronomy 12:2-5 begins the discussion of sacred space by negatively listing what does not belong in the worship of Yahweh, and then indicates that God will choose the place where he is to be worshiped.

> You must demolish completely all the places where the nations whom you are about to dispossess served their gods, on the mountain heights, on the hills, and under every leafy tree. Break down their altars, smash their pillars, burn their sacred poles with fire, and hew down the idols of their gods, and thus blot out their name from their places. You shall not worship the LORD your God in such ways. But you shall seek the place that the LORD your God will choose out of all your tribes as his habitation to put his name there. (Deuteronomy 12:2-5)

---

[1]Worship as service is well established in the biblical texts by the use of the single Hebrew word ʿābad. English translations of the Hebrew word ʿābad (pronounced aw-băd´) are rightly rendered either "serve" or "worship" because to worship the Lord is to serve the Lord. Joshua's famous declaration can be accurately translated using either "serve" or "worship": "choose this day whom you will [ʿābad]. . . . As for me and my household, we will [ʿābad] the Lord" (Joshua 24:15).

[2]For user-friendly cultural background summaries on the Hebrew scripture see John H. Walton, Victor H. Matthews and Mark W. Chavalas, *The IVP Bible Background Commentary: Old Testament* (Downers Grove, Ill.: IVP Academic, 2000).

It is clear that any syncretism or comingling of the remnants of pagan idol worship with the worship of Yahweh would compromise the proper worship of Israel's God. The demarcation of the profane from the sacred is important in order for worship to be holy and acceptable to God.

Setting apart sacred space is important to God, and Scripture has plenty to say regarding how this is to be done carefully and thoughtfully. Deuteronomy continues with this idea: "Take care that you do not offer your burnt offerings at any place you happen to see. But only at the place that the LORD will choose" (Deuteronomy 12:13-14). Scripture makes it clear that just any place will not do for the worship of God. Sacred space should reflect, even if imperfectly, God's holiness and character. This idea of God choosing a place is repeated for emphasis in Deuteronomy 12:18, 21, 26. The surprising thing about "the place that the LORD your God will choose" is that the place itself is never identified in Deuteronomy!

This lack of identification of a sacred place continues throughout the book of Joshua and into the early monarchy of Israel. It is important to note that even with David's conquest of Jerusalem as a capital city, the LORD graciously rejects David's desire to build a permanent place for the worship of Israel (2 Samuel 7:5-11). Even though God indicates that David's son will build the temple in Jerusalem, God's intention is to build a place for his name to dwell through the establishment of the Davidic kingdom (2 Samuel 7:11-13, 16, 25-29). So in the course of Israel's history, when God chose a site for the Jewish temple, Scripture repeatedly makes clear that setting apart sacred space for worship is more a matter of helping the worshiper respond to God's invitation to worship, but to do so with the freedom that comes from understanding divine boundaries. God's dwelling place is with his people, enthroned on their praises (Psalm 22:3).

The indeterminate particularity of a single place where God is to be worshiped is summarized well by professor J. G. McConville in his commentary on Deuteronomy when he writes,

> The "place" is an echo of the encounter between Israel and Yahweh at Horeb. . . .
> The oneness of it may have theological significance as a kind of ideal correlate
> of Yahweh's choice [and] more important, the fact that it is not named . . . has
> about it an irreducible openness. . . . The "place the LORD will choose" brings
> forever into Israel's life the principle that the covenant must always be re-

newed in a life of decision that finds itself constantly at Horeb, being called into covenant in an open history consisting of many times and (perhaps) many places.[3]

Indeed, creation is the arena of God's covenantal reality, the fullness of time and space where God chooses to reveal himself and redeem his people. But there is "more than meets the eye," more to divine reality than what can be known in time and space after the rebellion in Eden. In this "place" of time and space, there is an echo of longing, an existential ache of what was lost. The "place of meeting," the sanctuary set aside for worship echoes, too, with hope for what is and what will be. The apostle Paul understood this place-as-echo idea when he affirmed, "The God who made the world and everything in it, he who is Lord of heaven and earth, does not live in shrines made by human hands, nor is he served by human hands, as though he needed anything, since he himself gives to all mortals life and breath and all things" (Acts 17:24-25). In a similar way that the rhythm of the sabbath was made for human flourishing, sacred space helps people cultivate this grace and focus on offering worship that is pleasing to God and acceptable in his sight. Sacred space needs to be set apart for the service of worship both as an echo of God's invitation to come near and as a sense of care in how worshipers do this. In a great sense, Jesus, in the mediatorial role as our great high priest, becomes the "sacred place" within which Christian worship takes place. Christians are only able to "approach the throne of grace with

---

[3]J. G. McConville, *Deuteronomy,* Apollos Old Testament Commentary Series, ed. David W. Baker and Gordon J. Wenham (Downers Grove, Ill.: InterVarsity Press, 2002), pp. 231-32. The absence of site specificity in Deuteronomy for "the place the LORD will choose" is one of several reasons that McConville refrains from affirming what many other scholars posit as a contribution of Josiah's reform in the seventh century B.C. for much of Deuteronomy's writing. He writes, "The crucial premise that the narrative of Josiah's reform gives the clue to the setting of Deuteronomy . . . is based on a logical fallacy. From the fact that Josiah apparently read Deuteronomy and acted on it, it is inferred that Deuteronomy prescribed precisely what Josiah did." McConville goes on to say this ignores the "separate agendas" of each. In its relationship to the Pentateuch, McConville rightly considers that Deuteronomy is somewhat of a "pause" in the narrative that characterizes much of what comes before it, as it consists for the most part of Moses' speeches. He concurs with most scholars that Deuteronomy "bears a strong resemblance to that of an ancient treaty" but also asserts that the correspondence is not perfect. The content of Deuteronomy is somewhat a repetition of the laws and topics in Exodus, Leviticus and Numbers but is dealt with in distinctive ways, a major focus being the worship of Yahweh. The neglect of the biblical theology embedded within Deuteronomy, and chapter 12 in particular, contributed to the "swift reversal" of Josiah's reforms after him as Judah fell into defeat and exile.

boldness" because the Savior leads the way. This boldness is a work of God's grace on behalf of believers and is neither presumptuous nor expressed with care for the sacred nature of the divine invitation and need for mediation.

The important connection in Deuteronomy between the worship of Yahweh in the place of his choosing and the eradication of anything remaining in the place where other gods were worshiped is a pattern for biblical worship that may help congregations discern how best to develop the sacred space for their services of worship. Following the pattern in Deuteronomy, it may be helpful to first consider what does not belong and what should be eliminated or never included. An important question regarding worship is, "What is an intrusion of the world and its idols that may compete for a person's attention, even if some find it comfortable or enjoyable?"

Most importantly, sacred space needs to be space that helps the worshiper focus on the character of God. Christians in different cultures may define distractions differently, but it seems that the definition of sacred space should be space that helps worshipers worship and does not distract their attention from the worship of God. The need to focus on the presence of God and his pleasure is true whether one is in a twelfth-century Gothic cathedral or a gymnasium converted to a sanctuary for Sunday mornings. The question of how a community creates space for the sacred worship of God is vitally important for those who take God's character into account. Setting apart space that does not hinder one's service to God but enables attentiveness to God without distraction is essential for meaningful worship. God's concern for sacred space extends even down to the furniture, arrangement of space and use of particular items to help worshipers mature in spirit and their understanding of who God truly is. The arrangement of furniture and sacred symbols of faith were designed by God to help Israel's worship and can be significant aides in Christian worship. It is important to consider how God's design for the tabernacle and God's choice of its furniture and fixtures offers guidance for discerning biblical patterns for congregational sacred space today.

SACRED THINGS

Taking note of the sequence of law narratives in Exodus is helpful for understanding the texts in their initial context and then applying them in new and significantly contemporary settings. Upon reaching Sinai, Moses and the people are given the Decalogue and its initial exposition (Exodus 19:1–24:8). This part of Exodus ends with the building of a large altar at the foot of the mountain. Twelve pillars are erected corresponding to the twelve tribes of Israel. Burnt offerings and other sacrifices are made, followed by a first reading of the law and the inaugural establishment of the Mosaic covenant (Exodus 24:1-8).

Old Testament scholar Alex Motyer comments on this inaugural affirmation of the law when he writes,

> This basic relationship was now, as we would say, "set in concrete," and a stone altar was built to represent the Lord surrounded by the twelve tribes of his people. . . . The sacrificial basis of the inauguration of the covenant was now completed by the other two great categories of sacrifice: the burnt offering, symbolizing the holding of nothing back from God, . . . and the fellowship or peace offerings, symbolizing communion with God.[4]

This biblical pattern of the Godward "first function" of worship in Israel continued to be modeled in the early church and may still be seen in congregational worship today when a time for the confession of sin and a declaration of assurance based on God's sufficient grace takes place early in the service of worship. When communion with God is reaffirmed in this way, the people are prepared for the reading of God's Word.

The second part of the sequence of law narratives in Exodus begins with a vision of the LORD which is experienced with great joy by Moses, three priests and seventy elders of Israel (Exodus 24:9-11). This section continues with Moses being called up to the cloud-shrouded mountain for forty days and nights. The law Moses received during this time contains the details, design and purpose of the tabernacle, its sacred furniture and the sacred dress for Israel's priests. It includes how the priestly tribe of the Levites was to be set apart as worship leaders (Exodus 25:1–31:11). God's intention for doing things just the right way was an exercise in holiness, not the establishment of a repetitive routine leading to empty ritualism designed to achieve divine kudos.

---

[4]J. A. Motyer, *The Message of Exodus* (Downers Grove, Ill.: InterVarsity Press, 2005), p. 249. Motyer's commentary offers an exceptionally well done overview of the tabernacle and how it functions as a "visual aid" (p. 250) to guide and guard the worship of Israel.

The precision of detail in these chapters is given to counter the intention of pagan worship, which was an attempt to cajole the god(s) into an act of favor. Pagan rituals were often acts of imitation, such as sexual intercourse in order to prompt the gods of fertility to grant favor at harvest time or to give success in begetting children. Israel's God did not have to be cajoled in order to show mercy. As an act of grace, Yahweh called for space that invited the people to meet with God and yet was designed in such a way as to remind the same people of his unapproachable holiness. The tabernacle was a picture of both God's invitation to draw near and an admonition to take off one's shoes in doing so. This was built into the design of the tabernacle, which had an entrance into the worship space but also had curtains that delineated how far into the holy place a layperson or a priest could venture in order to worship Yahweh.

Peter Leithart, in his book *A House for My Name*, strikingly reminds readers that the tabernacle was a sacred place but that it was also designed like a house, Yahweh's house:

> A "sanctuary" is Yahweh's place, and holy things are Yahweh's things. This is why there are a lot of rules about what Israel may and may not do in the tabernacle: You shouldn't mess with Yahweh's things. In the New Testament, the church is the temple of God, made holy by the Spirit. If anyone messes with us, he is attacking God's holy things and messing around with the furniture of God's house. As the history of Israel shows, the Lord gets angry when people mess with his stuff.[5]

Leithart and other Old Testament scholars frequently observe that there are four layers of symbolism in the design of this "house" where God will dwell among his people. First, it is a dwelling place for God, a place of invitation for God to meet with his people. Second, it artistically replicates God's first place of meeting, the Garden of Eden. Third, this in turn is seen as an echo (or prototype) of God's eternal dwelling place in the heavenly realm. And fourth, the tabernacle is a reminder of where God revealed his desire to draw near and journey with his people: Mount Sinai itself. The layout of God's house has a "kitchen" (the courtyard), a "living room"

---

[5] Peter J. Leithart, *A House for My Name: A Survey of the Old Testament* (Moscow, Idaho: Canon Press, 2000), p. 83.

(Holy Place) and a "throne room" (Most Holy Place).[6]

The richness of theological symbolism reflected by the tabernacle layout and its pattern echoes between Eden, Sinai, Israel's journey, the church as the dwelling of God's Spirit and the eternal kingdom in the heavenly realm. This has particular implications for appreciating the importance of sacred space in understanding worship itself. First, worship is a great privilege because it occurs at God's own house. The invitation to enter sacred space is profoundly intimate. Second, entering the tabernacle is a gracious return to the promised restoration of edenic paradise. The intimacy with Yahweh that was lost in the fall is re-created in the tabernacle as a sign of God's ultimate restoration and renewal of God's creation. Third, worship is a sacred place where earthly life touches the hem of heaven's garment, where transcendence engages time and space, where God is present in the concrete reality of Word and sacrament by the Spirit. Fourth, worship is a return to Sinai where we can renew our identity as God's people and demonstrate our exclusive allegiance to the God who keeps his promise. It is the place where we gather to present ourselves and our offering to God. It is the place where, paradoxically, God presents himself to his people in that very offering of sacrifice.[7]

The ninth chapter of Hebrews is a New Testament midrash of the tabernacle law outlined in Exodus. A midrash is an exposition of an ancient text reexamined in the light of contemporary knowledge or events. The author of Hebrews considers how the tabernacle, where God meets his people, can now be identified with the Lord Jesus, the place where God and humankind have met in the incarnation of the Son. Hebrews reveals this insight with clarity:

> But when Christ came as a high priest of the good things that have come, then through the greater and perfect tent (not made with hands, that is, not of this creation), he entered once for all into the Holy Place, not with the blood of goats and calves, but with his own blood, thus obtaining eternal redemption. (Hebrews 9:11-12)

The tabernacle was a tent made to move and travel with God's people as a sign that God was both with them and set apart from them. The Gospel of

---

[6]Ibid. Leithart deals vividly with these many layers of symbolism in the details of Exodus 25–40 on pp. 82-86.

[7]I am grateful to Michael Farley for his help in directing me to the work of Peter Leithart and challenging me to articulate and include this theological summary of the tabernacle.

John gets at the depth of this idea in relation to the incarnation of God's eternal Word: "the Word became flesh and lived among us, and we have seen his glory, the glory as of a father's only son, full of grace and truth" (John 1:14). The word used for "lived among us" is from the same root word in the Greek used to translate "tabernacle" in the Hebrew Scriptures. God became human and "pitched a tent" to be present with his people. The two-fold nature of God's intimate presence and God's unique holiness that sets him apart are reflected in this verse in John. Jesus, as the incarnate Son, manifests the glory of God "full of grace and truth." The "grace and truth" in Johannine Greek reflects the Hebrew word pair, *ḥesed* and *ʾĕmet,* God's un-merited steadfast love and God's character as one who keeps his promises. Sacred space created by things set apart to aid in worship should reflect both the grace of God's steadfast love that calls us to turn aside for worship and the truth of God's character as he has kept his promise through the mediation of Christ Jesus.

SACRED PEOPLE

There is a chilling interlude in Exodus between Yahweh's directions for the tabernacle and the actual making of the tabernacle. If Exodus were an old wild west movie, chapter 32 would begin with the words, "Meanwhile back at the ranch." While Moses was on the mountain being schooled in how Yahweh desired to be worshiped, the restless people at the foot of the mountain decided to design worship in a way that made sense to them. In addition, their self-designed worship was intended to be more self-focused and "fun" than the law would allow.

The story of "the golden calf" (Exodus 32:2-18) is a portrait of how easy it is to neglect biblical patterns of worship that are reflective of God's char-acter. Motyer notes that the word "sin" is only found ten times in the first thirty-one chapters of Exodus, but it is found eleven times in chapters 32–34. Idolatry is sin. The people grew tired of waiting for Moses to return with God's design for worship, so they took (literally!) things into their own hands and fashioned an object of worship and a worship event that was satisfying to them. They wanted a god they could see and touch. They wanted a worship experience that was enthusiastic and designed to make them feel better about the situation in which they found themselves. Aaron and the people made a molten calf out of gold earrings worn by the wives, sons and daughters (Exodus 32:2) of Israel. When Aaron saw that the calf was heralded by the people as "your gods" who "brought you up out of the land of Egypt!" (Exodus 32:4, 8), Aaron tried to mitigate the idolatry by building an altar in front of the calf and proclaiming, "Tomorrow shall be a festival to the LORD" (Exodus 32:5). The next day the people "rose early" and brought offerings and sacrifices and then "sat down to eat and drink, and rose up to revel" (Exodus 32:6). Yahweh alerts Moses that the people "acted perversely" and rendered his verdict that the people "have been quick to turn aside from the way that I commanded them" (Exodus 32:7-8). R. Alan Cole makes the point that the "annexing" of behaviors common in the worship of Baal gods in the name of Yahweh was Aaron's greatest travesty. Cole writes, "open apostasy to Baal would have been less deadly than this 'syncretism.'" Cole also notes that the offensive nature of the Hebrew verb for "play" (v. 6) "suggests sex play, . . . drunken orgies. These, in a Baalized context, would have a religious, not an immoral, significance to the worshipper: but not so in [Yahweh's] sight."[8]

Up on the mountain, Moses could not see what the LORD could see, and he implored the LORD to be merciful with the people for the integrity of God's own name (Exodus 32:11-14). The text does not indicate that Moses understood the depravity of the situation or that he became angry until he "came near the camp and saw the calf and the dancing" (Exodus 32:19). At that point Moses broke the tablets of the law to indicate the people had broken the covenant they had made with Yahweh (Exodus 32:19). Moses then instituted a series of judgments on the people before returning to the mountain to intercede before God for them (Exodus 32:20-35).

Following this sobering episode, God commands Israel to leave Sinai and renews the covenant with them (Exodus 34). Before leaving the mountain, however, the people begin making the tabernacle and its furnishings (Exodus 35:4–39:43). The discipline of the people and their attention to detail in this effort stands in stark contrast to the frenetic activity and careless attitude they display in the episode of the golden calf.

The story of the golden calf can be compared to what one pastor has

---

[8]R. Alan Cole, *Exodus*, Tyndale Old Testament Commentary (Downers Grove, Ill.: InterVarsity Press, 1974), p. 216.

called "W.O.W.," shorthand for "Worship Our Way." It's pretty tempting in a world of technological gadgetry and a culture addicted to excitement to try to manipulate the feelings of worshipers or to elicit a particular kind of enthusiasm in order to let worship leaders know they are being effective. A worship leader who really believes that God is fully present by divine will wisely refrains from becoming the leader of a congregational pep rally by calling for a certain response from a congregation in order to stir up observable enthusiasm or contrition. Essentially, no matter how well intended, this can be an attempt to take over the work of the Spirit to guide the worship of God and the transformation of a person's heart and life. Leading worship biblically should be done with passion and excellence, but it should trust the response of worshipers to the Spirit of God.

The worship of Yahweh by his covenant people was set apart as exclusive. Worship was for God alone and needed to bear the mark of holiness. Holiness was to be demonstrated by the priests charged with leading worship. It was to be practiced by the people called to worship. Priestly apparel and ceremonial washings visually communicated the need to respond to Yahweh's call to worship in a thoughtful and careful way.

CONTEMPORARY CHALLENGES AND SACRED SPACE

It is understandable that Christians often struggle to appreciate the idea of sacred space outlined in the Mosaic law, which manifests both the invitation of God and distance between God and worshipers. However, Christians understand that the need for cleansing, forgiveness and holiness is mediated through the person and work of Jesus Christ on our behalf. The New Testament ultimately reveals that in Christ Jesus, through his life, suffering, death and resurrection, God came to be present among his people as Immanuel—"God with us." Further, the book of Acts describes the initial outpouring of God's Spirit on Jews, Samaritans and Gentiles, and the rest of the New Testament affirms that this indwelling of God's Spirit is a reality for the church today and forever. In the light of God's extraordinary nearness, is there any reason to value the "distance" as well as the "invitation" that sacred space provides?

Understanding God's closeness by the Spirit encourages believers to rest in the security of salvation through Christ, but this intimacy with God can lead to the presumption that God will accept any sincerely motivated idea someone wants to incorporate into worship. Many Christians who staunchly dismiss the idea that sincerity of belief, regardless of its truth, is adequate for salvation will also vigorously defend the idea that mere sincerity in the practice of worship is bound to please God. This inconsistency can be particularly common in evangelical congregations. And, not surprisingly, the reverse can often be the case in theologically liberal congregations. Both can be expressions of self-focused "worship our way."

A biblical pattern that should still mark Christian worship today is acknowledging that the presence of God creates "holy ground" that is set apart for worship. Part of responding to the invitation of God to draw near is also to acknowledge one's unworthiness to do so. This requires setting aside all distractions and divesting oneself of all that does not belong in worship. In western culture, a liturgical time for the confession of sin can be the practice of "taking off one's shoes." It might also mean turning off electronics, disposing of the coffee cup, dressing modestly or even wearing shoes! Coming prepared to be encountered by the Holy One in a service of worship might mean bringing a Bible, preparing your offering or, in certain traditions, fasting before the Lord's Supper. For parents it may mean consciously investing effort in helping young children participate in worship.[9]

One reason many Christians today are unaware of this inconsistency is because of the democratization of the faith which has deep roots in the Protestant Reformation. The Reformers rightly *reaffirmed* the biblical notion of the "priesthood of all believers" to counter the nearly exclusive empowerment of clergy in the church during the Middle Ages. The Reformers wanted to welcome the laity *back* to the table, *back* to the Scriptures and *back* to the assurance of salvation through faith in Christ Jesus. Take note of the italicized words in the preceding two sentences. What the Reformers were about was reintroducing the biblical faith of the early church

---

[9]Many people consider having children in the sanctuary for worship an unnecessary distraction, but the biblical pattern of worship included people of all generations gathered to hear and respond to the Word of God. Often children are either eliminated from corporate worship by offering alternative programs or they are given "worship aids" to keep them busy and quiet. However, these often merely distract children from and have nothing to do with what is going on in worship. Helping children learn to worship is an act of worship that is pleasing and acceptable (and encouraged!) by God. See Robbie Castleman, *Parenting in the Pew: Guiding Your Children into the Joy of Worship*, revised and updated ed. (Downers Grove, Ill.: InterVarsity Press, 2013).

that had grown up in the soil of Judaism. The Reformers carefully appealed to Scripture, to biblical doctrine shaped by the early church fathers and to early patterns of faith that encouraged all to draw near to God through faith in the Lord Jesus Christ. Although some of those who followed the Reformers introduced innovations that were not rooted in biblical patterns of the faith, the Reformers themselves did not start with an empty slate and reinvent Christian faith and practice to suit themselves.

In an effort to embrace the intimacy between the Savior and the sinner, the difference between the holy and the sinful was lost, the distinction between the sacred and the mundane was greatly blurred. To affirm that the Lord Jesus has gone before us so that believers might "approach the throne of grace with boldness" (Hebrews 4:16) doesn't make the "throne" a cozy loveseat or a beanbag chair. The only reason Christians can enter "with boldness" into God's presence is because they are invited and because Jesus, as the mediator of both the invitation and the distance, has gone before them. Access to the divine may be unfettered by the mediation of God's Son, but it is still access to the sacred, the holy.

CONCLUSION

The biblical pattern of worship has not changed. Worshipers respond to the invitation of God to come. In Christ Jesus and by the work of the Holy Spirit they even come close; but it is still the Holy God who is worshiped. One might ask, "But can't any space, any time, anything or anyone be set apart for worship?" Christians with a robust understanding of God's grace through the finished work of Christ will tend to answer this question with a quick "Yes!" These believers will also affirm the idea that worship itself can be expressed through anything that is done well and done "to the glory of God." It is true that a Christian is called to be a "living sacrifice, holy and acceptable to God" (Romans 12:1) so that all of life is, in one sense, an offering to God.

But the problem emerges when something is defined so broadly that it becomes either ill-defined or devalued. When "worship" means anything that anyone does, it tends to mean very little in terms of what pleases God. In Scripture, worship also has a narrow, restricted sense in which God defines how we are to come and how we are to act in his presence. The question and concern regarding worship need to focus on what the practice means to the One who is worshiped. In answering this question the biblical patterns for worship are quite particular, and the God of Scripture has a lot to say about what sacred space and service in worship is "holy and acceptable" to him.

Biblical patterns of worship do "set apart" time and space, people and things in order to take care that the worship of God is acceptable and pleasing to him. Holiness matters, and that means God designs worship to acknowledge what matters to him. We are wise when the worship we offer is shaped by the patterns evident in the light of God's word:

> The friendship of the LORD is for those who fear him,
> and he makes his covenant known to them. (Psalm 25:14)

WORKSHOP FOR CHAPTER THREE

1. Read Joshua 24:14-26 in the light of the Hebrew word *ʿābad,* and substitute the words rendered as a form of "to serve" with a form of "to worship" (or vice versa, depending on the English translation).

   - How does this idea help you understand Joshua's challenge and Israel's identity?

2. Think about the space in which you most often gather for worship.

   - What about that space helps or hinders your ability to give your full attention to serving the LORD in worship?

3. The tolling of bells or the sound of music is often used to signal the beginning of worship. These can be appropriate signals that the time of worship is different, a time intentionally set apart for the service of God. God needs no invocation to be present with his people; it is God who is already present who calls his people to worship. The lighting of candles at the beginning of worship has long symbolized the need for worship to be mediated by the presence of Christ Jesus through the Holy Spirit.

   - What is the signal that indicates the beginning of worship for your congregation?

   - Does the service itself reflect the biblical pattern for worship that begins with the declaration of God's inviting presence as well as God's defining holiness?

- Does the sanctuary space itself have furnishings or a layout that helps worshipers remember the tabernacle as God's house?

4. Think about how your congregation might enhance the sense of sacred space where it meets for worship.

   - What furnishings within this space help or hinder the congregation's awareness of God's holiness?

   - How might those who help lead worship enhance both the nearness of God and the holiness of God in what they do and how they do it?

5. Consider what one pastor has called "W.O.W.," shorthand for "Worship Our Way."

   - Have a free-for-all time with a small group and design a service of worship that is entirely focused on meeting all your needs, hopes, desires, style preferences and favorite theological ideas. This might be considered an exercise to get it out of your system!

   - When finished, critique the W.O.W. service in light of the story of the golden calf.

6. Read through the psalms and note ideas that relate to sacred space, things, people and time regarding the worship of God.

7. Read Hebrews 9–10 and note how a first-century Jewish Christian reflected on the biblical patterns of Israel's worship in the light of God's final work of salvation in Christ Jesus.

8. Consider practical things you might do to "prepare for worship" instead of just "getting ready for church."

   - Ask honest questions about your patterns of worship: are you more conscious of being on time for a job interview or a sporting event than you are for being on time to see and hear the call to sacred worship?

THE SHAPE OF
BIBLICAL WORSHIP

And one called to another and said:
Holy, holy, holy is the LORD of hosts;
the whole earth is full of his glory.

ISAIAH 6:3

Scripture from the Pentateuch to the parousia is embedded with both detailed instructions for worship and glimpses of how God's people have done well or poorly in the practice of worship in Israel and the church. The repetitive biblical patterns for divine liturgy are the focus of this chapter.

Life is liturgical. All people have life patterns that greatly shape how things are done, often for a lifetime. From the side of the bed one sleeps on to the sequence of getting dressed in the morning; from where one puts what on a hamburger to where one sits in a classroom, people are creatures of habit. Habits can be the supportive matrix for comfort zones as well as unhelpful addictions. The potency of habits and routines that shape our lives is evident in how easily they develop and how difficult they are to break. Rituals can be unconscious prompts for accomplishing what needs to be done, for reminding us what comes next. Often, however, habits, routines and rituals can also erode our understanding of *why* we do what we do.

Newlyweds who are combining life habits in a new household often experience a clash of habits that force an explanation long forgotten. Here are a few autobiographical illustrations:

Why do you fold towels the way you do?
Because that's how you're supposed to fold towels, sweetheart!

Why do you always cut that end stub off the turkey before you bake it?
Because my mother always cut it off and threw it away—you're not
supposed to eat it.
Why?
Because it's not good for you.
Why?
I don't know! It's just not.

They have catfish on this menu!
Yes, it's very good.
Catfish are garbage fish used for bait—they're not good for human
consumption!
I've been eating fried catfish my whole life; it's delicious!
Well, I'm not ordering it, and I'll never cook it. It's garbage fish!

During decades of a good marriage I found out that the real reason I fold towels the way I do is because that's how my mother folded towels to fit in the small cupboard of my childhood home. I found out that there's nothing really wrong about the stub at the end of a turkey. My mom cut the stub off because it didn't fit in her roasting pan if she left it on. And, after childhood and undergraduate years on the West Coast, even after more than three decades of married life in the South, I still don't order or fry catfish, but I no longer look aghast at folks who do.

Human beings are creatures of habit. Good, bad, silly, meaningful or meaningless—habits, routines, rituals shape our lives, mark its rhythm, and are rarely examined. They just are. But it is helpful to understand *why* we do what we do the way we do it. Life *is* liturgical, just like worship. It is no wonder that liturgies, the patterns of corporate worship, contribute more to the shape of one's faith than worshipers might ever realize.

One of the reasons worship wars are waged over the *style* of a service of worship is because people like what they like because they like it the way they like it! Worship wars aren't generally waged over the biblical understanding of the God who is worshiped, but over one's taste in church music, how Communion is served, and if the pastor wears a robe or not. However, the focus on the external styles of liturgy often distracts a worshiper from noticing the rhythm of a liturgy that really does shape faith, life and their understanding of God. Changes in liturgical style are often surprisingly uncomfortable because they touch something concerning the substantial shape of one's faith, what a person really believes.

In terms of style, different services of corporate worship can be very distinct. However, nearly all congregations that have any sort of intentional connection with historical faith formation and the worship development of the early church follow a pattern of worship that emerges in the scripture of the Old and New Testaments. The biblical patterns that emerge as liturgical patterns for worship underscore several ideas vital to the appropriate worship of God and essential for the formation of biblical faith in Christian congregations. These patterns, rhythms and holy habits also shape the everyday lives of individual believers.

GOD IS THE PRIMARY FOCUS OF WORSHIP

David's response to God's gracious call was to "bless the LORD, O my soul, and all that is within me, bless his holy name" (Psalm 103:1). The pleasure, blessing and glory of God should be the heartfelt desire of God's people through the service of worship. Even though it was emphasized before, to underscore this dominant idea can be helpful for recognizing bad habits that are hard to break. Worship is not a self-prompted, heartfelt effort that props up our self-esteem while praising God. Worship, in fact, is a gift of God's own grace, mediated by the Son and dependent upon the Spirit. It's all about God. Individuals and congregations may be blessed in the long run, but this can never be the goal if worship is a loving response to the God who loved us first.

Worship, like true love, is a gift shared within a relationship with no strings attached. True love gives itself for the simple pleasure of the other, not to coerce or manipulate the other's love in return. If a man or woman gives a gift with the intention of getting their spouse to do something in return, it is not true love; it's self-love. True love knows nothing of payback, ulterior motives or a return on the investment. And worship "in spirit and truth" (John 4:24) is a congregational gift given simply as a response to being loved first by God (1 John 4:19). Worship that is "holy and acceptable" to God (Romans 12:1) is what matters. And, as Sripture reflects, when it comes to the whole of our lives, the *means* matter to God as much as the ends because they are both mediated by God. In union with Christ by the Spirit, Christians enter the sanctuary to meet with God through worship that God designed to be "holy and acceptable."

EMERGING LITURGICAL PATTERNS IN ANCIENT ISRAEL

After Israel's exodus from Egypt, God's challenging word to Moses (Exodus 3:12) was fulfilled. Israel indeed was called to worship on Mount Sinai the God who had delivered them. The narrative story of Israel's experience of renewing the covenant with Yahweh when they reached Sinai is recorded in Exodus 19–24. Embedded within this narrative are the basic components that take shape in Israel's pattern for worship: God initiates worship by divine call, and those called respond with praise and thanks; worshipers confess their sinful unworthiness and need for divine forgiveness; God extends a means for forgiveness; God speaks; the people hear the word of God and respond to this word in a variety of ways, including sharing a community meal; and divine blessing then releases the worshipers to their homes and work.

This pattern is further embedded in one component of the sequence summarized above. The sequence of sacrifices as Israel's means of forgiveness also follows this broad liturgical pattern. In Leviticus 9 the pattern of sacrifices begins with God calling for a presentation of a sin offering by priests and people, then a burnt offering for the purpose of making atonement, followed by the response of the people in an offering of dedication, and finally the benediction of a peace offering or the offering of well-being.[1]

Many contemporary scholars agree that the consistency of this liturgical order is vital for the shape and practice of Christian worship. In a seminal article, A. F. Rainey noted that when texts provide a narrative description of the procedural order for offering different sacrifices together in the same liturgical event, the sacrifices always occur in the same sequence: sin/purification offering, (burnt) ascension offering and peace offering. The burnt offering (or whole offering) refers to the Hebrew word

---

[1]Allen Ross, *Recalling the Hope of Glory: Biblical Worship from the Garden to the New Creation* (Grand Rapids: Kregel, 2006), p. 98. Ross's book provides a compelling exegetical argument for these patterns.

meaning "that which ascends," a reference to the upward circulation of smoke that symbolically represented the connection of the worshiper to the presence of God.[2]

Again, the sequence in the Pentateuch that shapes the worship of Israel throughout its history begins with the initiating call of God, leads to the need for a recognition of sin followed by grace-given forgiveness which then enables the worshiper to hear the word of God, respond to that word in communion with God and receive God's blessing. Many narrative stories in the Scriptures, the furniture arrangement of the tabernacle, the details of Israel's sacrificial system, and the psalms and prayers used in early synagogues manifest a foundational pattern of biblical worship. This pattern, outlined in what follows, is evident in a variety of biblical texts and can still be seen in many services of Christian worship today.

CALLED TO WORSHIP

Recognizing that worship is a loving response to the God who loved us first fosters a sense of proper humility in the worshiping community. From the texts of origins in Genesis through the law given during the exodus from Egypt, to the establishment of Israel's monarchy, God is the one who calls his people to worship. Christians assemble at God's invitation, not their own initiative. The English word "worship" is related to the word "worthy"— to worship is to express that God alone is worthy of glory, adoration, praise, allegiance and sacrifice. This recognition is bound to remind worshipers that apart from God's grace we are unworthy people. It is the height of presumption to think anyone has the right or ability to initiate the worship of God. Only by God's preeminent call and grace, given to us through the person and work of Jesus Christ, can a congregation of God's people come to worship. Only through the Son of God who has gone before us can we dare approach the throne of grace (Hebrews 4:14-16).

This reality can be recognized in a variety of symbols evident in particular practices of some congregations in worship. Often the first act of

---

[2]Michael Farley, "What Is 'Biblical' Worship? Biblical Hermeneutics and Evangelical Theologies of Worship," *Journal of the Evangelical Theological Society* 51, no. 3 (September 2008): 605. Farley refers his readers to A. F. Rainey, "Order of Sacrifices in Old Testament Ritual Texts," *Biblica* 51, no. 4 (1970): 485-98.

worship is the lighting of candles meant to indicate that Jesus has gone before us to call us to worship. People enter the sanctuary to meet the God who is already present. Many congregations use a responsive reading from Scripture as a call to worship to indicate that it is God's Word that has called us to this hour. The pastor or worship leader might welcome the congregation, but it is God who has called us to assemble and who has gone before us as the mediator of all that is said and done.

At the beginning of many services of worship, music and singing is used to join the ongoing worship in the heavenly realm with those who eternally sing, "Holy, Holy, Holy" before the throne of God. John's account of heavenly visions in the book of Revelation gives us a glimpse of worship unconfined by time and space: "Day and night without ceasing they sing, 'Holy, holy, holy, the Lord God the Almighty, who was and is and is to come'" (Revelation 4:8). And again, "You are worthy, our Lord and God, to receive glory and honor and power, for you created all things, and by your will they existed and were created" (Revelation 4:11).

The back-and-forth antiphonal[3] nature of heavenly worship is why the liturgical call to worship is often a responsive reading (or singing) of Scripture, especially from the Psalms, between a leader and the congregation. An antiphonal call to worship is intended to reflect or echo the heavenly and eternal worship of God.

PRAISE THE LORD!

It should be no surprise that the first response to such a gracious call is gratitude manifest in the praise and adoration of the God who has invited his people to worship. The congregation's first response to God's presence with his people is praise! Who could not be thrilled by such an invitation? Psalm 100 expresses this well:

> Make a joyful noise to the LORD, all the earth.
>   Worship the LORD with gladness;

---

[3]*Antiphonal* means anything sung, said or chanted in alternating parts. In worship this alternating sequence can be between a worship leader and congregation, between right and left sides of a sanctuary, between men and women, or even young people and elders. The "holy, holy, holy" of heavenly worship mentioned in Isaiah and the Revelation appears to be the back-and-forth declaration of heavenly beings offering eternal praise to God.

come into his presence with singing. . . .
Enter his gates with thanksgiving,
and his courts with praise.
Give thanks to him, bless his name. (Psalm 100:1-2, 4)

Depending on the gifts within the congregation, other expressions of praise, like liturgical dance, testimonies of praise to God, thanksgiving for answered prayer and expressions that celebrate God's character can be offered to God.

CONFESSION OF UNWORTHINESS AND SIN

The recognition of God's ultimate worthiness and supreme glory also leads to a stark awareness of a lack of personal and corporate worthiness to offer such praise. Worshipers should rightly be aware that they fall short of the glory of God (Romans 3:23) and, if left on their own, are but sinful and fallen people. In ancient Israel the confession of sin even by the priesthood was mandatory before offerings and sacrifices were made. So in a service of worship modeled after the biblical pattern of Israel and the early church, unworthy people confess their sin to God corporately in the hearing of the whole congregation and silently within the meditation of one's own heart.

It is interesting how many psalms that begin with expressions of praise are followed by a section of self-reflection, sorrow or confession before ending with an affirmation of God's character or goodness. Psalm 19, Psalm 99 and Psalm 103 are examples of this pattern. The pattern of praise followed by confession is also seen in the Lord's Prayer (Matthew 6:9-13).

THE DECLARATION OF GOD'S GOOD NEWS

It is very common for the pastor or worship leader to cut the time of confession short with prayerful thanksgiving for God's forgiveness. The pastor's declaration is the rehearsal of the gospel, the good news that, in Christ Jesus and because of his work on the cross and final victory over sin and death in the resurrection, we are God's forgiven people. The timing of this "habit" is actually quite meaningful. It might be assumed that a worship leader would cut confession short in a service of worship for the sake of time management, but it is actually a biblical idea. The interruption of a time of confession is exactly what the father of the wayward "prodigal son" did as his son headed for home (Luke 15:11-32). Grace always interrupts our best efforts at contrition. Paul celebrates this when he writes, "God proves his love for us in that while we were still sinners Christ died for us" (Romans 5:8). Our utter unworthiness is addressed by God's salvation through the life, suffering, death, resurrection and ascension of Jesus Christ. "God, who is rich in mercy, out of the great love with which he loved us even when we were dead through our trespasses, made us alive together with Christ—by grace you have been saved—and raised us up with him and seated us with him in the heavenly places in Christ Jesus" (Ephesians 2:4-6). The news doesn't get any better that this. So is it any wonder that after the declaration of God's power to save, the congregation rises to sing a song of doxology? *Doxa* is the Greek root for the word "to praise"!

THE WORD OF THE LORD

As God's forgiven people, the congregation can now hear the Word of God with hearts and ears cleansed anew by God's grace. This is the point in the service when passages from the Hebrew Scriptures and the New Testament are read. Have you ever wondered why, in this day of high literacy, the Word of God is still read aloud for the whole congregation to hear? Certainly this is helpful for the very young, but there's more to this custom than its historical roots in the days when few could read. This practice of hearing God's Word does have deep roots in the Shema of Israel. *Šĕma͑* is a Hebrew word meaning "Hear!" and is the first word of Deuteronomy 6:4, which begins the great section of God's address to Israel calling them to obedience by restating the Mosaic law. God's people always hear the Word read aloud in the congregation as a symbol that we, as the people of God, are all accountable to each other for acting on the Word that we have heard together.

The reading of Scripture in a Christian service of worship often includes readings from the Hebrew Scripture and one from the New Testament. Some liturgies always include readings from the Gospels and add third readings from the New Testament Epistles or Psalms. These readings can be arranged in a variety of ways to include congregational singing or special music that reflect on the texts. The sermon is an exposition of the Scripture that has been read and a proclamation of how the Word of the Lord is to challenge and direct the lives of those who have heard it.

Jesus ended his own exposition of Torah, the Sermon on the Mount (Matthew 5–7), with this very idea. After teaching the Word of God, Jesus ended his sermon with the admonition that wisdom is the fruit of life for those who hear the Word of God and then obediently do the Word of God (Matthew 7:24-27). The famous simile that begins "like a wise man who built his house on rock" is too often thought of as a cute children's song with hand motions. However, the illustration of houses being built wisely on rock or foolishly on sand is, in fact, the crescendo of Jesus' challenge to his congregation that they obey the words they have heard him speak.

The hearing and preaching of God's Word in a service of worship always follows the confession of sin and the declaration of God's grace in Christ Jesus. And the hearing and preaching of God's Word in worship is always followed by the congregation responding to that Word in a variety of ways.

RESPONDING TO GOD'S WORD

Obediently responding to the Word of God is a great joy in a service of worship and can take shape in a variety of ways. Some responses will be a part of every service and some only on occasion, depending on the gifts of the Spirit, and how the Spirit prompts the worship of God in each congregational community. The following are just some of the responses to God's Word that a congregation can offer in a service of worship:

- People are initiated into the body of Christ and the community of the church in baptism. The congregation sings songs that cement and celebrate the challenge of obedience to the Word that has been heard.

- Christians affirm their reconciliation and unity in Christ by blessing each other with the peace of Christ.

- Testimonies of faith and life are given as a way to honor God's faithfulness in individual lives.

- The community presents tithes and offerings for the ongoing work of the congregation's witness and mission.

- Prayers of intercession are offered.

It is important to remember that in all the ways a congregation responds to God's Word, the focus must remain on God's glory and honor. The congregational responses are still intent on God's divine majesty. The gifts of God's Spirit, as they are manifest in the congregation, are used for the sake of God's pleasure through worship. Indeed, the congregation presents itself as a "living sacrifice, holy and acceptable to God, which is your spiritual worship" (Romans 12:1). The New International Version wrongly uses the word "sacrifices" (plural). The Greek work is singular and points to the fact that only "in Christ" and by the "mercies of God" can right worship be offered. Only Christ is the acceptable sacrifice.

It is also important to recognize that all that is done in a service of worship is a corporate gift to God, the stewardship of a community's life together in the Spirit. This is symbolized in worship in a variety of ways. Individuals put their money in a plate or basket with the gifts of other worshipers in order to present the offering as that of the *congregation*. It is *our* gift to God, not just the contribution of separate individuals. This corporate practice underscores that both the widow's small offering as well as the wealthy person's tithe are simply contributions given together as people who belong to each other through their belonging to God. In the light of Romans 12:1, it is clear that a congregation gathers together in Christ by the Spirit to worship and present ourselves, making one "sacrifice" to God.

Congregations need to think biblically about why they do what they do in corporate worship and take care not to lose the richness of historical patterns of worship that have shaped the people of God. Liturgical habits need to be understood. Just like newlyweds, congregations need to look into the reasons we do what we do the way we do it.

The people of God are called by God to worship *together* as the body of Christ. Each act of worship symbolizes the congregation's unity in Christ by the Spirit. The congregation responds to such a grace-given invitation with praise and thanksgiving *together*, not as individual believers. The community of faith recognizes its sin and unworthiness to worship such a holy God as a body confessing sin *together*, bearing one another's burdens, not just one's own. Corporate confession is interrupted by the good news of God's grace and the salvation secured for all of God's people through the life, suffering and work of God's Son. A congregation hears the word of God read and preached as a community of believers accountable to each other for obedience and steadfastness (Hebrews 10:23-25). *Together* the congregation hears the Word of God and responds to God's Word through joyful obedience.[4] More is lost than one might know when a box is placed in the back of the sanctuary as a receptacle for an individual's offering. Great theological richness and understanding is blotted out when individuals in a worship service take the elements of the Lord's Supper on their own initiative at any time. The congregation of brothers and sisters in Christ are brought together as one body for the communal meal instituted by Christ (Matthew 26:26-28; Mark 14:22-25; Luke 22:19-20; 1 Corinthians 11:23-33). So this meal of grace should be served one to another or by congregational leaders. All of this is a response of the body of Christ through the agency of the Holy Spirit to give glory and honor to the head of the church, the Lord Jesus Christ.

THE BENEDICTION

The service comes to a close with a reminder that the triune God, who has mediated the worship of the congregation and has received the "good and acceptable" offering of his people, blesses all those gathered for the mission to which they are called to engage together. The congregation, having responded to God's Word, receives God's blessing for their ongoing mission in the world. The congregation is commissioned for the work and witness of the gospel in the world in God's name: Father, Son and Holy Spirit. By God's grace, the congregation receives the blessing of God to bear God's Spirit together as the church into a world that needs to hear and see and experience the presence of the God we have worshiped.

A PICTURE OF BIBLICAL LITURGY

This sevenfold pattern marks worship in the Scriptures from Sinai to the exilic synagogue, from the early church to the Roman Mass, from the liturgies of the Reformation to the frontier communities birthed through the church's mission. From call to praise, from praise to confession, from confession to forgiveness, from forgiveness to the Word, from the Word to response, from response to benediction, the rhythm of biblical liturgy shapes

---

[4]Ephesians 4:1-16 and 5:15-20 provide rich biblical guidance for the corporate nature and practice of Christian faith, life and worship.

our faith as the people of God. This rhythm is embedded in biblical narratives and in the whole canonical story of Scripture. One of the places in God's Word where this pattern is most evident is in Isaiah's experience of worship, described in Isaiah 6.

> In the year that King Uzziah died, I saw the Lord sitting on a throne, high and lofty; and the hem of his robe filled the temple. Seraphs were in attendance above him; each had six wings: with two they covered their faces, and with two they covered their feet, and with two they flew. And one called to another and said:
>
> > "Holy, holy, holy is the LORD of hosts;
> > the whole earth is full of his glory."
>
> The pivots on the thresholds shook at the voices of those who called, and the house filled with smoke. And I said: "Woe is me! I am lost, for I am a man of unclean lips, and I live among a people of unclean lips; yet my eyes have seen the King, the LORD of hosts!"
>
> Then one of the seraphs flew to me, holding a live coal that had been taken from the altar with a pair of tongs. The seraph touched my mouth with it and said: "Now that this has touched your lips, your guilt has departed and your sin is blotted out." Then I heard the voice of the Lord saying, "Whom shall I send, and who will go for us?" And I said, "Here am I; send me!" And he said, "Go and say to this people:

'Keep listening, but do not comprehend;
keep looking, but do not understand.'
Make the mind of this people dull,
        and stop their ears,
        and shut their eyes,
so that they may not look with their eyes,
        and listen with their ears,
and comprehend with their minds,
        and turn and be healed."
Then I said, "How long, O Lord?" And he said:
"Until cities lie waste
        without inhabitant,
    and houses without people,
        and the land is utterly desolate;

until the LORD sends everyone far away,
>   and vast is the emptiness in the midst of the land.
Even if a tenth part remains in it,
>   it will be burned again,
like a terebinth or an oak
>   whose stump remains standing
>   when it is felled."
The holy seed is its stump.

Isaiah 6 is an important transitional chapter that stands in stark contrast to the picture of Israel in the chapter before and the chapter that follows. The sixth chapter of Isaiah is actually a contrast between the "success" of Uzziah's kingship and the complacency of Israel in the eigth century B.C.[5] and the "unsuccessful" mission of Isaiah that unfolds after chapter 6. Isaiah 6:1 begins abruptly and may indicate that Isaiah was surprised by this rather transcendent experience in worship.

In fact, this is the only time in Scripture that an event is dated in relation to the death of someone. It would have been something like saying "on 9/11" this happened. Depending on one's age at the time, people remember where they were and what they were doing when terrorists attacked the World Trade Center on September 11, 2001. It's like recalling where you were when President John F. Kennedy or Martin Luther King Jr. were assassinated. The "year King Uzziah died" was a sad memory for Isaiah's readers because Uzziah had been a beloved king who ruled during a time of great prosperity and national achievement. He was the king of Judah for fifty-two years, the longest reign of any monarch of Israel or Judah. (You can read the story of Uzziah's great success in 2 Chronicles 26:1-15.)

Not only that, everyone knew how Uzziah died. He died about two years after contracting a particularly virulent case of leprosy. And Isaiah's readers knew how he contracted this fatal illness: it was divine judgment for trying to manufacture a spiritual experience in a way that was forbidden by God (2 Chronicles 26:16-21). "In the year King Uzziah died" would have been a poignant reminder of a tragedy for Isaiah's first readers. A great king died because Uzziah had tried to worship God on his own terms instead of by

---

[5]The description of Israel prior to chapter 6 testifies to the self-satisfaction of Israel that Yahweh considered perilous to the nation and an affront to his divine rule and holiness.

God's direction. The king entered the temple where only the priests were allowed to "make offering on the altar of incense" (2 Chronicles 26:16). As a king of Judah, Uzziah was not a Levite, the tribe of Israel's priests. However, Uzziah became proud and decided he had earned the right to worship the LORD any way he wanted to, even go behind the curtain where only the Levites of the priesthood were allowed.

When Isaiah wrote, "In the year that King Uzziah died, I saw the Lord sitting on a throne" (Isaiah 6:1), the prophet knew his first readers would understand the contrast. In the year that King Uzziah died, Isaiah had a worship experience far greater than anything Uzziah tried to manufacture for himself. The contrast here between Uzziah's self-designed effort and Isaiah's grace-given vision is intentionally stark. God's willingness to meet with his people and call them to worship is a surprise that should mark the astounding privilege that is worship. First, notice that Isaiah is *called to worship*. Isaiah enters into the worship of God that is already ongoing. The prophet's experience is initiated by God's grace, not his own effort or an attempt to manufacture a spiritual high or divine blessing.

Isaiah enters into the ongoing *praise* of God (Isaiah 6:2-3), which was and is led eternally by seraphs (literally "flaming ones"). The next time the Greek word in the Septuagint for "seraphs" is used in the Bible is at Pentecost (Acts 2:3) which may indicate that, like Israel, the identification of the church as God's people is profoundly marked by the Spirit's agency to bring God praise. The trifold "Holy, Holy, Holy" is fit praise for the God who continues to reveal himself through the Scriptures as Father, Son and Holy Spirit. Also notice that Isaiah actually describes the scene and its surroundings, but not the Lord himself. What Isaiah sees when he sees the LORD himself is indescribable.

Isaiah is increasingly aware of his own unworthiness as he offers praise in God's presence (Isaiah 6:4-5). Isaiah's *confession* is heartfelt, not just for his own sinfulness, but for that of all God's people. Worship that is aware of God's nearness should always remind us of our unworthiness to be in the place of worship where God has called us.

The recognition of his own unworthiness brings Isaiah to the brink of despair and, interrupting the prophet's confession, God takes the initiative and extends his cleansing grace (Isaiah 6:6-7). The "flaming ones" are directed to bring the fire of divine atonement and render the unclean prophet clean. Isaiah's lips are cleansed in order to open his ears to hear the word God wants Isaiah to hear.

Then Isaiah hears the *word of God*, and it is a word hard to hear (Isaiah 6:8-13). God's word to Isaiah is an invitation to a ministry of hardship and suffering. Unlike Uzziah, Isaiah will not be popular. Unlike Uzziah, Isaiah will not be considered successful. But also unlike Uzziah, Isaiah will prove himself faithful.

Notice, too, that in verses 8 and 11, as God speaks, Isaiah *responds* to God's call. He testifies that he is willing to obey. And when the difficulties of God's call become clear, Isaiah struggles with its demands and honestly asks just what we would in Isaiah's place: "How long, O Lord?"

At the end of this divine liturgy God blesses Isaiah with a promise: "The holy seed is its stump" (Isaiah 6:13). Four chapters later Isaiah relates, "A shoot shall come out from the stump of Jesse" (Isaiah 11:1). Embedded in the *benediction* of Isaiah 6 is the promise of the Son of David, the Messiah of Israel, and the One who is the Alpha and Omega of Isaiah's ministry and mission.

This sevenfold sequence of biblical liturgy (call→praise→confession→ forgiveness→hearing God's Word→responding to God's Word→ blessing) is the rhythm of worship that has shaped the faith of God's people for God's mission in the world. Worship like this can help the church, as it did Isaiah, to say yes and keep saying yes to a hard work and witness in a world that can turn a deaf ear to the Word of God. The holy "habit" of the biblical liturgy that shapes worship is pleasing and acceptable to God. There are biblical reasons for biblical worship. When congregations ask why we do what we do the way we do it, pastors and worship leaders need to offer explanations reflected in the patterns of worship found in God's Word and indwelt, enabled and made acceptable by the triune God of grace.

LITURGY FOR A LIFETIME

In fact, this liturgy is a godly rhythm for the whole of life. What if every day this sevenfold rhythm marked our life and shaped our faith? When we awake, we realize we've been *called* into wakefulness and enter into the *praise* of God for new day. There is humility and wisdom when we are quick to *confess* that sin is crouching nearby and that we are "prone to wander," as the hymn says. But, dependent on Jesus by the Spirit for *forgiveness* and wisdom, we hear the *Word of God* as we take time for reading Scripture. We *respond* throughout the day, "building the house" on the rock of God's Word with obedience and joy. And when our heads hit the pillow, we receive the *blessing* of God in sleep (Psalm 127:2) until the new day begins. This is the rhythm of a believer's life. It is the holy habit for congregations who present themselves to God, a people indwelling the one sacrifice holy and pleasing to God.

Conclusion

The rhythm of biblical liturgy isn't confined to a style. Pipe organs can help a congregation worship God as well as praise bands. Praise and confession can be offered by God's people in sanctuary pews or chairs in a gymnasium. Pastors can wear robes or not, as long as they don't make themselves the center of attention. Where a person stands to read the Scriptures to the congregation may be different in various congregation settings, but it must be read. How Communion is served to the congregation may differ from congregation to congregation, but it must be *served*—offered as a symbol of God's grace and experienced as the community of God's people. The congregation may participate in the confession of sin in a variety of ways, but the declaration of the efficacy of God's grace must contain the announcement of the good news of Christ Jesus. In order to worship "in Spirit and truth," we must follow the Spirit into the Word of God that tells us the truth about why we do what we do the way we do it. This liturgy, this rhythm, this repetition of a holy habit shapes us as God's people for the whole of life.

Workshop for Chapter Four

1. Take some time to look in New Testament prayers for the pattern of prayer discussed in chapter four. Look for such prayers in Acts, Paul's letters and some of the general epistles. Examples to consider might be Acts 4:24-30 and Colossians 1:9-12.

   • Write some prayers of your own using this pattern.

2. One way prayer is often organized, especially corporate prayer, is

known as the fivefold form of the collect. The pattern of prayer is as follows:

1. **The Invocation**: how God is addressed
   "Almighty God," "Our Father," "O Triune God of Grace"
2. **Basis** of the (1) address that reflects the character of God
   "You are powerful to save," "You are our only perfect parent," "You who dwell as a community of light and love"
3. **Petition** based on or reflective of (1) the address and (2) God's character
   "We have need of your strength . . . ," "As your children, we need your wisdom . . . ," "In our community we need unity . . . "
4. **Stated purpose** building on the (3) petition
   "So that we will not grow weary in well-doing," "So that we can better shepherd those in our care," "So that all will know we belong to you by how we love one another"
5. **Ending** that is fitting for all of the above
   "In the name of Jesus, whose power is perfected in weakness," "In the name of Jesus the Son through whom we call you Father by the Spirit," "In the name of the Father, Son and Holy Spirit, who makes us one"

- Write several prayers using this pattern.
- Write prayers in this pattern for specific services of worship, such as for a funeral or a wedding, for baptismal prayer or a time of commissioning for church leaders or missionaries.

3. What are ways a congregation might respond to hearing the Word of God read and preached other than those mentioned in chapter four?

4. Using the canonical liturgy outlined in chapter four, design several services of worship that incorporate a variety of congregational gifts and styles of worship.

- *Call*
- *Praise*
- *Confession*
- *Declaration of Absolution*

- *Hearing God's Word*
- *Responding to God's Word*
- *Benediction*

5. Note the sequence of what happens in a service of worship with the same congregation for at least a month.

   - Note what parts of the service stay the same or change within this sequence.

   - Note if there are any changes in the sequence, the basic framework for the service.

   - Consider why changes may or may not take place.

   - Consider a variety of biblical texts that may or may not be reflected in your month-long experience of worship with this congregation.

6. Make time to sit down with the pastor or worship leader to talk about "why we do what we do the way we do it." Ask questions about how congregational or denominational history might influence the liturgical shape of worship.

WORSHIP BY THE BOOK

*David was afraid of the L*ORD *that day; he said,*
*"How can the ark of the L*ORD *come into my care?"*

2 SAMUEL 6:9

The main focus of God's people after the institution of the law and the conclusion of Israel's refinement in the wilderness was the conquest of the land promised to Abraham under Joshua's leadership. The establishment of Israel's borders continued throughout the turbulent time of the judges, which led up to the reign of Israel's first king, Saul. During the period of the judges and the kingship of Saul, the worship of Yahweh that engaged Israel was primarily offered in households as part of sabbath observance and with extended families and in tribal gatherings at the times and places designated for keeping the Mosaic festivals. Most notable of these places in biblical narrative texts for such gatherings were Gilgal, Mizpah, Shechem and Shiloh. It seems that it was fairly rare for all of Israel or even designated leaders to meet at one place and time once the tribal areas were settled. The Levites were not given tribal territory and were spread throughout the tribal holdings to regulate the proper worship of Yahweh and to serve as spiritual guides and teachers of the law for Yahweh's people.

Weak leadership and poor oversight of Israel's spiritual life had led to a relative fluidity in worship practice during the transition of Israel's leadership from judges to kings. This is clearly seen in the early chapters of 1 Samuel. These narrative accounts center on the call and early spiritual and leadership formation of Samuel as Israel's last judge against the backdrop of the poor spiritual leadership of the priest Eli and his sons. In his book *The Religion of Ancient Israel*, Patrick Miller describes the function of religious observance during this period as a defining feature despite the uneven quality of Israel's religious and civic leaders. Miller summarizes this dynamic well when he writes

> The worship of Yahweh was not confined to domestic and local expressions. The tribes of Israel were joined together not only around the need for security and protection but more importantly around their common allegiance to the covenant god of the league, Yahweh. The union of the tribes had its primary expression in the all-Israel cult of the tribal confederation. . . . Centralized expressions of Israelite religion, whose locus was not the family or geographically related communities but the larger trans-tribal community defined as the "people of Yahweh," continued beyond the time of the tribal league and into the monarchical period so that many features of the all-Israel cultus did not cease with the rise of kingship. From that time on, however, they became a part of the state religion. . . . In both contexts, there was a clear relationship between the cultus with its central focus on the all-Israel festivals and the solidarity of the confederation or the nation. That is, the cohesiveness and the unity of the community rested on and was regularly rearticulated, reactualized, and thus solidified by theological and liturgical means rather than coercive ones.[1]

Not only was there no movement to unify the worship life of Israel during the period of the judges, but the army tended to be composed of tribal regiments and quasi-independent leaders. The lack of national unity and authoritative leadership during the period of the judges weakened both Israel's military and spiritual life. Both of these weaknesses come together in a pivotal episode near the end of this period when "all the people did what was right in their own eyes" (Judges 21:25).

In the early chapters of 1 Samuel, the event that vividly demonstrates the disunity and spiritual weakness of Israel during the period of the judges is the capture of the Ark of the Covenant during a battle with the Philistines.

---

[1]Patrick D. Miller, *The Religion of Ancient Israel* (Louisville: Westminster John Knox Press, 2000), p. 80. For more on the development of religious practice in Israel, see pp. 80-87, where the author discusses the period of tribal confederation prior to the monarchy. The term "cultus" refers to the actual rituals and practices of a religious community and does not necessarily imply any inclusion of the hidden or occult.

Concerning the need to discern the biblical patterns for corportate worship, this event exposes the perils of "using God" or the worship of God as a means to other ends. The narrative lesson on worship that begins with the capture of the ark in 1 Samuel 4 does not come to an end until 2 Samuel 6 with the return of the ark during the time of David's reign. For the purposes of this book, the central point in this complex military and religious story is to be aware of how easy it is to let one's good intentions manipulate worship for one's own purposes. Both the capture of the ark and its retrieval nearly seventy years later by David are marked by good intentions but are, in fact, contrary to how God designates the boundaries of worship and to an understanding of holiness in Scripture.[2] Israel and David both learned the hard way why paying attention to God's word is of first importance for maintaining a right relationship with God and for offering worship that honors God's character. Worship "by the book" helps God's people steer clear of the ambiguity of using worship as a tool to fulfill their own desires.

The importance of God's unrivaled sovereignty and the primacy of God's prerogative in initiating divine directives is central to the lessons to be learned from the narrative of the ark's capture. The presence of the ark in military campaigns was not prohibited by the law. However, prior to this episode in 1 Samuel 4, the inclusion of the ark in military campaigns was initiated by Yahweh, not the people (see Joshua 6 for a clear example). It is important to note that after being defeated by the Philistines in a preliminary confrontation (1 Samuel 4:1-2), the elders of Israel ask one question,

---

[2]The length of time between the capture of the Ark of the Covenant and its retrieval by king David can only be approximately determined. First Samuel 6:1 states that the ark was in Philistia proper for seven months. It was then returned by a new cart to the border town of Beth-shemesh, a residence designated for Levites (Joshua 21:16), where the priestly tribe brought it under their care for an indeterminate amount of time (1 Samuel 6:13-21). The ark was eventually sent farther into Israelite territory to lodge at Kiriath-jearim (later termed Baal-Judah) where "a long time passed, some twenty years" (1 Samuel 7:2). Saul's kingship lasted forty years, during which the ark was ignored. (The account in 1 Samuel 14:18 refers to the use of the ephod, not the ark, for purposes of divination. See Old Testament commentaries to further understand the translation of this text.) David began his forty-year reign in Hebron as only the "king of Judah" (2 Samuel 2:11) during a power struggle with the house of Saul. David's coronation as king of "all Israel" was delayed during this time, and only afterward did his campaign to unite the tribes into a real nation commence with the reunification of the army and the conquest of Jerusalem, which took place over several years. So the total time between the capture of the ark and its being brought into Jerusalem under David's kingship was at least sixty-eight years and possibly as many as seventy-five years.

"Why has the LORD put us to rout today before the Philistines?" (1 Samuel 4:3). Having asked this question, however, they do not look to the possibility of their own failure for the answer, nor is there any indication in the text that they consider Israel's relationship with Yahweh under the sinful influence of Eli and his sons to be part of the problem. Instead, the elders decide to bring the ark more than twenty miles from Shiloh to the battle site in the ill-founded hope that the presence of Yahweh will assure their victory over the Philistines (1 Samuel 4:3).

In this attempt, Israel treated a sacred object and, by extension, Yahweh as a means to other ends, their need for a military victory. In using the ark as someone today might use a "lucky" rabbit's foot, Israel treated the ark like an idol. This subtle perversion of Yahweh's promise and favor into an expression of idolatry is clearly seen in Psalm 78:56-66 in its reflection on this story. The Philistines' reaction when they hear Israel's celebration as the ark enters the camp is meant to help the readers of the narrative understand how close Israel had come to resembling the idolatrous nations that surrounded its borders (1 Samuel 4:5-9). A series of divine judgments fall upon Israel for their presumption of Yahweh's favor: the defeat of Israel and the death of Eli's sons (1 Samuel 4:10-11); the death of Eli; the death of Eli's daughter-in-law during childbirth; and the foreboding name Ichabod given to Eli's grandson (1 Samuel 4:12-22). Ichabod means "the glory of Israel has departed," and betrays Israel's ultimate concern for the nation's own glory, which brought Israel perilously close to full-blown idolatry.

The ark (literally a box or chest) was designed as a sacred repository of Yahweh's covenant with Israel and a symbol of Yahweh's presence with and mercy on Israel (Exodus 25:10-22). The ark with its empty space, the "mercy seat," between the cherubim was understood as only a footstool (or throne) for the sovereign LORD but was not in any way an image or idol of Yahweh. Nevertheless, as a sacred (set apart and holy) object used in worship, the law mandated its care, use and transport very specifically. Indeed, the glory of Yahweh could never be confined to the hollow box or the empty space between the gold angelic wings on its lid (the mercy seat) or the tabernacle (the tent which was to house the ark). The real presence of Israel's God was necessarily aniconic because no physical representation could adequately reflect, let alone contain, God's glory.

Dressing idolatry in the garb of religious fervor and self-serving ideas of worship is an impotent attempt to coerce the favor of God who alone is sovereign. The ensuing duel between Yahweh and the Philistine gods (1 Samuel 5) underscores the absolute sovereignty of Israel's God. The outbreak of disease and the "unexplainable" destruction of Philistine idols when in proximity to the ark caused the Philistine leaders to move the ark from Ashdod to Gath and then to Ekron and finally back "to its own place, that it may not kill us and our people" (1 Samuel 5:11). So after seven months (1 Samuel 6:1) the ark ended up in the Israelite village of Beth-shemesh just over the border from Philistia, and they sent it on to Kiriath-jearim where it remained under the care of local Levites until David, at least sixty years later, decided to retrieve the ark in order to help centralize the worship life of Israel in Jerusalem. From beginning to end, this narrative lesson is meant to remind God's people that the God revealed in Hebrew and Christian Scripture is never a means to an end, even "good" ends. Self-styled worship designed as means to other ends, especially those driven by human needs, personal desires or political agendas are devoid of God's glory. With the capture of the ark, the glory departed from Israel. The self-styled attempt to retrieve the ark during David's kingship reminded Israel of the vital importance of shaping worship carefully by knowing God's Word.

THE STORY CONTINUES

Samuel was the last judge of Israel, and under his leadership the nation established a monarchy to help Israel develop a more robust national identity. However Saul, as Israel's first king, did very little to unify the confederation of Israel's tribes into a nation. The narrative texts that describe Saul's life (1 Samuel 9–31) reveal a leader who craved the affirmation of Israel as a whole but surrounded himself, for the most part, with only those from his own tribe of Benjamin. He was a man who seemed hesitant at times to assert himself when strong military leadership was needed and at other times would take on spiritual leadership that was the province of the priestly tribe alone. Although Saul reigned for approximately forty years, he did little to effect the worship life of Israel. But the last half of his reign did shape the next king who would be "a man after [God's] own heart" (1 Samuel 13:14).

David's slow and tumultuous ascent to the kingship of all Israel (well over twenty years from the time of his anointing to his coronation) helped David gain both spiritual wisdom and a vision for Israel as a unified nation. Soon after David's coronation, he unified the tribal armies into a national army and conquered and established Jerusalem as a city that functioned as a center for both civic and religious authority. David's conquest of Jerusalem was politically helpful because the city was not situated on territory occupied by any tribe of Israel. Establishing Jerusalem as a neutral capital helped to change Israel's understanding of itself as a confederation of tribes, often with competing agendas, to that of a nation united by their king under the sovereign rule of Yahweh. This latter idea concerning the ultimate identity of Israel as the people under Yahweh's rule and care was forged during the many years David spent as a fugitive during the reign of Saul. However, even David was not immune to attempting to incorporate a personal and political agenda into his design for Israel's national worship. The difference between Saul and David lies in the fact that, although David learned the hard way, he did learn.[3]

When David decisively defeats the Philistines (2 Samuel 5) the story of the ark is finally continued. The retrieval of the ark in 2 Samuel 6 is tied directly to the loss of the ark in 1 Samuel 4. David's plan to bring the Ark of the Covenant out of its long hiatus near the border of Philistia was as much a patriotic pep rally as it was an act of worship, and this was more perilous than David realized. One Old Testament scholar comments, "David will also discover that honouring Yahweh while extending one's own position creates dangerous ambiguity."[4]

DANGEROUS AMBIGUITY

The "dangerous ambiguity" of David's desire to bring the ark from Baal-Judah (formerly Kiriath-jearim) to Jerusalem is reflected in the number of "men of Israel" David took with him. In the earlier battle, when the ark was

---

[3]A study of the life of David through Scripture is a worthwhile enterprise. For an inductive study in two volumes that includes all of the narrative texts from 1 Samuel 16, all of 2 Samuel and 1 Kings 1:1–2:12, see Robbie F. Castleman, *David, Man After God's Own Heart*, Fisherman Bible Study Guide (Wheaton, Ill.: Shaw Books, 2000) and *King David: Trusting in God for a Lifetime*, Fisherman Bible Study Guide (Wheaton, Ill.: Shaw Books, 2000).

[4]David G. Firth, *1 & 2 Samuel*, Apollos Old Testament Commentary (Downers Grove, Ill.: InterVarsity Press, 2009), p. 375.

captured by the Philistines, thirty thousand Israelite foot-soldiers lost their lives (1 Samuel 4:10). It is no coincidence that when David goes to retrieve the ark he calls up a matching thirty thousand soldiers (2 Samuel 6:1). This replication in the biblical account, no matter how one interprets the way numbers are used in Scripture, clearly indicates that David knew about the defeat of Israel on the day the ark was captured. David engineered a show of national bravado near the border of this defeated enemy while at the same time bringing the neglect of the ark to an end as part of his plan to reinvigorate the worship of Yahweh in Israel. The retrieval of the ark and celebration that David planned was more focused on David's success as a warrior and the military strengthening of Israel than it was on the glory of Yahweh returning to center stage in Israel's worship life. This is evidenced by the fact that David knew more about the military losses when the ark was captured than he did about the Levitical law concerning the actual transportation of the ark.

In 2 Samuel 6:2 the ark is described as "the ark of God, which is called by the name of the LORD of hosts who is enthroned on the cherubim." In this story, which spans two Old Testament books, the last time the ark was described this way was in 1 Samuel 4:4. The repetition of this language is used by the story writer to clearly tie the lesson of the ark's loss to the events of the ark's retrieval. The literary details of this story of the ark in Scripture is meant to highlight the importance of God's presence, power and glory concerning the worship life of Israel. David may have researched the battle when the ark was captured, but he failed to study God's law when it came to the ark itself. The question David asked in 2 Samuel 6:9, "How can the ark of the LORD come into my care?" should have been asked long before the journey to retrieve the ark began.

The transportation of the ark on a "new cart" (2 Samuel 6:3) mimicked the way the Philistines had returned the ark to Israel (1 Samuel 6:7-8). The Philistines were not held accountable for the way they transported the cart because they did not have the law to provide the guidelines for the ark's care and transport. Israel did have the law and, to Yahweh, this made all the difference. The common expression "ignorance is no excuse" is highly applicable for God's sudden judgment that interrupted David's celebration. David and the priestly descendents of Abinadab did not design a service of worship guided by the Word of God, but one that modeled itself after what seemed to work in the Philistine world. Uzzah's effort to steady the ark on the cart was well-intentioned, but God's holy wrath brought a sudden and severe judgment upon Uzzah and brought the celebration to a halt. David's attempt to combine a military and political agenda with a celebration of Yahweh as Israel's God created ambiguity that proved quite dangerous, especially to Uzzah![5]

David's initial reaction to Uzzah's death is a good indication that David was more concerned about his reputation as a warrior and king than he was about the care he needed to exercise in order to honor Yahweh. "David was angry because the LORD had burst forth with an outburst upon Uzzah" (2 Samuel 6:8). However, David's initial anger gave way to a proper fear of the LORD. "David was afraid of the LORD that day; he said, 'How can the ark of the LORD come into my care?'" (2 Samuel 6:9). This fear of the Lord was, as Proverbs indicates, the beginning of wisdom (Proverbs 1:7). For the next three months David and the priestly leadership apparently did their homework (2 Samuel 6:11; see 1 Chronicles 15:2-15) and studied the law concerning the ark and its care and transport. What they discovered was that the law commanded that the ark be transported only by the Levites using long poles (Exodus 25:10-20).

The contrast between the first attempt to bring the ark to Jerusalem that ended in Uzzah's death and the second attempt, which followed the instructions in the Mosaic law, are as clear as they are significant. One of the most obvious changes is that the ark is no longer transported on a cart but, according to the law, by "those who bore the ark" (2 Samuel 6:13). Joy, dancing and singing mark both celebrations (compare 2 Samuel 6:5, 14-15), but the care of the ark acknowledges the supreme power of Yahweh with due reverence. The way the story is told makes clear the distinction between the ark and Yahweh himself. Patrick Miller notes this when he writes, "Even when Uzzah was killed for having touched the ark of the covenant to steady it, the

---

[5]Patrick Miller, in *The Religion of Ancient Israel*, comments on David's dual intention for the event when he writes, "Here a shrewd political act takes place in the context of a religious occasion to cement futher the support of the people" (p. 255 n. 236). Miller's comprehensive account of the development of worship practice in Israel is an excellent source for the particularities of the long process, especially in contrast to the worship practices of Israel's neighbors.

destruction is described as being due to the wrath of God who struck him down (2 Sam. 6:7). . . . That happened because of Uzzah's apparent violation of the line between the holy and the common rather than because of an inherent danger in the ark itself. . . . The danger came explicitly from divine decision."[6]

Another contrast that gives evidence to David's "learning curve" regarding God's holiness is evident when the narrative states, "when those who bore the ark of the LORD had gone six paces, [David] sacrificed an ox and a fatling" (2 Samuel 6:13). It must have been such a relief when no one died after six careful steps! With this assurance that they had finally followed the divine instructions, a sacrifice is offered to acknowledge their need for and recognition of Yahweh's favor. David Firth comments on 2 Samuel 6:12-13 and connects it to the idea he termed "dangerous ambiguity" when he writes,

> David's mixed motives in bringing the ark are clarified here. News that Obed Edom's house was blessed by Yahweh because of the ark's presence became the trigger for David's bringing it from there to Jerusalem. The rejoicing associated with this is less defined than the first attempt [suggesting that] . . . his fear of the ark has been overcome.[7]

THE FEAR OF THE LORD IS THE BEGINNING OF WISDOM AND WORSHIP

The proper "fear of the LORD" is the beginning of worship as well as wisdom. Allowing the Word of God to guide the design of worship and honoring the holiness of God by all that is done in worship are guardrails that make possible the joy of the LORD expressed in worship by God's redeemed people. That was certainly true for David and Israel, and it is still true for God's people in services of worship today. Good intentions do not make anything and everything done in worship acceptable to God. David had good intentions. David wanted to help Israel celebrate God's faithfulness and goodness to his people. David wanted to celebrate before the LORD. David wanted to please God. But David neglected to study the Word of God that set the

---

[6]Miller, *Religion of Ancient Israel*, pp. 132-33. Miller's comment is intended to differentiate Israel's understanding of Yahweh's presence from any "mechanistic or animistic kind of sacrality."

[7]Firth, *1 & 2 Samuel*, pp. 376-77.

parameters for worship that is acceptable and pleasing to God. David designed a service of worship that pleased himself and served his own needs and favored agenda. David was like a friend who gives a gift they themselves would like to receive, regardless of the likes and dislikes of the one to whom the gift is given.

Worshipers today need to know the Word of God in order to know how best to honor God in worship. Too many people today offer worship to a god of their own making, a god more shaped by culture and personal needs than by the revelation of God in the Scriptures. A service of worship is a gift to God from a congregation. Knowing God's Word and allowing it to guide the planning and offering of the service are vital to giving a gift that is delightful and pleasing to God, because it shows we know God in a deep and personal way. Beyond this, the recognition and understanding of God's own mediation of worship that is designed to acknowledge God's holiness as well as God's mercy and grace is vital if God's people are to offer honor, reverence, joy and adoration that is fitting for who God is.

As the story in 2 Samuel 6 continues to unfold, the ark of the LORD is finally brought into Jerusalem, the city of David, and it is "set in its place, inside the tent that David had pitched for it" (2 Samuel 6:17). The preparation of a tent is also a result of David's belated study of the law concerning the care and transport of the ark. It is clear in the text that this tent was fashioned like the tabernacle in the wilderness since "burnt offerings and offerings of well-being" (2 Samuel 6:17) were offered to the LORD. God was pleased, the people were blessed, and the king of Israel must have breathed a sigh of contentment and relief. But this didn't mean that everyone was happy.

SOME PEOPLE MIGHT NOT LIKE WHAT PLEASES GOD

If personal agendas within worship can corrupt the service of God, those with agendas outside of worship can attempt to cut short the joy of biblical worship. Michal, David's wife and the daughter of Saul, Israel's first king, was not a part of the entourage of worshipers that entered Jerusalem with the ark of the LORD. She observed the service from a distant window and judged David's "leaping and dancing before the LORD" (2 Samuel 6:16) as "vulgar" and "shameless" (2 Samuel 6:20). The text indicates that Michal's criticism was rooted in her status-conscious pride that *her husband's* behavior was unfit for a king of Israel. The text makes it clear that David's behavior was "*before the LORD*" (2 Samuel 6:16, emphasis added) as the ark came into the city, and this assertion is repeated in David's reply to Michal after the service was over. In fact, this phrase is repeated for emphasis in David's reply. "It was *before the LORD* . . . that I have danced *before the LORD*" (2 Samuel 6:21).

It is notable in the text that Michal is not described as David's wife but as "the daughter of Saul" (2 Samuel 6:16, 20, 23). David does point out to Michal that Yahweh chose him "in place of your father and all his household, to appoint me as prince over Israel" (2 Samuel 6:21), but David's reply focuses on his relationship to the LORD, not his status within Israel. This is clear when David continues his response to Michal's criticism by highlighting his own willingness to be humble before the LORD and to worship as one of the people (2 Samuel 6: 22). David Firth makes this point well in his commentary when he writes,

> Unlike the narrator, who noted that David danced before Yahweh, Michal does not speak of his dancing, but claims he has exposed himself before the lowest of the low: the handmaids of his servants. This, she claims, is something only the most vulgar Israelite would do. The emphasis upon exposure is so marked that *glh* (uncover) is used three times. . . . David takes Michal's sarcastic jab about honour and turns it around. An Israelite king is honoured because he worships enthusiastically with the people, not by behaving like traditional kings.[8]

This exchange with Michal shows how well David learned a hard lesson about how "honouring Yahweh while extending one's own position creates dangerous ambiguity." David will no longer allow his own agenda within worship, nor Michal's opinion as an outsider looking in, to shape the worship he offers to the LORD.

Humility is always a mark of biblical worship. Historically, one of the reasons pastors wore robes was to indicate the power and authority to preach was not found in them but in the Word of God. The early vestments of the Roman and Eastern rites "covered" the priest in their service as a sign that their authority was not their own, but from Christ and his church. The

---

[8]Ibid., pp. 378-79.

academic gown that was the robe of later medieval preachers and the Reformers was still intended to "cover" the teacher and draw attention to what was taught. The wearing of robes by those who sing in a choir is not only grounded in the scriptural references concerning the singers who helped lead the worship of Israel (Psalm 29:2; 2 Chronicles 20:21) but in the idea that the rich and the poor can stand side by side in a choir and look the same. David's assertion that he would intentionally be humble in his own eyes was his affirmation that Yahweh was his LORD and Israel's true king. It's interesting that many medieval cathedrals built niches into one side of the nave within which rulers could worship unobserved by the congregational commoners. This practice had both positive and negative aspects. On one hand, it was understood that it was right for a ruler to kneel in worship. But on the other hand, many kings, emperors and rulers did not want the peasants to see them kneel! It takes thought to think through "worship by the book" in different situations and the practices that grow from adopting certain patterns. On one hand, it may be good to provide a monarch a place to be unobserved in worship to shelter them from peasants or paparazzi. On the other hand, the monarch is a sinner called to worship like anyone else, and it may be wrong to enable a practice based on pride or sense of elevated entitlement.

Worship is an exercise of humility because it reminds God's people who is really on the throne and in charge. Biblical worship is a humbling reminder to Christians that they are one body under Jesus Christ who alone is head of the church. When anyone thinks their own good intentions are good enough for God, humility is a lesson yet to be learned. David learned humility the hard way. But what about Uzzah, whose death led David to study God's Word? If such divine judgment fell on everyone with mixed motives in worship that led to "dangerous ambivalence," graveyards would fill up far faster than sanctuaries without a doubt!

The text gives no clear hint that the way Uzzah tried to steady the ark as it threatened to topple on the cart was any more than an instinctive gesture. But Uzzah belonged to a family of priests from the tribe of the Levites. Uzzah's unintentional but careless action highlights the neglect of Israel's spiritual leaders lasting from the time of Eli and his sons to the Davidic kingship. The ark had been in the care of this family for decades and the Levitical descendents of Abinadab should have known better. God's judgment that resulted in Uzzah's death was actually a judgment on the negligence of Israel's spiritual leaders to shepherd the worship life of Yahweh's people.

While trusting that God's character was not compromised in Uzzah's death, one must accept God's right to bring such a judgment as a wake-up call to Israel's people, priests and king. David was called to the kingship of Israel as a man after God's own heart (1 Samuel 13:14), and the time had come for the revival and reformation of Israel. Uzzah's death was the spark that ignited a holy fire that renewed Israel's worship as a nation, increased David's contributions to the Psalms, and eventually would result in the glory of Solomon's Temple. The glory of Israel may have departed when the ark was captured, Eli died and Ichabod was born, but the glory of God began to shine when the ark made its way to Jerusalem celebrated by a king who had learned the importance of planning worship by the book!

A New Testament Lesson Learned the Hard Way

There is a startlingly similar incident in the New Testament story of Ananias and Sapphira (Acts 5:1-11) that echoes the perils of "honouring Yahweh while extending one's own position" and thus creating "dangerous ambiguity." When Ananias and Sapphira presented their offering, like David, they participated in an act of worship also designed to elevate their own status among God's people. Unlike David, they died for their duplicity. In the light of God's forgiveness through the finished work of Christ, God's people *again* needed a reminder that God's grace does not negate God's holiness. The religious fraud perpetrated by Ananias and Sapphira was actually lying to God (Acts 5:4), an act that did not treat God as holy.

The unsettling story of Ananias and Sapphira ends with an astute, and probably understated comment: "great fear seized the whole church and all who heard of these things" (Acts 5:11). It is important to note that this is the first time in the book of Acts that the word for "church" occurs. Just as the worship of the holy God defined by Scripture was the identifying mark of Israel as the people of Yahweh, so worship designed within the parameters of God's Word is still the defining mark of the church of Jesus Christ. God still calls his people to worship in Spirit and in truth with uncompromised holiness.

CONCLUSION

Those who plan and lead worship today need to bear in mind how easy it is for the subtleties of dangerous ambiguities to influence the design of a service. Many worship leaders guard the story-shape of worship by having announcements and informal times of greeting placed before the call or after the benediction. Many also take great care in how, when and even if the recognition of national holidays or personal days (anniversaries, birthdays, Mother's and Father's Day) are included in the liturgy.

Even though evangelism, discipleship training, and local and global missions are all a part of healthy congregational vision and witness, thought must be taken of how these good intentions relate to corporate worship liturgy. Within the sevenfold pattern of biblical worship the gospel is proclaimed, disciples are shaped, and saints are equipped to participate in the ongoing mission of God in the world; but the focus of this pattern is God's story of redemption. Too often other worthwhile agendas encroach on the time set aside for the congregation to "just" worship God with joy, repentence, thanksgiving, attention to the Word and participation in sacramental practice.

Worship is uniquely the province of God's people. Good works with good intentions can be accomplished through all sorts of programs in the congregation and in secular society. There are plenty of other venues and no end to congregational programs that can "equip the saints for the work of ministry" (Ephesians 4:12), but worship is unique in that it has no other end in sight but its own means, mediated by God's Spirit, to bring glory and honor to the God who has invited us to celebrate his story as our story. The time given for worship should be guarded from other agendas lest good, but still dangerous, ambiguities displace God's intention for calling his people to worship.

WORKSHOP FOR CHAPTER FIVE

1. Consider this account from 1 Samuel 2:12-17: "Now the sons of Eli were scoundrels; they had no regard for the LORD or for the duties of the priests to the people. When anyone offered sacrifice, the priest's servant would come, while the meat was boiling, with a three-pronged fork in his hand, and he would thrust it into the pan, or kettle, or cauldron, or pot; all that the fork brought up the priest would take for himself. This is

what they did at Shiloh to all the Israelites who came there. . . .Thus the sin of the young men was very great in the sight of the LORD; for they treated the offerings of the LORD with contempt."

- In the light of this passage, consider the importance of accountability and self-giving in congregational leaders and worship leaders today.

- Consider both negative and positive examples of congregational leaders in your experience and that you know of in the broader culture. Bear in mind the situation of monarchs being provided a measure of privacy in worship in the Middle Ages. A sense of self-empowerment can lead to unwise practices in the church for both clergy and laity that have the potential to lead to sin that is "very great in the sight of the LORD."

2. Think about how services of worship are sometimes used as a means to an end other than the glorification and pleasure of God. Consider how easy it is to use human needs, personal desires or political agendas as "good" ends that might influence the design and content of worship.

- How would you define the line between God-defined and God-initiated biblical worship and idolatry?

- What might help congregations, worship leaders and pastors discern this line?

3. Identify ways that a service of worship might be compromised by "good intentions" that might create a "dangerous ambiguity" by mixing human agenda with the honor and holiness of God.

- Why would God's judgment through the death of Uzzah be particularly important to congregations today in order to reinvigorate and refocus worship planning and practices?

4. Consider how "outsiders" shape and influence services of worship in different faith communities.

- Consider as outside influences not just people who want to protect their own status or position within society but also expectations of visitors, seekers or others who may not understand what worship is.

- Also consider how cultural influences, media and technology tend to shape worship from the "outside."

5. Thoughtfully reread the Scripture passages from this chapter, comparing and contrasting details that help each episode relate to the other.

6. Think about how you might be more mindful of God's holiness in your practice of worship.

   - Consider what you can do to strengthen your knowledge of God's Word.

   - Discuss with others the tension experienced between affirming both the demands of God's holiness and the gifts of God's grace in the Christian life.

WORSHIP AND HOLINESS

O Lord, who may abide in your tent?
Who may dwell on your holy hill?
Those who walk blamelessly, and do what is right.

PSALM 15:1-2

Both the fear of the Lord and the sevenfold pattern of worship embedded in biblical texts shaped the worship practices of Israel throughout its history. This sevenfold pattern took shape over a long period of time. From the sabbath rhythm of creation itself and the early practices of Israel's patriarchs to the initiation of the law at Sinai, which mandated the exclusive nature of Israel's fidelity to Yahweh, this sevenfold pattern characterized the rhythm of Israel's worship. During the subsequent regulation of Israel's worship under the kingships of David and Solomon and the further development of liturgical practice under the pre-exilic prophets to the inauguration of synagogues during the exile of Judah, this sevenfold pattern consistently and creatively framed the worship of God's people. The further development of this pattern for worship was reinvigorated during the post-exilic period and contributed to the dynamics of Israel that eventually culminated in the new community of God's people that composed the early church of the first century.

The historical breadth and depth of the sevenfold pattern that emerges in the Old Testament and is manifest in many traditions today in a variety of forms and styles for corporate worship indicates its importance as a framework for biblical liturgy. However, Scripture makes it clear that God has an overriding concern for the character of those he calls to worship and sends from worship into his ongoing mission in the world. The holiness and integrity of the worshiper is vital to the dynamic of the worship God himself mediates.

The Scriptures clearly make the integrity and holiness of the worshiper of paramount importance. Not only did king David learn lessons about worship hard way, he reflected on them in psalms he wrote for the use of God's people in worship. In Psalm 51, David addresses God:

> For you have no delight in sacrifice;
>> if I were to give a burnt offering, you would not be pleased.
> The sacrifice acceptable to God is a broken spirit;
>> a broken and contrite heart, O God, you will not despise. (Psalm 51:16-17)

Another "hymnwriter" of Israel reflected on the importance of the worshiper in the prophetic role of speaking on God's behalf:

> Not for your sacrifices to I rebuke you;
>> your burnt offerings are continually before me. . . .
> Those who bring thanksgiving as their sacrifice honor me;
>> to those who go the right way
>> I will show the salvation of God. (Psalm 50:8, 23)

God's glory is rightly, in the words of the Westminster Assembly,[1] the

---

[1]One task of the Westminster Assembly was to help organize and educate the "Christian Church in England" a century after the English Act of Supremacy (1534). The first two questions of the Westminster Shorter Catechism (1647) underscore the concern for God's glory as central for Christian faith and life and the idea that this can only be understood in the light of Scripture. Although dated in format and language, these questions affirm the primary focus of the present text. God's glory is the central concern of worship, and Scripture is the primary resource for understanding what God finds pleasing and acceptable in this pursuit.
Q. 1. What is the chief end of man?
A. Man's chief end is to glorify God, [a] and to enjoy him forever. [b]
    [a]. Ps 86:9; Is 60:21; Rom 11:36; 1 Cor 6:20; 10:31; Rev 4:11
    [b]. Ps 16:5-11; 144:15; Is 12:2; Lk 2:10; Phil 4:4; Rev 21:3-4
Q. 2. What rule hath God given to direct us how we may glorify and enjoy him?
A. The Word of God, which is contained in the Scriptures of the Old and New Testaments,
 [a] is the only rule to direct us how we may glorify and enjoy him. [b]
    [a]. Mt 19:4-5 with Gen 2:24; Lk 24:27, 44; 1 Cor 2:13; 14:37;
     2 Pet 1:20-21; 3:2, 15-16
    [b]. Deut 4:2; Ps 19:7-11; Is 8:20; Jn 15:11; 20:30-31; Acts 17:11;
     2 Tim 3:15-17; 1 Jn 1:4

Christian's "chief end," the ultimate focus not just for the cosmos and the whole of human life but also for the service of worship. Worship that glorifies God is worship that transforms the worshiper. If our chief end is the glory of God manifesting itself in a joyful, right and unending relationship with God, then God's chief end is the redemption of those created to bear his image and likeness. Worship focused on God's character, God's integrity, radically reorders the life of the worshiper. For Christians, biblical worship is one way God shapes our lives to more clearly bear the divine image. Jesus, in the full humanity of the incarnation, displayed the divine image perfectly as the "image of the invisible God" (Colossians 1:15). Simply put, worship that glorifies God makes us more like Jesus.

This dynamic is only possible because worship is mediated through the eternal priesthood of Jesus. Only in Jesus, the great high priest, is worship perfected as an acceptable offering, holy and pleasing. Only in union with Christ by the Spirit is the integrity of the worshiper possible. This dynamic is parallel to the reality of God's righteousness for the Christian. Only in the righteousness of Christ given by faith through God's grace is one made right with God. Only through the Savior's work, not our experience of that work, is salvation accomplished. Only through the mediation of Christ Jesus in his priestly office is worship made worthy for God's glory.

James Torrance summarizes this parallel between salvation through Christ alone and the mediatorial role of Christ as high priest when he writes,

> As Paul expounds justification by faith by contrasting life in the Spirit—the way of grace—with false self-confidence in the flesh, so the epistle to the Hebrews contrasts two forms of worship: true worship, which means reposing on and participating in the self-offering of Christ who alone can lead us into "the Holy of Holies"—the holy presence of the Father—and false worship, with its false reliance on what we do by following our own devices or traditions. In other words, when we take our eyes off Jesus Christ and that worship and offering which God has provided for us in Christ, which alone is acceptable to him, we fall back on our "religion."[2]

---

[2]James B. Torrance, *Worship, Community & the Triune God of Grace* (Downers Grove, Ill.: InterVarsity Press, 1996), p. 59.

Just as our salvation is accomplished through the work of God in the incarnation of the Son—his suffering, dying, rising and ascending—so only in union with the Son by the Spirit is our "liturgy" (literally the "work of the people") true worship. The transformation of our lives, like our salvation, isn't grounded in our work, our effort, but in God's grace through the work of God the Son. Both salvation and sanctification are gifts of grace through faith.

CONNECTING WORSHIP, WORK AND WITNESS

G. K. Beale's book *We Become What We Worship: A Biblical Theology of Idolatry* makes this same point in the negative. Essentially any sort of idolatry has our own glorification as its chief end. When God is glorified through worship that is pleasing and acceptable to him, God's people are not morphed into some sort of divine essence, but they do become who they were always meant to be: truly human, people who bear the image and likeness of God (Genesis 1:26). God's redemption of fallen and sin-fractured humanity becomes increasingly manifest in the realities of everyday life. The integrity between who a person is and what a person does becomes increasingly seamless. Instead of disintegration (the opposite of integrity), Christians become who they are in Christ. While we are working to glorify God through the liturgy of worship, God is at work to bless us and make us better at being his image-bearers in the world.[3]

Jesus understood the need for seamless integrity between who a person is and what a person does and repeatedly addressed this challenge in the Sermon on the Mount (Matthew 5–7). In this seminal teaching of Jesus, he denounced those who thought of themselves as "the righteous" for actually being "the hypocrites." Over and over again Jesus challenged his hearers not to be "like the hypocrites" who give alms, pray, fast, make judgments and all sorts of good things *to glorify themselves* (Matthew 6:1-18). The problem with hypocrites is that, even in doing good things, their aim is that others recognize them and glorify their efforts. Jesus goes further when he stunningly warns his hearers to not be like the fraudulent "many" who, in fact, do very good things. "On that day [of judgment] many will say to me, 'Lord,

---

[3]G. K. Beale, *We Become What We Worship: A Biblical Theology of Idolatry* (Downers Grove, Ill.: IVP Academic, 2008).

Lord, did we not prophesy in your name, and cast out demons in your name, and do many deeds of power in your name?'" (Matthew 7:22). Even though these are things Jesus himself was known to do, Jesus continued his warning, "Then I will declare to them, 'I never knew you; go away from me, you evildoers'" (Matthew 7:23). Looking at what these "many" claim to have done, one must ask why Jesus denounces them as "evildoers." It is because there is disintegration (a lack of integrity) between the good they have done and the persons they really are. Like the hypocrites, the "many" are concerned about their own glory in the kingdom of God. And Jesus reveals that he does not know them, does not recognize them, does not regard or look at them. This disregard is a New Testament echo of God's disregard for Cain's offering (Genesis 4:4-5) discussed in chapter one. Like Cain, whose protest to God betrayed his self-concerned pride, the "many" clamor at the narrow gate of the kingdom in an attempt to draw attention to their own efforts done outwardly in Jesus' name though inwardly they intend to bring glory to themselves.

When the church enters into worship through Christ, focused on God's glory by the mediation of the Spirit, God's people learn better how to center on God's glory as the intention of the church's mission, which is also mediated by the Son through the Spirit. This God-centered focus can help sustain a believer's contribution to the work and mission of God for a lifetime. When God's glory and pleasure are the focus of one's work and witness in the world, God's people are less prone to give up when the response of others to our efforts or the appreciation for our sacrifices is disappointing. When obedience to God is motivated by the utmost desire to please God, believers are less prone to bear the burden of meeting all the expectations of others, less likely to burn out from frenetic efforts to satisfy everyone's needs.

The model for such carefully focused obedience is Jesus' own obedience to the Father in the self-emptying dynamic of the incarnation (Philippians 2:5-8). Jesus didn't meet the needs of everyone he encountered as he walked the dusty roads of Palestine. When Jesus cried "It is finished" from the cross, the beggar who sat at the Gate Beautiful near the temple still couldn't walk. Even after the resurrection and ascension, there were still many blind, lame or demon-possessed people with great needs. The Spirit was sent after the glorification of Jesus (John 7:39) in order to empower the church for the ongoing mission of God in the world. Worship focused on the glory of God can help prepare the church to participate in mission with this same chief end.

Burning out, giving up or complaining about a lack of appreciation for how one serves the congregation or the world can all be symptoms of self-concern. When believers are tempted to protest like Cain or complain like "the many," Jesus intends his startling rebuke at the end of the Sermon on the Mount to provoke self-examination and subsequent repentance that keeps his hearers from the edge of the abyss that is the end of self-glorifying pride. The ending of Jesus' sermon was meant to sober his first hearers and those who read the sermon in Matthew's Gospel today.

TRUE WORSHIP AND THE MISSION OF GOD

The challenge of *doing* the Word of God is the ending of Jesus' Sermon on the Mount.

> Everyone then who hears these words of mine and acts on them will be like a wise man who built his house on rock. The rain fell, the floods came, and the winds blew and beat on that house, but it did not fall, because it had been founded on rock. And everyone who hears these words of mine and does not act on them will be like a foolish man who built his house on sand. The rain fell, and the floods came, and the winds blew and beat against that house, and it fell—and great was its fall! (Matthew 7:24-27)

The ending of Jesus' sermon is often thought of only as a simple illustration, but for Jesus, the admonition to his first listeners to actively respond to what he taught them was vital for judging the genuine maturity of their relationship to God. For Jesus, obedience is the mark of truly hearing the Word of God—doing the Word is the manifestation of genuine faith. And the tell-tale sign of biblical worship is a congregation leaving the sanctuary to continue bringing glory to God by engaging in God's mission in the world.

The end result of a service of worship, like the ending of a sermon, is focused on answering one question: So what? The question is meant to focus the congregation on how to respond to the God who has called them to worship. This concern brings the worshiper full circle. The integrity and holiness of the worshiper, called and sent, is vitally connected to how God considers the integrity and holiness of the service of worship itself.

Mark Labberton summarizes the connection between worship and the integrity of the worshiper when he writes,

> Scripture calls us to worship that affirms and demonstrates the right ordering of all of reality. Faithful worshipers kneel to receive and then enact the story of God's re-creation of all things. God's purpose is for us to "love the Lord your God with all your heart, and with all your soul and with all your strength, and with all your mind," then go on to love "your neighbor as yourself" (Luke 10:27). This is God's right ordering of reality. By God's grace, what sin has distorted and injustice has desecrated begins to reappear in the ordinary lives of God's faithful worshipers and the world at large.[4]

A significant part of the historical context for Isaiah's vision of heavenly worship in Isaiah 6 was the fifty-two years of Uzziah's "successful" kingship over Judah. Like Uzziah, God's people had become prosperous, independent and unrighteous. Right before his experience of heavenly worship in Isaiah 6, Isaiah reflects on the status of Israel's pride and self-sufficiency in chapter 5: "Ah, you who join house to house, who add field to field, until there is room for no one but you. . . . Ah, you who call evil good and good evil, who put darkness for light and light for darkness. . . . Ah, you who are wise in your own eyes, and shrewd in your own sight" (Isaiah 5:8, 20-21). Israel's affluence, moral perversion and arrogance are, as Labberton writes, "what sin has distorted and injustice has desecrated." The first chapter of Isaiah reflects on the disconnect between the worship and justice as the prophet speaks for God:

> When you come to appear before me,
>   who asked this from your hand?
>   Trample my courts no more;
> bringing offerings is futile;

---

[4]Mark Labberton, *The Dangerous Act of Worship: Living God's Call to Justice* (Downers Grove, Ill.: InterVarsity Press, 2007), p. 39. Mark Labberton is the Lloyd John Ogilvie Chair for Preaching at Fuller Theological Seminary in Pasadena, California. Prior to this appointment, Labberton was the senior pastor at First Presbyterian Church in Berkeley, California, for sixteen years. This book addresses both the biblical texts dealing with the connection between worship and social justice and its contemporary challenges with significant theological depth and antidotal illustrative application.

incense is an abomination to me.
New moon and sabbath and calling of convocation—
    I cannot endure solemn assemblies with iniquity.
Your new moons and your appointed festivals
    my soul hates;
they have become a burden to me,
    I am weary of bearing them.
When you stretch out your hands,
    I will hide my eyes from you;
even though you make many prayers,
    I will not listen;
    your hands are full of blood.
Wash yourselves; make yourselves clean;
    remove the evil of your doings
    from before my eyes;
cease to do evil,
    learn to do good;
seek justice,
    rescue the oppressed,
defend the orphan,
    plead for the widow. (Isaiah 1:12-17)

Worship that is pleasing and acceptable to God is offered by worshipers who are obedient to God's will and dependent on God's grace. The idea of displeasing God through the very practices he commanded cuts to both the seriousness and the subtlety of hypocrisy. Doing the right things for the wrong reason and without dependence on the mediation of God is rejected by God in both worship and mission. Again, the parallel between this dynamic in Isaiah and the end of the Sermon on the Mount is startling. Just before the metaphor of the wise and foolish who build on rock or sand, Jesus speaks an unsettling word against the hypocrisy of self-deception in the context of divine judgment: "Many will say to me, 'Lord, Lord, did we not prophesy in your name, and cast out demons in your name, and do many deeds of power in your name?' Then I will declare to them, 'I never knew you; go away from me, you evildoers'" (Matthew 7:22-23). The "many" replicated things that Jesus himself was known to do, but they did so like the false prophets who spoke their own word for pride, self-promotion and the notice of others. Mission, like worship, must be done "in Christ." The integrity needed between being and doing must be mediated by divine grace for it to be pleasing and acceptable to God. Jesus affirms that "true worshipers will worship the Father in spirit and truth, for the Father seeks such as these to worship him" (John 4:23). True worshipers are those whose whole life is shaped by the will of God and dependent upon the Spirit of God. True worship itself is manifest only through the work and person of Christ Jesus. The same dynamic is true for the church's engagement in God's mission in the world. The liturgy of worship that is shaped by God's word helps prepare the worshiper for mission shaped by God's character. The spirit and truth of God-pleasing worship is the spirit and truth of God-focused mission. Those who obediently *do* in mission the Word of God they *hear* in worship are the people God will know in "that day."

Jesus also relates the importance of the disciple's transformation through union with him ("abiding"), knowing God's word, obedience and mission in the Upper Room Discourse in the Gospel of John.

> Abide in me as I abide in you. Just as the branch cannot bear fruit by itself unless it abides in the vine, neither can you unless you abide in me. . . . If you abide in me, and my words abide in you, ask for whatever you wish, and it will be done for you. . . . If you keep my commandments, you will abide in my love, just as I have kept my Father's commandments and abide in his love. (John 15:4, 7, 10)

OBEDIENCE GROUNDED IN GOD'S GRACE

Christians robustly (and rightly) affirm that salvation is achieved only through the work and person of Christ Jesus, and we receive God's salvation as a gift of God's grace through faith alone. The mediation of the Son by the Spirit is why true worship is also a gift of God's grace. Evangelical Christians who trace their history and theological formation from the retrieval of patristic biblical theology during the time of the Reformation tend to be keenly suspicious of any idea that juxtaposes obedience and faith, lest it lead to the erosion of *sola fide, sola gratia, sola scriptura.* "Only faith, only grace, only Scripture" is the famous trifold summary of the sixteenth-century reformulation of Christian doctrine. However, it is neither helpful nor biblical to distance the affirmation of salvation by faith alone from obedience, which is the fitting *response* to salvation as the unmerited gift of God. In fact, the New Testament (*sola scriptura*) affirms the relationship between faith, grace and obedience very clearly.

The ending of the Sermon on the Mount has already been highlighted as an example of how seriously Jesus related obedience focused on God's glory as the proper manifestation of salvation. In John's Gospel, Jesus clearly teaches the relationship between salvation that rests in the love and grace of God and obedience as the fitting response of the believer.

> My Father is glorified by this, that you bear much fruit and become my disciples. As the Father has loved me, so I have loved you; abide in my love. If you keep my commandments, you will abide in my love, just as I have kept my Father's commandments and abide in his love. (John 15:8-10)

Again, the relationship of hearing God's Word (*sola scriptura*) and resting (*sola fide*) in the love (*sola gratia*) of God manifests itself in the obedience of lives centered on the glory of God. Worship that is centered on glorifying God (*soli Deo gloria*) yields worshipers who invest in the mission of God (*missio Dei*) with the same purpose. Radical dependence on God's grace is absolutely necessary for salvation and mission, faith and obedience. Salvation by faith alone needs to be affirmed as more than just correct doctrine; it must manifest itself as Christ's presence in the church by the Spirit through the church's participation in the mission of God. Only then is the worship of the church acceptable and pleasing to God. Again, a challenge from Mark Labberton: "Worship and justice both depend on acknowledging true desperation."[5] Both the faith and the work of the church are utterly dependent on God's grace.

When worship is disconnected from God's mission in the world, it easily becomes the self-soothing practice of contemporary religious disembodied spirituality. When worship is focused on the spiritual revival of the congregation or individual believers, our well-being, or our inward and invisible lives, it is nothing more than a functional means to ends of self-help or self-esteem. When worship is disconnected from the mission of God, it easily becomes entrenched in its own quest for a pleasant, com-

---

[5]Ibid, p. 89.

forting and joyful spiritual experience. What is startling about this manifestation in evangelical faith communities is how this parallels the ahistorical faith of the Protestant liberalism that flourished during the Enlightenment. When the "Christ of faith" was disconnected from the "Jesus of history," one's religious experience became all that mattered. Humankind then became the measure of all things, rather than God's Word, and not God's incarnate Son. This last point leads directly to the notion that people can self-determine what is good and not good, that humanity no longer needs the mediation of God regarding the "knowledge of good and evil." When justice, like righteousness, is no longer dependent on God and God's Word, the integrity of both God's people in worship and God's mission in the world is lost.

The prophet Amos highlights the bifurcation of worship and justice when he declares as the voice of the LORD:

> I hate, I despise your festivals,
>   and I take no delight in your solemn assemblies.
> Even though you offer me your burnt offerings and grain-offerings,
>   I will not accept them;
> and the offerings of well-being of your fatted animals
>   I will not look upon.
> Take away from me the noise of your songs;
>   I will not listen to the melody of your harps.
> But let justice roll down like waters,
>   and righteousness like an ever-flowing stream. (Amos 5:21-24)

God's people have long struggled to unite worship and mission and to focus both on God's glory. It is no small comfort and encouragement to know that "the Lord disciplines those whom he loves, and chastises every child whom he accepts" (see Proverbs 3:12 LXX and Hebrews 12:5-6). In part, Christians experience God's grace because God is patient. Time and again God rebukes his children in order to restore them to a right and good relationship with him in love, faith and obedience.

Worship engages the whole of life. Worship that is acceptable and pleasing to the Lord is shaped by biblical liturgical patterns, but it blooms into a life of holiness and wholeness beyond liturgical limits. The integrity of worshipers, not just the shape of a service of worship itself, is a central concern to God and the bedrock of what is needed to glorify God. The integrity of being and doing is only possible through union with Christ by the Spirit. Only in this union can one understand the admonition of James to "be doers of the word, and not merely hearers" (James 1:22). The integrity of the Christian is grounded in the imputed righteousness of Christ mediated by the Holy Spirit. It is impossible by our own effort to come to worship to be shaped by the Holy One and at the same time to acquire the necessary holiness sufficient for worship that pleases God. Apart from God's grace, God's call, God's mediating presence, we "can do nothing" (John 15:5). When we realize the necessity of abiding "in Christ" alone, we also realize that the integrity of being and doing is found only in the perfection of the Lord Jesus. In Christ we come, in Christ we stay, in Christ we go.

ABIDING IN GOD'S PRESENCE

Psalm 15 is a foundational text for understanding the connection between worship and personal integrity, between liturgy and life. This psalm offers an important description of a worshiper who is responding fully to the truth and reality of who God is. Psalm 15 is a repository of wisdom God's people need to learn in order to be those who build on solid rock and stand in glory on the Day of the Lord.

> O LORD, who may abide in your tent?
> Who may dwell on your holy hill?
> Those who walk blamelessly, and do what is right,
> and speak the truth from their heart;
> who do not slander with their tongue,
> and do no evil to their friends,
> nor take up a reproach against their neighbors;
> in whose eyes the wicked are despised,
> but who honor those who fear the LORD;
> who stand by their oath even to their hurt;
> who do not lend money at interest,
> and do not take a bribe against the innocent. (Psalm 15:1-5)

The questions that begin this psalm of David can be considered in a variety of ways. Is this the question of a priest to approaching pilgrims at the entrance to a well-known place of worship? Or are these the questions of pilgrims on a journey about entrance requirements at an unknown sanctuary? For the former, pilgrims would be expected to know the right answer, the "password," for a lifestyle that would grant them entrance. For the latter, the response of the welcoming priest makes clear to those who would worship rightly what is required. Scholars have wrestled with understanding the sequence of the psalm's ambivalent question-and-answer structure for centuries, but one thing is clear regardless of how one considers the structure: coming into the presence of the LORD is not something done casually or hypocritically.

After considering a myriad of ways of understanding the structure and intended use of the Davidic psalm, Old Testament scholar Ronald E. Manahan summarizes the basic structure and broad intention of Psalm 15:

> Psalm 15 is structured as a question-answer-observation sequence. There is an absence of cultic and liturgical detail. The piece is instructional, giving evidence of wisdom influence. . . . Worship is the central focus of the psalm. *Entrance into the Lord's presence is not to be to a casual matter.*[6]

The first question of the psalm, "who may abide in your tent?" can also be translated, "who may sojourn . . . ?" reflecting the idea of the Hebrew verb *gûr*, which carries the idea of staying put in a place (thus the term "abide" in the NRSV) whether for a long or fairly short period of time. Manahan rightly submits that the noun form of this verb is "often rendered 'resident alien.'" So these pilgrims find themselves in a place that is not their home but want to stop for some time and find welcome in the house of their God that they might offer worship. No wonder the sacred space for worship is termed a *sanctuary*!

So who can enter this sanctuary? In typical Hebrew parallelism that emphasizes both poetic form and relative importance, the text asks who can dwell on the LORD's "holy hill." Those whose lives reflect the God they have come to worship. The sanctified may enter the sanctuary. God's people set apart for his service may enter the space set apart for attending to his glo-

---

[6]Roland E. Manahan, "The Worshiper's Approach to God," in *Authentic Worship: Hearing Scripture's Voice, Applying Its Truth*, ed. Herbert W. Bateman IV (Grand Rapids: Kregel, 2002), pp. 55-77; emphasis in original.

rious presence. Now, stating this idea of worthiness can sound unsettling to believers who are aware of their unworthiness and sin-marred lives. By this criteria, who *could* enter the place of God's dwelling? Only those who are known to this God, who can stand in the day of God's judgment on the day of his coming. Worship is primarily about being *known by God*, the one whose house his people enter. The question here is not "What do I know about God?" but "Does God know me?" Jesus underscores this dynamic reality at the end of the Sermon on the Mount when he says, "I never knew you; go away from me you evildoers"(Matthew 7:23). Only "in Christ," our mediator and high priest, can we enter the sanctuary.

Manahan summarizes this challenging dynamic in Psalm 15 by concluding,

> This wisdom piece mirrors the covenant relationship between God and the worshipers. That relationship is not held together by cultic rituals. No, those will not do. They are not enough. Rather, the covenant-making God holds the relationship together. In our psalm, relationship is stressed, not liturgical details.

Like worship itself, the ethical life of the worshiper is a response to God who has established his covenant with his people. The epistle of 1 Peter holds this idea together when discussing the identity of God's people, their status as "resident aliens," and the need for integrity and ethical behavior to reflect that very identity:

> But you are a chosen race, a royal priesthood, a holy nation, God's own people, in order that you may proclaim the mighty acts of him who called you out of darkness into his marvelous light.
> Once you were not a people,
>   but now you are God's people;
> once you had not received mercy,
>   but now you have received mercy.
>
> Beloved, I urge you as aliens and exiles to abstain from the desires of the flesh that wage war against the soul. Conduct yourselves honorably among the Gentiles, so that, though they malign you as evildoers, they may see your honorable deeds and glorify God when he comes to judge. (1 Peter 2:9-12)

The ethical parameters of Psalm 15 are specific and clearly stated. They include behaviors that reflect the worshipers' relationship with God, but also affect the worshipers' relationship with those in their own households, those who live near them, those in the fellowship of God's people and those in society at large.

The New Testament is no stranger to the dynamics of a life that "gives what it gets." The covenant of mercy that 1 Peter refers to above is not only an echo of Hosea 1:9-10, but a reflection of Jesus' teaching at the beginning of the Sermon on the Mount that those who have been merciful will receive mercy (Matthew 5:7). Notice that Jesus' teaching connects giving and getting mercy from another direction. This is similar to what Jesus does (in both directions!) with love and obedience in the Upper Room Discourse. If one loves and abides in Jesus, one obeys his word. If one keeps his commandments, then they truly love and abide in him.

So who can answer the call to worship with holiness and integrity? Psalm 24 is closely related to Psalm 15 and asks and answers this question like this:

> Who shall ascend the hill of the LORD?
>   And who shall stand in his holy place?
> Those who have clean hands and pure hearts,
>   who do not lift up their souls to what is false,
>   and do not swear deceitfully.
> They will receive blessing from the LORD,
>   and vindication from the God of their salvation.
> Such is the company of those who seek him,
>   who seek the face of the God of Jacob.
> (Psalm 24:3-6)

Indeed, worshipers do become like the God who is worshiped, a God who allows no fissure between who he is and what he does. Integrity in all areas of life is a mandate for those who would worship in spirit and in truth. Like these psalms, Jesus dismissed liturgical and cultic details to get at the heart of the matter, the heart of worship, the heart of what it means to be known by God. "Woman, believe me, the hour is coming when you will worship the Father neither on this mountain nor in Jerusalem," he said. "But the hour is coming, and is now here, when the true worshipers will worship the Father in spirit and truth, for the Father seeks such as these to worship him" (John 4:21, 23).

The worshipers God seeks will find kind welcome at the entrance to that sanctuary. Psalm 24 celebrates such a merciful God of glory who welcomes the resident alien to enter into his presence:

> Lift up your heads, O gates!
>   and be lifted up, O ancient doors!
>   that the King of glory may come in.
> Who is the King of glory?
>   The LORD, strong and mighty,
>   the LORD, mighty in battle.
> Lift up your heads, O gates!
>   and be lifted up, O ancient doors!
>   that the King of glory may come in.
> Who is this King of glory?
>   The LORD of hosts,
>   he is the King of glory. (Psalm 24:7-10)

WORKSHOP FOR CHAPTER SIX

1. Mark Labberton asks in his book *The Dangerous Act of Worship,* "Where is the evidence that we are scandalized before God when we hunger for worship that almost never leads us to have a heart for the hungry?"[7]

   - Consider a variety of ways for a congregation to invite and include the poor and hungry in the life of the congregation.

   - Think through what it would take to help the unchurched poor and hungry understand the meaning and practice of Christian worship.

   - What are things your community of faith does or can do to strengthen the integrity of the worshiper and the mission of the congregation?

2. Pause and take a moment to observe the specifics of Psalm 15:2-5 concerning the ethical behavior of those desiring to worship God.

   - Which behaviors relate to those near you—family, close friends, one's neighbors?

   - Which behaviors relate mostly to more distant relationships, in business dealings and truth-bearing in the world at large?

---

[7]Labberton, *Dangerous Act of Worship,* p. 38.

- Consider your strengths and weaknesses in these relationships and how they help or hinder your preparedness for worship.

3. The word *selāh* noted at the ending of each refrain in Psalm 24 is a Hebrew word that may mean "pause and think about this for a while" and may include the idea of bowing while one does this.

   - Take some time to do just that in the light of worship in God's presence and the integrity of your life.

4. Read James 1:22-27 and consider the connection between worship, life, ethics, justice and personal integrity in this passage. Consider ways your congregation attends to the moral integrity of pastors, worship leaders, teachers and the congregation as a whole with both grace and truth.

   - Talk to your pastor, a worship leader and a person involved in mission outreach about enhancing the connections between the congregation's worship and work.

5. Think through the typical liturgical practices in your congregation. Is there evidence of an "only the spiritual is really important" tendency in the service? How are incarnation, embodiment and obedience included in the service?

6. Consider people in your congregation who are known for their holiness of character or particular kind of obedience in their lives (like people who are retired or long-term missionaries, those who work with the poor, people who suffer physical ailments with faith, etc.).

   - How might some of these people share their stories as a part of worship? How might these people be connected with others in the congregation across cultural or generational lines?

WORSHIP IN EXILE,
SYNAGOGUES AND THE
EARLY CHURCH

When he came to Nazareth, where he had been brought up, he went to
the synagogue on the sabbath day, as was his custom. He stood up to read,
and the scroll of the prophet Isaiah was given to him. He unrolled the
scroll and found the place where it was written. . . . And he rolled
up the scroll, gave it back to the attendant, and sat down.
The eyes of all in the synagogue were fixed on him.

LUKE 4:16-17, 20

When Jesus entered his hometown synagogue, a place where Jews prior to
the destruction of Jerusalem in A.D. 70 gathered for prayer, reading Torah and
other community events, he was initially welcomed and felt right at home.
Jesus knew what to do. He knew the prayers that would be prayed at a certain
time with the gathered community of Jews, his family and local friends. Jesus
knew to stand to read from the Hebrew Scripture and how to turn to the
passage to be read from the scroll handed to him by the ḥazzān, the synagogue
official who was charged with the upkeep of the synagogue and its furnishings
and scrolls. After he read and returned the scroll, Jesus knew to sit down, as
was the custom of rabbis, in order to expound on the text.

There is no clear mention of synagogues in the Old Testament, but synagogues were well established and robustly functioning centers at the time of
the New Testament. The prominence of the synagogue as a center for Jewish

communities in the New Testament is clear. From the synagogue of Nazareth where faithful Jews gathered on a certain sabbath to hear a hometown rabbi named Jesus read from the Isaiah scroll, to the synagogues of the diaspora where Paul began his proclamation of the good news of Messiah Jesus,[1] the synagogue can be recognized in significant ways in the New Testament as the cradle of the early church.

However, prior to the events of A.D. 70, the synagogue was a community center that served a variety of functions, prominent among them the nurture of God's people by the reading of God's Word. After the destruction of the temple, the reading of Scripture in synagogues continued, but there was also a "rapidly developing prayer liturgy" and evidence of the synagogue's identification as sacred space, including the orientation of later synagogues toward Jerusalem and the standardization of Torah shrines with sacred Torah scrolls.[2]

The patterns of the Christian church that developed from the synagogue, the communal reading of Scripture and times of prayer, and the nurture of a common faith seem to parallel the activities within the synagogue prior to the destruction of the temple. As Christian Jews were put out of synagogues, and as the inclusion of Gentiles within Christian fellowships accelerated, gathering in homes for the reading of the Scriptures, prayer and community meals (whether sacred or not) paralleled the activities of Jewish communities in synagogues. Most research indicates synagogues were not set apart as sacred space in the more formal sense until after the fall of Jerusalem and the significant differentiation of the Christian faith that accelerated after that time. While acknowledging the fluid nature of the development of synagogue practices between Palestine and the diaspora, as well as the significant difference in the centrality of the synagogue before and after the fall of Jerusalem in A.D. 70, there are more than a few reasons why the Jewish synagogue was a template for early Christian communities, leadership and

---

[1]The only exception to this pattern in the New Testament is in Philippi, where there was no synagogue (Acts 16:11-13). In this case Paul went to find the Jewish community on the sabbath day by the river because he knew that's where they would gather for the ritual washings required before such prayer. *The IVP Bible Background Commentary: New Testament* by Craig Keener (Downers Grove, Ill.: InterVarsity Press, 1993) has a concise summary of Jewish practice in the diaspora.

[2]See Rachel Hachlili, *Ancient Jewish Art and Archaeology in the Land of Israel* (Leiden: Brill, 1988), pp. 141ff.

liturgy. However, the development of Christian worship involves more than the worship practices of early house churches that were greatly shaped by the patterns of Israel's weekly gatherings in the synagogue. The synagogue was not the temple—and there was more to Israel's worship that contributes to the biblical patterns of Christian liturgical development.

It is not unusual for scholars to make fairly direct connections between the patterns of worship in synagogues and the development of Christian worship in the early church. The significance of this influence can be affirmed with confidence regardless of the exact genesis of the synagogue's historical development. However, the biblical patterns for Christian worship should not be limited to the textual glimpses the New Testament offers of synagogue, and by extension, house church practices. It is important when considering the Jewish influence on Christian worship to consider why these "gathering places" became increasingly important for the Jewish community sometime during the post-exilic or intertestamental period.

PATTERNS OF WORSHIP IN THE NEW TESTAMENT: GOSPELS

Very few worship patterns are explicit in the New Testament Gospel accounts. It is not surprising that Luke's account includes more details of Jewish synagogue practices and temple ritual than the others, because Luke was concerned to "set down an orderly account" (Luke 1:1) for his patron, the "most excellent Theophilus" (Luke 1:3), thought by most New Testament scholars to be a Gentile unfamiliar with Judaism, the gospel story and the history of the early church (Acts 1:1-4). Luke notes the priestly rotation for service in the temple (Luke 1:5), the prophecies of Anna and Simeon at the circumcision of Jesus in the temple (Luke 2:21-38), Jesus' attendance and teaching at the Passover when he was twelve years old (Luke 2:41-51), but records these events with a focus on the narrative of Jesus' life, and there is scant mention, if any, of liturgical practice itself.

All the Synoptic accounts include the regular practice of Jesus reading and teaching Scripture and healing in the synagogue (see Matthew 12:9-13; Mark 3:1-5; Luke 6:6-10; 13:10-17; and the non-Synoptic John 6:59). These accounts routinely take place on the sabbath, not because that is the only time Jesus participated in synagogue life, but because how Jesus and his disciples kept the sabbath was under scrutiny by the Pharisaical leaders of Judaism, especially in Galilee.

Patterns of worship are important not just to external structures but also to the interior life of the worshiper. Implications of the need for holiness and biblically mandated justice for the poor and oppressed also surface in the Gospel writings. Matthew (as part of the Sermon on the Mount) and Luke include the stark teachings of Jesus concerning pride in the practices of piety, almsgiving, fasting and prayer (see, for example, Matthew 6:5-18; Luke 11:42-44; 18:9-14). The importance of humility in giving to God tithes and offerings is emphasized by both Mark (12:41-44) and Luke (21:1-4). The cleansing of the temple is a significant event that highlights Jesus' concern to eliminate merchandizing religious practice that catered to the rich, exploited the efforts of the poor, and marginalized the simple devotional practices of Palestinian Jews and Jewish religious pilgrims from the diaspora (Matthew 21:12-17; Mark 11:15-19; Luke 19:45-48; and John 2:13-22). Jesus' act of cleansing the temple was an act of judgment on Israel's failure to embody the story of Yahweh's covenant to bless all the nations of the world through the seed of Abraham. This judgment was not about the abuse of merchandizing per se but about how that practice thwarted the ultimate mission of God for the salvation of the world.

The devotional and worship practice of prayer is addressed negatively not only in Jesus' cleansing of the temple but also in the Sermon on the Mount (Matthew 6:5-15) and in Luke (11:1-13). The elevation of humility in the practice of prayer is accompanied by an example of prayer and the structuring of prayer that is meant to guide the disciples of Jesus. Far from being completely original, the "Lord's Prayer" is very Jewish in its praise, petition, and sequential shape and intention. According to New Testament scholar Craig Keener, "the overall links between the Lord's Prayer and the Kaddish are too close for coincidence."[3] A Jewish Kaddish is a prayer of praise that addresses God and extols God's attributes directly. Jesus does give a distinctive context for praise—that of the kingdom both present and coming—in his prayer. In addition, the Lord's Prayer does give New Testament readers an idea of one Jewish prayer practice that Jesus both af-

---

[3]Craig S. Keener, *A Commentary on the Gospel of Matthew* (Grand Rapids: Eerdmans, 1999), p. 215 n. 26.

firmed and practiced in his ministry life with the disciples.[4] In Jesus' prayer, both the fatherhood of God and the rightness of God's kingdom begin the prayer and precede the supplications of need concerning those who pray. The latter elements are not typical of a Kaddish, but this prayer of Jesus in Matthew and Luke is more than a prayer to be prayed. It is a pattern of prayer to be used by Jesus' followers, in which he commends the inclusion of supplication and intercession.

The integrity of the worshiper, especially concerning the offering of tithes and sacrifices, factors into Jesus' teaching just as it did in the Hebrew Scriptures. In the Sermon on the Mount Jesus admonishes his listeners, "So when you are offering your gift at the altar, if you remember that your brother or sister has something against you, leave your gift there before the altar and go; first be reconciled to your brother or sister, and then come and offer your gift" (Matthew 5:23-24). This clearly undergirds a central teaching of Jesus that sums up all the Law and the Prophets: "'You shall love the Lord your God with all your heart, and with all your soul, and with all your mind.' This is the greatest and first commandment. And a second is like it: 'You shall love your neighbor as yourself'" (Matthew 22:37-39; see also Mark 12:30-31 and Deuteronomy 6:5). For those who are true worshipers, it is necessary that the love for God must be extended to loving relationships and manifested in patterns of reconciliation and peace-making efforts. Jesus' teaching is underscored in New Testament teaching outside the Gospels. Romans 12:16-18; 1 John 2:7-11; 3:16-17; 4:9-11 are good examples of how loving one another in the body of Christ and those in need are necessary if one claims to love God.

Jesus consistently used Jewish patterns and practices and gave them a new focus, context and intention for use by his disciples. With his disciples in the upper room before his arrest and betrayal, Jesus took the symbolic elements used to remember Israel's exodus from bondage in Egypt and elevated this reenactment to embody his own sacrifice that would liberate his followers from bondage to sin, death and the clutches of the evil one (Matthew 26:26-29; Mark 14:22-25; Luke 22:15-20; 1 Corinthians 11:23-26). Jesus' segue from Passover Seder to the Lord's Supper is a good example of

---

[4]Ibid., pp. 215-26.

how New Testament authors often offered only a glimpse of Jewish religious observance because they assume their readers had a certain level of familiarity with Jewish customs. This glimpse and the understanding and practice of the first Jewish Christians gain clarity only as they are explicated in the late first century and the first half of the second century when regulation becomes necessary.

Patterns of Worship in the New Testament: Acts

The lack of explicit descriptions of corporate worship in the Gospels is extended to the book of Acts. Much is assumed by Luke about the practices and general rhythms of Jewish religious life that are incorporated into Christian faith communities. These emerging messianic communities embrace a new designation for their identity as non-Jews begin to swell their ranks. Luke relates that "it was in Antioch that the disciples were first called 'Christians'" (Acts 11:26).

During the time the apostles centered their work and witness in Jerusalem, the fledgling community of disciples grew in numbers from about one hundred twenty-five people to several thousand who "devoted themselves to the apostles' teaching and fellowship, to the breaking of bread and the prayers. . . . Day by day, as they spent much time together in the temple, they broke break at home and ate their food with glad and generous hearts, praising God and having the goodwill of all the people" (Acts 2:42, 46-47). Attending to "the prayers," spending time in the temple, teaching, eating community meals and the breaking of bread in the Lord's Supper were all familiar habits of faith rooted in Judaism.

Prayer is one act of worship prominent in Acts. Acts 3:1 mentions the apostles' habit of saying "the prayers" in the temple at the set hours established for the liturgical prayers of Israel's common worship. Acts 4:23-26; 12:5; 12:12 clearly indicate that believers gathered in homes for extended times of prayer that centered around the felt needs of the community and not the formal liturgy of Jewish worship life. Both types of prayer were valued and practiced by the early church. Acts notes both the unity of the body and the diversity of expressions of faith apparent in the early church: "And every day in the temple and at home they did not cease to teach and proclaim Jesus as the Messiah" (Acts 5:42). As the church spread geographically, diversified ethnically and began to suffer increasing persecution, the church moved prayer meetings, preaching, teaching, evangelism, community meals and the reading of scripture from the synagogue (Acts 9:20; 13:14; 14:1; 15:21; 17:1; 18:4) to houses (Acts 18:7; 20:7-8, 20).

The shift in meeting as Jewish and Gentile believers on the "first day of the week," either in addition to the Hebrew sabbath or as its substitute, is only mentioned once in the book of Acts: "On the first day of the week, when we met to break bread . . ." (Acts 20:7). The significance of this isolated mention in Acts is due to its relationship to Pentecost. The Jewish feast of Pentecost was celebrated fifty days after Passover and also fell on the first day of the week. This is implicit in the account of Acts 2. Daily gatherings are more apparent in the early days that were centered in Jerusalem and only became more designated and intentionally focused as the church mission spread to "the ends of the earth" (Acts 1:8).

The oversight of baptismal practice and the administration of the Lord's Supper in the book of Acts is a work in progress, much like the emergence of church leadership itself. The "laying on of hands" to set apart leaders was simply an extension of this practice in Judaism (see Acts 6:6; 13:3, for example) and continues to this day in Christian services of ordination for setting apart pastors, elders, deacons, missionaries, bishops and other leaders for kingdom work. The need for the regulation of baptism and the Lord's Supper surfaced rather early in Acts. Philip's ministry in Samaria (Acts 8:4-25) illustrates clearly the importance of oversight, regulation and accountability for the sacred practices of the church. The accountability of local communities to the apostolic leadership of the church helped bring wisdom in both faith and practice to the early church. After their first missionary journey was complete, Paul and Barnabas gave a report to the congregation that sent them (Acts 14:27) and to the apostolic leadership council in Jerusalem (Acts 15:1-35).

It is interesting that the first time the word for "church" (*ekklēsia*) is used in the book of Acts, it is associated with the "great fear" that "seized the whole church" after the corruption introduced by the duplicity of Ananias and his wife Sapphira in the giving of offerings (Acts 5:1-11). God's people are, as an echo of Yahweh's promise to Moses, still defined by the God who alone initiates the call to worship and the holiness that befits such a call.

The book of Acts, like the Gospels, offers only glimpses of the shape of Christian worship in the early church. But the grounding of Christian worship in the soil of Hebrew faith and practice is assumed by Luke and clearly apparent in his account written for Theophilus (Acts 1:1) and, since then, for all "friends of God" by faith. A fine summary of God's faithfulness through the Spirit that empowered the church for witness, work and worship is found in Acts 9:31: "Meanwhile the church throughout Judea, Galilee, and Samaria had peace and was built up. Living in the fear of the Lord and in the comfort of the Holy Spirit, it increased in numbers." God used the judgment on Ananias and Sapphira, like the judgment on Uzzah, during a time when a movement of God's Spirit was inaugurating something new for his people. The establishment of Jerusalem as focal point of the sacrificial rite of Israel and the birth of the church under the headship of Christ Jesus were pivotal points in the identification and renewal of God's people at those times. "Living in the fear of the Lord" was a costly and important lesson in both cases. The story-shape of biblical worship needed correction as well as grace at key moments, and this in itself indicates how important this was and is to God.

In all of this, the church is God's new covenant temple, God's new creation, God's house, the place where, as in the tabernacle, heaven and earth meet. The church draws near to God through sacrifice, the ultimate and final sacrifice of the Lamb of God (Romans 3:25; 8:3; Ephesians 5:2; Hebrews 9:12-14, 23-26; 10:5-22; 1 Peter 1:18-21; 1 John 2:2). The sacrificial language of the Old Testament is incorporated into New Testament ideas. The Word of God is like a sacrificial sword that divides bones and marrow (Hebrews 13:15; 1 Peter 2:5, 9). The fragrance of the church as the "aroma of Christ" (2 Corinthians 2:15) is akin to the incense that was part of various offerings in the priestly service of the tabernacle and a connection to eternal worship in the heavenly realm (Revelation 5:8; 8:3-4). Material gifts for the work and mission of the church are described as a pleasing sacrifice (Hebrews 13:16). The great thanksgiving included in the Lord's Supper is linked not only to the Passover but also to the peace offering.[5] The pervasive use of Old Tes-

---

[5]Thanks to Michael Farley for directing me to an essay by John Collins, "The Eucharist as Christian Sacrifice: How Patristic Authors Can Help Us Read the Bible," *Westminster Theological Journal* 66 (2004): 1-23, which helped me summarize this typology.

tament typology (a comparison or link between the Old Testament and New Testament that denotes the continuity of the biblical story) in the New Testament helps one to discern how Christian worship emerged from the story of Israel even as it became a distinctive story with a christological center and climax.

EPISTLES:
THE CHURCH AS THE DWELLING PLACE OF GOD BY THE SPIRIT

Despite the continuity between synagogue worship and that of the early church, there was one crucial difference. The New Testament describes the transformation of Israel's relationship with God from a place to a person. Jesus himself inaugurates this transformation by refocusing the worship of God from a place to the saving work of the Messiah:

> Believe me, the hour is coming when you will worship the Father neither on this mountain nor in Jerusalem. . . . But the hour is coming, and is now here, when the true worshipers will worship the Father in spirit and truth, for the Father seeks such as these to worship him. God is spirit, and those who worship him must worship in spirit and truth. (John 4:21, 23-24)

Jesus' new and dynamic reorientation of worship took place near Jacob's Well in Sychar of Samaria and was directed to a person who was tired of "coming here to draw water" (John 4:15). Indeed, the living water Jesus offered would spring from a person, not a place: "The water that I give will become in them a spring of water gushing up to eternal life" (John 4:14). This new "place" is foreshadowed in this passage as the *people* who come to believe that the rabbi, who had been thirsty and tired by the well of Sychar in the heat of the day, is the source of living water and the "Savior of the world" (John 4:42).

The New Testament tells the story of how the people of God become the "true worshipers" that the Father seeks. The sign of salvation is no longer an exclusive worshiping community brought to the mountain of God as a fulfillment of Yahweh's promise to Moses "you shall worship [me] on this mountain" (Exodus 3:12), but one body of people—Jews, Samaritans and Gentiles—out of whom gushes the life of the Savior. That's what it means to be "true worshipers [who] worship the Father in spirit and truth." The salvific and sanctifying work of the Messiah are included in his mediatorial role as the great high priest of worship.

The variety of metaphors employed in the epistles of the New Testament highlight this new dwelling place of God by the Spirit. Paul's preferred metaphor for the church is the "body of Christ" in whom the fullness of God dwells (Romans 8:9, 11; 12:5; 1 Corinthians 10:16-17; 12:12-27; Ephesians 1:22-23; 2:16; 3:6; 4:4, 12, 16; 5:30; Colossians 1:18; 2:17-19; 3:15). Peter compares the church to a building, a temple in fact, made of living stones—"a spiritual house, to be a holy priesthood, to offer spiritual sacrifices acceptable to God through Jesus Christ" (1 Peter 2:5). This text focuses on the transformation of identity from place to community and redefines the people of God as a "chosen race, a royal priesthood, a holy nation, God's own people" (1 Peter 2:9). This celebration of God's redemptive work extends to Israel's experience of alienation during exile and conquest and the struggle for holiness of those who would worship Yahweh rightly that is so notable in the prophets (see 1 Peter 2:9-10).

The zenith of this transformation is described near the end of New Testament, in the Revelation of John:

> Then I saw a new heaven and a new earth; for the first heaven and the first earth had passed away, and the sea was no more. And I saw the holy city, the new Jerusalem, coming down out of heaven from God, prepared as a bride adorned for her husband. And I heard a loud voice from the throne saying,
>
> > "See, the home of God is among mortals.
> > He will dwell with them;
> > they will be his peoples,
> > and God himself will be with them;
> > he will wipe every tear from their eyes.
> > Death will be no more;
> > mourning and crying and pain will be no more,
> > for the first things have passed away."

And the one who was seated on the throne said, "See, I am making all things new." Also he said, "Write this, for these words are trustworthy and true." Then he said to me, "It is done! I am the Alpha and the Omega, the beginning and the end. To the thirsty I will give water as a gift from the spring of the water of life. Those who conquer will inherit these things, and I will be their God and they will be my children." . . .

I saw no temple in the city, for its temple is the Lord God the Almighty and the Lamb. And the city has no need of sun or moon to shine on it, for the glory of God is its light, and its lamp is the Lamb. The nations will walk by its light, and the kings of the earth will bring their glory into it. Its gates will never be shut by day—and there will be no night there. People will bring into it the glory and the honor of the nations. But nothing unclean will enter it, nor anyone who practices abomination or falsehood, but only those who are written in the Lamb's book of life. (Revelation 21:1-7, 22-27)

True worship offered in spirit and truth with holy hands by the church, the community of those redeemed by the salvation of God the Son and indwelled by God the Spirit, is the crescendo of the New Testament. And it is important to notice that the shape of this worship is informed by the story of God's people in the Old Testament and how God made himself known through the very practice of Israel's worshiping life, the theology of the canon that is centered on God's desire to dwell intimately with his people, and the Light and Lamb and Living Water revealed in Jesus, the beginning and the end of all that was, is and will be.

CONCLUSION

The connection between ecclesiology and worship, the connection between who the church is and how the church glorifies the Lord and attends to God's pleasure, cannot be separated. The history, practice, theology and transformation of God's people from beginning to end need to shape the praise, prayers, songs, confessions, offerings, doxologies, liturgies, initiation rites, meditations and reenactments of God's salvation in sacrament and the hearing and the preaching of God's Word. The canon and its theology, the history and practices of Israel and the early church, and lessons learned by God's people from the first Garden of Eden to the last garden in the New Jerusalem reveal what it means to worship in spirit and truth.

The canonical-theological approach to liturgical study can help the church and its congregations discern the "spirit and truth" of true worship. Biblical parameters that give definition to the *truth* of what God has revealed concerning what is pleasing to him are as important as the dynamic of *spirit* that transforms the people of God into true worshipers. Like David, who only learned to dance freely in a way that pleased the Lord when he learned God's truth about the transportation of the Ark of the Covenant, the church can only enter into true worship when it is fettered wisely and safely in the Word of God through the incarnate Word of God by the Spirit. When the *fear* of the Lord binds the people of God by the Spirit to our great high priest, the church can, paradoxiacally, follow him behind the curtain and "approach the throne of grace with *boldness*" (Hebrews 4:16).

WORKSHOP FOR CHAPTER SEVEN

1. Consider how the words, sequence and pattern of this prayer Jesus taught his disciples help shape the prayers you pray both privately and in corporate worship.

   He was praying in a certain place, and after he had finished, one of his disciples said to him, "Lord, teach us to pray, as John taught his disciples." He said to them, "When you pray, say:
   Father, hallowed be your name.
      Your kingdom come.
      Give us each day our daily bread.
      And forgive us our sins,
         for we ourselves forgive
            everyone indebted to us.
      And do not bring us to the time of trial." (Luke 11:1-4)

   Pray then in this way:
   Our Father in heaven,
   hallowed be your name.
   Your kingdom come.
   Your will be done,
      on earth as it is in heaven.
   Give us this day our daily bread.
   And forgive us our debts,
      as we also have forgiven our debtors.
   And do not bring us to the time of trial,
      but rescue us from the evil one. (Matthew 6:9-13)

2. Rewrite the Lord's Prayer in your own words.

3. Think through how the Lord's Prayer might be used to structure an entire sevenfold service of worship.

   • Construct a liturgy based on this idea.

4. Consider how the practice of worship in your congregation reflects the "true worship" Jesus delineated as needing both "spirit and truth, for the Father seeks such as these to worship him. God is spirit, and those who worship him must worship in spirt and truth" (John 4:23-24). The need for spirit communicates a conscious dependence upon God as the mediator of that which pleases him; the need for truth grounds worship on the foundation of God's word.

   • Consider how this consciousness of divine mediation and the word of God are evident (or less than evident) in the service of worship in your congregation.

   • Think about the liturgy of the service of worship you attend most often. Is this service fairly balanced? If not, in what area is it imbalanced?

5. Read through the book of Acts and make a list of comments concerning corporate worship that might help inform and shape your understanding and leadership of worship.

6. Read through Paul's letter to the Ephesians and make a list of comments concerning corporate worship.

   • Design a service of worship using the text of Ephesians 1:3-23.

7. Select one practice that is outlined in the Mosaic law concerning worship (like a memorial observance or particular sacrifice) and trace its development in Scripture.

   • Include lessons learned through Israel's failure or disobedience.

   • If possible, trace the transformation of this Old Testament observance in the practice and theology of the early church through the New Testament.

EXCURSUS: HISTORY AND DEVELOPMENT OF THE SYNAGOGUE

From Luke 4:16-17, 20 it is apparent that some patterns of activity for observing the sabbath in first-century Palestinian synagogues seem to be clearly set. However, the historical development of the synagogue itself is actually unclear. Some scholars suggest a date and place for the inaugural development of the synagogue as early as the Babylonian exile. Others think there is more robust evidence for the emergence of the synagogue in Judea shortly after the post-exilic revival of the prophet Ezra. Still others support the idea that the synagogue developed during the intertestamental period in the diaspora. During my work on this chapter, I did an informal survey of the three Old Testament scholars at my university where I teach, and each of them summarized the initial emergence of the synagogue at three different times; two placed the inaugural locus within Palestine and one within the eastern diaspora. From the current state of research concerning the history and function of the synagogue, it must be clearly acknowledged from the outset that the careful consideration of how the worship within Jewish synagogues influenced the early development of Christian worship is more complicated than one might expect.

Lee I. Levine, the Rev. Moses Bernard Lauterman Family Chair in Classical Archaeology, Hebrew University of Jerusalem, summarizes the breadth of scholarship concerning the history of the synagogue when he writes,

> What factors were decisive in its development, who was responsible for it, and where exactly this "creation" took place, the sources at our disposal are simply oblivious to these issues. . . . Most opinions . . . place the synagogue's origins in a sixth-century setting related to the reforms of Ezra and Nehemiah, specifically the Torah-reading ceremony. . . . Still others posit either a fourth-century, . . . third-century . . . and even a second- or first-century date (resulting from the developments in Judea) for the emergence of the synagogue. This spectrum of opinion relates not only to the dating of the synagogue's origin but also to its geographical setting. Some locate the first appearance of the synagogue in Babylonia, others in Egypt, and still others in a Judean setting.
>
> For all their diversity, the above theories, almost without exception, share at least two common assumptions—that the religious component of the ancient synagogue was primary and that dramatically new religious circumstances were what gave rise to the innovations in this area. Implicit in most of these theories is the view that some kind of liturgical activity, be it listening to God's word from a prophet, the recital of public prayer, or the introduction

of scriptural readings, played a crucial and definitive role in the formation of the early synagogue.[6]

Levin's work builds on patterns discerned by a wide field of scholars that note the presence of synagogues in the diaspora, as well as Palestine, in villages and walled cities, by the first century B.C. Most often these meeting places in Palestine were called synagogues or "place of gathering" (Levine notes only one exception), but in the diaspora, "place of prayer" (*proseuchē*) was the dominant term. Other names used included "sanctuary" or "place of instruction." Overall, the synagogue was a community gathering place that could be used in a variety of ways, from political activity to education, charitable work, celebratory meals, or liturgical functions such as community prayer and the reading and teaching of Scripture.

It is important to note that even though synagogues during the Second Temple period played a significant role in Jewish religious life, the buildings themselves lacked a discernible religious character early on. Levine notes that there was "no clear-cut orientation toward Jerusalem, no place for a Torah shrine, no decorative element of religious significance, and no dedicatory inscription noting a special status accorded the building." However, "the regular communal reading of scriptures" was the unique feature of worship that took place in the synagogue even as it developed over a fairly long period of time. Many scholars determine that the centrality of this practice had its beginning in the reforms of Josiah and in the post-exilic revival of Ezra. Some scholars suggest that the practice of reading the Scriptures in community settings may have developed as a parallel practice to the sacrificial cult of the temple even before the destruction of the second temple.[7]

Scholars generally date the writing of the Gospel According to John near the last decade of the first century. John's focus audience lived at least twenty years after the fall of Jerusalem when the centrality of the synagogue for Israel's worship life became, understandably, increasingly important. After the fall of Jerusalem, the religio-political leadership of the Pharisees also

---

[6]Lee I. Levine, "The Nature and Origin of the Palestinian Synagogue Reconsidered," *Journal of Biblical Literature* 115, no. 3 (Autumn 1996): 425-48.
[7]See Michael A. Fishbane, *Biblical Interpretation in Ancient Israel* (Oxford: Clarendon, 1985), p. 113.

increased in prominence, when the need for a functioning priesthood and the demise of the Sanhedrin Council and its leadership, which had been dominated by the Sadducees, had been eliminated. John's Gospel highlights Jesus' anticipation of these changes by including narratives that focus on the reality of God's salvation encountering people outside Judaism (the Samaritan woman and her village in John 4), and outside the synagogue system. Examples of this emphasis can be noted in Jesus' teaching in John 16:2: "[The Jews] will put you out of the synagogues. Indeed, an hour is coming when those who kill you will think that by doing so they are offering worship to God." The widening gulf between Jewish synagogue and Christian church is also anticipated in the concern of the parents of a man healed of congenital blindness that they would be "put out of the synagogue" (John 9:22). After all, Jesus found this man outside the temple area after he had, in fact, been excommunicated for his witness concerning Jesus (John 9:34-38). It is telling that this man's declaration of faith—"Lord, I believe"—culminates in "worship" (*proskuneō*) outside Judaism proper (John 9:38).

PART TWO

HISTORICAL PATTERNS

The Interpretations of Worship

EARLY PATTERNS FOR CHRISTIAN WORSHIP

CLARIFYING THE FAITH

Remember, Lord, your Church, deliver her from all evil,
make her complete in your love, and gather her from
the four winds, into your kingdom which you have prepared for her,
for yours is the power and the glory for ever.

DIDACHE 10.5[1]

Early Christian worship practices were greatly shaped by the words of Jesus as they were remembered and recited, written and copied by the original eyewitnesses. The sayings, teachings and practices of Jesus were treasured by the early disciples. It is clearly demonstrable that there was plenty of encouragement and support for incorporating imitation and re-enactment into the patterns of teaching, mission and worship that were developmentally integrated into the early church. The stories of events, as well as Jesus' teaching and practices, were rehearsed over and over again by eyewitnesses who wanted to pass them on to those who had not heard or seen Jesus themselves. Eventually these accounts were written down for use in congregations as the church spread throughout the Roman Empire. This chapter will consider only a few of the earliest extra-canonical documents that offer examples of how the earliest Christians remembered, regulated

---

[1]Thomas O'Loughlin, *The Didache: A Window on the Earliest Christians* (Grand Rapids: Baker Academic, 2010), pp. 161-71. All quotes from the *Didache* are from O'Loughlin's translation.

and reenacted the patterns of worship set in the canon of Scripture.

A good example of this is the post-resurrection story of the two disciples[2] from Emmaus who only came to recognize Jesus by the familiar way he "took bread, blessed and broke it, and gave it to them" (Luke 24:30). It was this practice of Jesus connected to his teaching that led these disciples to exclaim, "Were not our hearts burning within us while he was talking to us on the road, while he was opening the scriptures to us?" (Luke 24:32). It's only natural that the wording of Luke's account for the supper in Emmaus is nearly identical to Luke's wording of the Lord's Supper before the crucifixion (Luke 22:19), but Mark's wording of Jesus' "Last Supper" is also identical to that found in Luke (Mark 14:22). Most biblical scholars recognize that both Matthew and Luke used the Gospel According to Mark for their own work. The Synoptic accounts of the Lord's Supper, first Mark, followed by Luke (written shortly before the fall of Jerusalem) and then Matthew (written shortly after the fall of Jerusalem) are all very similar, which indicates not only that the account was given by eyewitnesses but also that the early church understood the importance of this story as the prototype for the Eucharistic meal as a part of the early worship life of the Christian community.

What is exceptionally notable, however, is Paul's explicit rendering of the reenactment of the Lord's Supper in 1 Corinthians, an epistle that may have been written even before Mark's Gospel and certainly before the Gospel accounts of Luke, Matthew or John. Paul writes:

> For I received from the Lord what I also handed on to you, that the Lord Jesus on the night when he was betrayed took a loaf of bread, and when he had given thanks, he broke it and said, "This is my body that is [broken] for you. Do this in remembrance of me." In the same way he took the cup also, after supper, saying, "This cup is the new covenant in my blood. Do this, as often as you drink it, in remembrance of me." (1 Corinthians 11:23-25)

Paul, of course, was not a disciple until after the ascension of Jesus and did not participate in any meal with Jesus, let alone the Last Supper. But in this passage, Paul relates that he "received" this tradition by means of direct

---

[2]One disciple is Cleopas (Luke 24:18), and the invitation is extended to Jesus as, "Stay with us" (Luke 24:29), which may indicate these two disciples were a married couple.

revelation "from the Lord." Paul's emphasis on this teaching of Jesus as a first-hand account implies that Paul understood the importance that the early church placed on the words and practices of Jesus in the formation of Christian teaching, mission and liturgical practices. In fact, the Gospel of John, probably written in the last decade of the first century, does not include an account of the inaugural supper of the Lord because the wording and practice of this reenactment were already very well known in the Christian communities across the empire. The careful reenactment of the event was instituted by Jesus and this pattern for the Eucharistic meal was practiced in the worship life of the earliest Christian communities. In addition, the Gospel According to John does recount Jesus' washing the disciples' feet "during supper" (John 13:2-5). It is interesting to note that Jesus intentionally invited the disciples to imitate his teaching and practice, saying, "So if I, your Lord and Teacher, have washed your feet, you also ought to wash one another's feet. For I have set you an example, that you also should do as I have done to you" (John 13:14-15). The practice of foot-washing in conjunction with the Lord's Supper or as a practice of community initiation that accompanied baptism may have been limited to some early Johannine communities.[3]

The recital and reenactment of the story of Jesus, like the reenactment of the story of the exodus for Israel in its festivals, was central to the development not only of Christian worship practice but of the canon (the uniquely authoritative apostolic writings) of the New Testament. The vital connection between the early church and Judaism is manifest in their shared story, not just the truth embedded within the story. The story-shape is seen in the church's need for a gathering place and authoritative, defining documents and worship practices.

First, this Jewish-Christian faith needed a place to tell its story. After the destruction of Jerusalem in A.D. 70, the need for a new central identity for non-Messianic Jewish communities radically changed the practices within synagogues. Synagogues in Palestine, as well as the diaspora, became sacred spaces for worship (without the sacrificial cult rites) and

---

[3]Geoffrey Wainwright and Karen B. W. Tucker, *The Oxford History of Christian Worship* (New York: Oxford University Press, 2006), p. 37. The editors of this comprehensive dictionary note the work of Martin F. Connell, n. 17, in this regard.

not simply gathering places for the Jewish community. The expulsion of early Christian communities from synagogues made it necessary for these fledgling congregations to meet in private homes and occasionally in public meeting places (see Acts 18:5-7 and 19:8-10 for clear examples of this shift). The differentiation of the Christian church from Judaism is seen in the canonical Gospel accounts and is clearly accented in the book of Acts. This differentiation continues to accelerate after the catastrophic events of A.D. 70 that reduced Jerusalem to rubble, destroyed the sacrificial temple cult, and effectively ended the Sanhedrin council and the power of the Sadducees. This subsequently empowered the religio-political party of the Pharisees, who furthered the effort to distance traditional Judaism from the new Christian communities.

Second, this Jewish-Christian faith needed uniquely authoritative documents in which the story was set in concrete for those who were not eyewitnesses to the original events. Including the story context for the teachings of Jesus was one way the apostolic writings that end up as the New Testament were underscored as *eyewitness* accounts. The inclusion of the story in which the truth was revealed was something the early church simply continued from Judaism. Some early documents contained the sayings of Jesus but without narrative context.[4] It is telling that these documents are never admitted into the canon even though they appear to quote Jesus accurately. Why? Because these documents lack the story, the narrative context, that embodies the truth of the teaching. The story-shape is important to the record of God's revelation just as it is for worship. The Old Testament is a story—a story of God's faithfulness to his people. Through this story, not just the truth it tells, we learn who God is, who we are, what

---

[4]This appears to be the case for one written source that scholars have named "Q" for the German word *quelle* which means "source." This Q document of Jesus' sayings without the story of Jesus may have been used by Matthew and Luke, but not by Mark. It's interesting to note that all Q sayings are nearly identical in Matthew and Luke, which indicates the likelihood of a written account. However, the narrative context for these Jesus sayings is different every time. Like most public speakers and teachers, it is not unusual to say nearly the same thing in several different venues, especially if what is said is foundationally important for the speaker. Noticing the distinctions between Gospel accounts is no threat to their reliability but underscores their authenticity as eye-witness accounts and treasured (and accurate) memories of those who heard Jesus during the years of his public ministry. For a summary of this dynamic see Robert H. Stein, *Studying the Synoptic Gospels: Origin and Interpretation* (Grand Rapids: Baker Academic, 2001).

went wrong and how God will make it right. The narrative context for the revelation of God is of prime importance for determining the unique authority of Scripture as *inspired*, as "God-breathed" (2 Timothy 3:16 NIV). This pattern for the eventual formation of the New Testament canon was particularly important as the church grew and Christian communities became increasingly differentiated from Judaism. However, one early church document that lacks narrative context provides a particularly transparent window through which one can glimpse the teaching and practices of the early church.

THE *DIDACHE*

The *Didache* is a fascinating document with an equally fascinating history that indicates how the earliest Christian communities used the teachings of Jesus and reenacted Jesus' most prominent practices with the first disciples. These practices led to patterns of teaching, mission and liturgical practice in first-century Christian congregations. In discerning biblical patterns for shaping and informing Christian worship today, it is helpful to consider how the earliest Christians actually did this.

The importance of story is underscored by Thomas O'Loughlin in his book *The Didache: A Window on the Earliest Christians*. O'Laughlin indicates the importance of grounding imitation and reenactment on the historical foundations of the Christian faith when he writes, "Christianity is an explicitly historical religion: it is based on a historical individual, Jesus, and what he did and taught. Christianity is also the community descended from the community that Jesus formed around himself; it treasures its past and its memories."[5]

It seems that the *Didache* was used in a variety of congregational settings to function as a basic primer for the leaders of congregations as they were newly established throughout the empire. Although compiled in Greek, a fairly wide number of versions in different translations make it impossible to "isolate its place of origin" with any confidence.[6] Introductory infor-

---

[5]O'Loughlin, *The Didache*, p. xv.

[6]Ibid., pp. 22-26. O'Loughlin's work on the *Didache* is an engaging primer on this text used by first-century Christians. O'Loughlin submits that new scholarship over the last fifty years points positively to a date prior to A.D. 70 (as early as A.D. 50) and maintains that many copies and a variety of versions of the text were broadly used in congregations by A.D. 80–90.

mation on the *Didache* and its basic outline is provided in an appendix at
the end of this chapter. For our purposes, the content concerning worship
practices will be the central focus.

A major section of the *Didache* (chapters 7-10) addresses liturgical praxis
regarding baptism, fasting, prayer and the Eucharistic meal. It is interesting
to note how the *Didache* includes both pattern and flexibility as it serves
as a resource for early Christian church communities. The following is
O'Loughlin's translation of chapter 7, which addresses the practice of baptism:

> 7.1 With regard to baptism, here is the teaching: You are to baptize in this way.
> Once you have gone back over all that is in the Two Ways, you baptize in
> the name of the Father and of the Son and of the Holy Spirit in living
> [running] water.
>
> 7.2 However, if you do not have access to living water, then baptize in some
> other water; and if you do not have any cold water, then you can use
> warm water.
>
> 7.3 And if you cannot get access to either [running or still], then pour water
> three times on the head in the name of the Father and of the Son and of
> the Holy Spirit.
>
> 7.4 Moreover, before the baptism takes place, let both the person baptizing
> and the person who is going to be baptized fast—along with as many
> others as are able to do so. Indeed, you must instruct the person who is
> going to be baptized to fast for one or two days before baptism.[7]

The importance of baptism in the triune name is very clear in this short
chapter, but there are no stipulations included concerning the person who
is doing the baptism. This omission of detail, just as we find in the New
Testament, is probably due to the assumption that those with recognized
authority in the community to baptize are conducting this rite of cleansing
and initiation. The episodes in the book of Acts that deal with the baptism
of early converts, either as households or as individuals, make a fascinating
survey of both particular patterns as well as flexible practice.

Baptism in Acts is often associated with the conviction of those who

---

O'Loughlin indicates that the noncanonical status of the *Didache* is due to its genre as a
"training manual" and states, "it was not the sort of document that was held as precious but
simply useful."
[7]Ibid., pp. 166-68.

have heard the gospel (in a wide variety of ways), with an expression of repentance (in a variety of ways), baptism by water in the name of Jesus for individuals as well as households (which may or may not have included young children), accompanied by what seems either a little or a fair amount of instruction depending on the circumstance, and the oversight of recognized church leaders. The following summary of water baptism in the book of Acts indicates both the patterns and the flexibility within the patterns for this rite of Christian initiation.

- Acts 2:38, 41—on the day of the Jerusalem Pentecost

- Acts 8:12, 14-17—the initiation of the Samaritans by Philip and follow-up ministry of Peter and John

- Acts 8:34-38—the baptism of the Ethiopian eunuch by Philip

- Acts 9:17-18; 22:12-16—the accounts of Paul's baptism

- Acts 10:46-48 (repeated in Acts 11:15-18; 15:7-11 without specific mention of baptism)—the conversion and initiation of Cornelius and the first Gentiles

- Acts 16:14-15—the conversion and baptism of Lydia and her household in Philippi

- Acts 16:32-34—the conversion and baptism of the Philippian jailer and his household

- Acts 18:8—the baptism of Crispus and others in Corinth

- Acts 18:24–19:7—the baptism of twelve persons in Ephesus; this is the only account in the NT of "rebaptism" and gives insight into the relationship of baptism in Jesus' name and the Holy Spirit.[8]

Note both the patterns (for instance, water is always used) and the flexibility (for instance, where baptism happens, the timing of baptism as related to the dawning of a person's faith).

The *Didache* differs from this summary of water baptism in Acts in two

---

[8]Everett Ferguson comments in *Baptism in the Early Church: History, Theology, and Liturgy in the First Five Centuries* (Grand Rapids: Eerdmans, 2009) that Acts 18:24–19:7 "provides one of the more difficult baptismal texts in Acts" (p. 180). Ferguson summarizes well, however, "three distinguishing marks of Christian baptism [that] come out in this passage: baptism is connected with faith in Jesus, . . . baptism is associated with receiving the Holy Spirit, . . . [and] baptism into the name of the Lord Jesus (19:5) is specifically contrasted with John's baptism and so marks the new baptism as Christian baptism" (p. 181).

ways. First, the *Didache* clearly states that baptism is to be done "in the name of the Father and of the Son and of the Holy Spirit." Second, a certain amount of teaching identified as "the Two Ways" (chapters 1-6 of the *Didache*) is expected. Both of these differences may be either rooted in or reflected by the Gospel of Matthew.[9] Matthew 28:19-20 renders the baptismal formula found in the *Didache* in the commissioning of Jesus' disciples to, "Go therefore and make disciples of all nations, baptizing them in the name of the Father and of the Son and of the Holy Spirit, and teaching them to obey everything that I have commanded you." Like Matthew, the *Didache* links baptism to both the initiation of disciples of Jesus and learning the fundamental teachings of Jesus.

In his book *Introducing Early Christianity*, Laurie Guy offers a good summary of the contrasts and connections between Matthew and the *Didache*:

> The Didache shows a number of signs of significant influence from Matthew's Gospel; so unsurprisingly it indicates that baptism is to be into the threefold name, a universal practice in the later church. Baptism in the *Didache* was to be in "living," that is, in running water. This suggests that baptism at this time was normally by immersion. Such a conclusion is based on the emphasis placed on the nature of the water medium, and the acknowledgment that if living/running water is not available then pouring is a valid alternative (*Did.* 7.1-3). At the same time one should note that the language echoes that of the Torah, where ritual purity commonly required use of living/running/pure water (Lev 14:5-6, 50-51; 15:13; Num 19:17).
>
> This underscores an aspect of the significance of baptism: it is the instrument of cleansing. The *Didache* also demonstrates a solemnity regarding the administration of baptism: the baptizer, the baptized and others are to fast one or two days prior to the baptism (*Did.* 7.4).[10]

---

[9]The Matthean patterns of Jesus' teaching and baptismal formula seen in the *Didache* are reasons why some scholars date the *Didache*'s compilation after the fall of Jerusalem and after the circulation of Matthew's Gospel; some say as late as circa 100 to 130. In the long run, the dating of the *Didache*'s compilation matters very little as both Matthew and the *Didache* are representative of Jesus' teaching, the former with unique inspiration, narrative context and canonical authority.

[10]Laurie Guy, *Introducing Early Christianity: A Topical Survey of Its Life, Beliefs & Practices* (Downers Grove, Ill.: InterVarsity Press, 2004), p. 33. Guy's wording makes it clear that he considers the *Didache* to be influenced by the Gospel According to Matthew and dates the *Didache* circa A.D. 100 (p. 31). That both the *Didache* and Matthew helped bridge the gap between Jewish-Christian believers familiar with Judaism and new Gentile converts is clear in both texts.

What is notable about the *Didache* throughout the document is not only its lack of narrative context but its lack of theological reflection. The *Didache*, especially the content presented after the Two Ways, reads like a how-to manual. The document reflects the fact that as the church established itself within the heritage of Judaism it was, at the same time, increasingly differentiated from Judaism; theological explanation was secondary to daily faithfulness to Jesus. As the church was increasingly ostracized from the nonbelieving Jewish community, it was also subject to the ebb and flow of persecution by the Roman Empire. Church councils would not convene openly until the fourth century, and only then would the protection of the emperor afford the church the opportunity to put on paper the theology of the faith built upon the apostolic teachings and expressed in its worship. Documents that offer glimpses of worship practices in the early church are invaluable not just for helping inform worship practice throughout church history but also for appreciating the work of the Spirit in bringing understanding to faith.

The teaching of Arius denied the equality of being of the Father and the Son and was denounced as heresy at the Council of Nicaea in A.D. 325. However, the heresy of Arius had *already been defeated* in the worship of the church. The church for nearly three and a half centuries had remembered, regulated and reenacted the patterns of worship set in the canon of Scripture through hymns and early creedal summaries of the faith, such as Philippians 2:5-11, 1 Timothy 3:16 and the worship songs in the Revelation to John. The church had already entered into God's story of salvation through the waters of baptism and used the baptismal formula that recognized God's salvation through Jesus the Son in the presence of the Spirit. The church had regularly (daily or weekly) reenacted the Lord's Supper to remember God's saving work in the death and resurrection and ascension of Christ Jesus and to anticipate the future reign of the church with Christ in his coming kingdom.

Baptism still should be practiced as an initiation rite that both reenacts and remembers God's work of salvation through the person, life, death, resurrection and ascension of Jesus. The *Didache*, in both its mandatory patterns and its flexible practices, is a good model of both grace and truth in how Christian communities have adopted particular worship patterns and expressions of faith concerning baptism throughout church history. That baptism is entrusted to the church as a community of believers for its regulation and accountability is uncontested in Scripture and should be reflected in the practice of Christian communities today. Privatized baptisms for a family photo opportunity, a youth group "ocean dunking," or friends "baptizing" friends in college fountains or motel swimming pools apart from the community of faith, without any sort of accountability to the greater body of Christ, have no biblical foundation. Paul's summary of baptism in Galatians makes it clear that being baptized into Christ is being baptized into the body of Christ:

> for in Christ Jesus you are all children of God through faith. As many of you as were baptized into Christ have clothed yourselves with Christ. There is no longer Jew or Greek, there is no longer slave or free, there is no longer male and female; for all of you are one in Christ Jesus. And if you belong to Christ, then you are Abraham's offspring, heirs according to the promise. (Galatians 3:26-29)

Everett Ferguson notes that

> the passage continues in chapter 4:1-7 by affirming that those in Christ have received adoption as God's children, and because they are children they have received the Spirit of the Son enabling them to address God as "Abba, Father" (4:6). Note that here the sequence is not that the Spirit comes to make persons children of God but that because they are children they receive the Spirit. They become children because they are in Christ, the Son. And they enter into Christ at baptism.
>
> Baptism did not make them children of God. Faith did this (3:26).[11]

James B. Torrance notes with succinct clarity that "the efficacy of baptism is not in the rite or in the water, but in the faithfulness of Christ," and that for the community of believers baptism "marks the frontier between the church and the world."[12] The reality is that baptism is a sign of God's covenantal faithfulness fulfilled in Christ Jesus. We are baptized into Jesus' baptism, not our own. By the Spirit, we participate in what Jesus has done for us "to fulfill all righteousness" (Matthew 3:15). God keeps his promises

---

[11]Ferguson, *Baptism in the Early Church*, p. 147.
[12]James B. Torrance, *Worship, Community and the Triune God of Grace* (Downers Grove, Ill.: InterVarsity Press, 1997), p. 81.

without fail. The church believes this by faith which is itself a gift of God's covenantal grace. What is actually signified in baptism is understood by paying attention to the sign itself as remembrance and reenactment of Christ's own baptism on our behalf. The *Didache* mainly addresses the "how" and a bit of the "who," but the "why" of baptism, the meaning of baptism, is left embedded in the story of God's promises to his people kept supremely and completely by God the Son in the power of God the Spirit. Most disputes over the practice of the sacramental signs happen when the reality of what is depicted in the story is marginalized or forgotten, when reality is separated from the sign itself and all that is left is "how" and "who" and "when." Torrance comments on this cautionary idea when he writes, "In any discussion of baptism, the first question to be asked is not who should be baptized—infants or adults or both—nor how it should be administered—by sprinkling, pouring or immersion—nor whether it may be repeated. These are important questions, but they can only be answered when we have first asked what the meaning of baptism is."[13]

Paul's identification of baptism as a rite of initiation into Christ through God's grace by God's gift of faith given by God's Spirit is one reason the church moved quickly to reflect this understanding by using the triune name of God in the rite. When the *Didache* particularizes the baptism formula as "in the name of the Father and of the Son and of the Holy Spirit," this early church manual is keeping sign and story together. Torrance addresses the importance of why the church baptizes in the triune name by focusing clearly on who Jesus is in his relation to the Father and the Spirit, which makes the necessary connection between sign and the reality conveyed in the story. Being baptized into Christ's baptism ought to be trinitarian because his baptism was trinitarian.

[The church baptizes in the triune name] not just because of our Lord's missionary command in Matthew 28:19, but because these words enshrine the good news of grace. The mission of the church in the world is grounded in the mission of the Son and the Spirit from the Father to bring us to sonship and communion. Our Lord began his ministry for us in his vicarious baptism in the waters of the Jordan when, as the Son, he received from the Father the

---

[13]Ibid., p. 74.

baptism of the Spirit for us in our humanity and set his face to the cross. His own baptism was trinitarian.[14]

The church's longstanding struggle concerning believer's baptism and paedobaptism is evidence of what can happen when story and sign are disconnected. Paedobaptism can become a rite of superstition or family tradition, and believer's baptism can become a heartfelt but essentially self-dependent effort to "get right with God." In both cases the reality of God's salvation is lost in the shadowy darkness of our own small story and concerns. Neither the infant nor the believer is saved when sprinkled, poured or immersed in water with or without the triune name. The moment of salvation is in the heart of the Father who "chose us in Christ before the foundation of the world" (Ephesians 1:4). The moment of salvation is achieved for us only through the life, death, resurrection and ascension of Jesus the Son in obedience to the Father (Philippians 2:5-11; Romans 6:3; Galatians 2:19-20). The moment of salvation is secured by the Spirit, the "pledge of our inheritance" (Ephesians 1:13-14) and the "spirit of adoption" that identifies us as belonging to God as his children (Romans 8:15). The signifier of this story—God's great story, not ours—focuses on the reality of salvation grounded in God's saving work in Christ Jesus, not one's experience of that salvation. Communities of faith have been and are free to identify themselves by practices that reflect their participation in God's story. Both Scripture and the *Didache* leave plenty of room for variety within the biblical pattern that embodies the divine drama of God's faithfulness.

THE *DIDACHE* AND THE LORD'S SUPPER

The *Didache* also focuses on the how-to of the Lord's Supper for early church communities and recognizes that, as in life, what a person does shapes what a person believes. The Latin expression *lex orandi, lex credendi* (literally "the law of prayer is the law of belief") is an ancient shorthand summary for the idea that how a person prays expresses what a person actually believes. Jesus was no stranger to connecting behavior with belief. "Do this," Jesus said, to remember what he was about to do on the night he was betrayed. In the accounts of the crucifixion of Jesus in the four Gospels,

---

[14]Ibid., p. 75.

none explain how Jesus achieved atonement, salvation, redemption, propitiation, justification or any other element of soteriology that the historically orthodox Christian faith holds as central. The church finds the explanation of the meaning of the cross, resurrection and ascension of Jesus outside the accounts of the four Gospels in the rest of the New Testament. However, on the night when he was betrayed and arrested, Jesus gave the disciples a practice to prepare them to reflect on and understand the story that they would be commissioned to teach the rest of the world after his glorification when the Spirit was sent to empower their witness. Jesus prepared his followers for a thanksgiving expressed through reenactment that would signify God's great work of redemption on the cross of Calvary.

Again, the concern of the *Didache* is that the reenactment helps keep story and sign together. Following the chapter on baptism there is a very short chapter that deals with new days of fasting for the church and instructions on praying the Lord's Prayer. Then chapters nine and ten deal with the how-to of the Eucharistic feast.

> 9.1 Now this is how you should engage in giving thanks, bless God in this way.
>
> 9.2 First, at the cup, say: We give thanks to you, our Father, for the holy vine of David, your servant, which you have made known to us. Through Jesus, your servant, to you be glory for ever.
>
> 9.3 Then when it comes to the broken loaf say: We give thanks to you, our Father, for the life and knowledge which you have made known to us. Through Jesus, your servant, to you be glory for ever.
>
> 9.4 For as the broken loaf was once scattered over the mountains and then was gathered in and became one, so may your church be gathered together into your kingdom from the very ends of the earth. Yours is the glory and the power through Jesus Christ for ever.
>
> 9.5 Only let those who have been baptized in the name of the Lord eat and drink at your Eucharists. And remember what the Lord said about this: do not give to dogs what is holy.
>
> 10.1 After you all have had enough to eat, give thanks in this way:
>
> 10.2 We give you thanks, Holy Father, for your holy name which you have made to dwell in our hearts, and for the knowledge and faith and immortality which you have made known to us. Through Jesus, your servant, to you be glory for ever.
>
> 10.3 You are the mighty ruler of all who has created all for your name's sake,

and you have given food and drink to human beings for their enjoyment so that they might give thanks to you. But to us, from your generosity, you have given spiritual food and drink, and life eternal, through your servant.

10.4 Above all things we give thanks to you because you are mighty: to you be glory for ever.[15]

10.5 Remember, Lord, your church, deliver her from evil, make her complete in your love, and gather her from the four winds into your kingdom you have prepared for her, for yours is the power and the glory for ever.

10.6 May grace come and may this world pass away. Hosanna to the God of David. If anyone is holy, let him advance; if anyone is not, let him be converted.[16] Maranatha. Amen.

10.7 However, permit the prophets to give thanks in whatever manner they wish.[17]

There are several notable things about this instruction. First, the prayers are all directed to "our Father" and the doxologies focus on the "glory and the power" due him. The *Didache* seems to reserve the idea of the kingdom for the Son and his church both in chapters nine and ten and in the doxology of the Lord's Prayer (*Didache* 8.2). Second, the repetition of "Jesus, your servant" and his identity as the "holy vine of David" (9.2) coupled with "Hosanna to the God of David" (10.6) underscore the effort the *Didache* makes to help the church recognize and appreciate its Jewish foundation while the nations (Gentiles) are increasingly included in the story. Unlike Pauline writings, the focus of the *Didache* is on the Davidic covenant that anticipates the kingdom, not the Abrahamic covenant that anticipates the

---

[15]The three expressions of thanksgiving in *Didache* 10:2, 3, 4 are modeled after Jewish prayers of thanks during and after meals. They have been adapted for Christian use in the celebration of the Eucharist. For further detail of the adaptation of the Jewish *Birkat ha-Mazon* in the *Didache*, see Frank C. Senn, *Christian Liturgy: Catholic and Evangelical* (Minneapolis: Fortress, 1997), p. 65.

[16]In distinction from the pattern here in the *Didache* there are communities of faith that do not insist that one must be baptized prior to participation in the Lord's Supper. Wesley believed that the Lord's Supper could be a converting ordinance. One could convert (repent and believe) on the way to the table to "receive Christ." However, it is important to affirm that baptism is not a *condition* that must be fulfilled before one can take one's first communion. This would make baptism, and by extension, partaking of the Lord's Supper, a practice to gain merit and not an expression of faith in the grace of God found in the work of Christ Jesus. The reality of the sacraments is found in Jesus, to receive life from him, to be joined to him by the Spirit.

[17]O'Loughlin, *The Didache,* pp. 166-68.

blessing of the nations. The emphasis on the Davidic covenant in this context is important because in the Gospels, the last supper with Jesus was an inaugural feast instituted in anticipation of the eternal kingdom. Mark and Matthew render the anticipation as a kind of fasting for Jesus: "Truly I tell you, I will never again drink of the fruit of the vine until that day when I drink it new in the kingdom of God" (Mark 14:25; Matthew 26:29 is identical, except that Matthew avoids the use of the divine name for his readers). Luke records Jesus' words after the supper, "I confer on you, just as my Father has conferred on me, a kingdom, so that you may eat and drink at my table in my kingdom" (Luke 22:29-30). The *Didache* carefully helps the church both remember the great gift of salvation in the sacrifice of Jesus and anticipate the fulfillment of the kingdom in the fullness of time. Both the ideas of remembrance and anticipation are to be reflected in the prayers of thanks offered during the meal.

Third, like the earliest glimpses of the Eucharistic meal in Acts and earlier writings in the New Testament, most notably 1 Corinthians, the celebration of the Lord's sacrifice and coming kingdom is generally in the context of a regular meal shared by the gathered community. The tenth chapter of the *Didache* begins, "After you all have had enough to eat, give thanks," and this reflects community meals in Acts, which were themselves reflections of weekly Jewish home-based sabbath meals and the yearly Passover feast (Acts 2:46; 20:7). The 1 Corinthians text, written only ten to fifteen years after Jesus' death, makes it clear that because of the abuse of the meal by excessive consumption and social-class discrimination (1 Corinthians 11:17-21), the separation of the Lord's Supper from the family or community meal begins very early. Paul asks the Corinthian Christians,

> Do you not have homes to eat and drink in? Or do you show contempt for the church of God and humiliate those who have nothing? . . . So then, my brothers and sisters, when you come together to eat, wait for one another. If you are hungry, eat at home, so that when you come together, it will not be for your condemnation. (1 Corinthians 11:22, 33-34)

It is interesting that the emphasis of the *Didache*, possibly written close to the time of Paul's letters to the churches of Corinth, focuses in some detail on how to pray, how to give thanks for the elements, which are signifiers set apart to commemorate the sacrifice of Jesus and anticipate the kingdom to come.

Fourth, the *Didache*, in contrast to the Gospel accounts (Matthew 26:26-29; Mark 14:22-25) begins with the celebration of the cup which is followed by that of the bread (*Didache* 9.2, 9.3). This may simply be ordered because of the comment in 9.4 which follows, a simile using the loaf that focuses on the unity of the church. The ordering in *Didache* 9 is the same as 1 Corinthians 10:16 and Luke 22:17-19, which reflect the Jewish order of blessing first the cup, then the bread.[18] Frank Senn comments,

> However, in the Synoptic tradition Jesus identified his blood of the new covenant with the final cup of blessing *after* the meal, and Paul does the same with his tradition in [1 Corinthians] 11:23-25. So it is possible that Paul has deliberately inverted the order in 10:16 in order to connect the oneness of the sacramental body of Christ with the oneness of the ecclesial body of Christ.[19]

This Pauline order and ecclesial connection is exactly what the *Didache* accomplishes in its order and subsequent connection. The church throughout its history has, for the most part, shared the loaf first and then the cup. Even so, to rigidly fix the order of the Eucharistic elements would contradict the very flexibility of practice common in this ancient text.

Finally, *Didache* 9.5 makes it clear that the Eucharistic meal is only to be shared by those who are members of Christ's body by rite of baptism. This certainly reflects the care and oversight that the rite receives in the New Testament, especially the accountability for holy conduct in Paul's admonition to the Corinthian Christians (1 Corinthians 11:17-34). The exclusionary nature of the Lord's Supper is apparent in other ancient documents of the church, including Justin Martyr's *First Apology* (A.D. 150), which makes clear the community meal and the Lord's Supper were joined as one ritual very early in Christian history.[20]

---

[18]However, the Lukan account which begins with the cup (Luke 22:17) and is followed by the bread (22:19) ends with "And [Jesus] did the same with the cup after supper, saying, 'This cup that is poured out for you is the new covenant in my blood.'" The inclusion of the "new covenant" is only found in Paul's account in 1 Corinthians 11:23-25.

[19]Senn, *Christian Liturgy*, p. 96.

[20]See Justin Martyr's *First Apology* 66.1 in *Early Christian Fathers*, ed. Cyril C. Richardson

Justin Martyr wrote in his *First Apology* to the emperor Antonius Pius and the senate of Rome, "When the president has given thanks and the whole congregation has assembled, those whom we call deacons give to each of those present a portion of the consecrated bread and wine and water, and they take it to the absent."[21] This emphasis on the unity of the body, like the loaf in the *Didache*, is important. The meal of the Lord is always served by leaders to the community, not taken on one's own initiative; the meal is an expression of God's grace, never deserved, never taken for granted. Also, the Lord's Supper is always shared by the community, not privatized for a personal act of piety. Historically, the only exception to this is when a pastor with a member of the congregation and/or elder takes the elements of communion to the sick, incarcerated or others whose absence is not voluntary.

Laurie Guy summarizes several aspects of the Lord's Supper in the *Didache* when he writes,

> There is repeated focus on giving thanks (*eucharisteō*), indicating that the primary focus is on gratitude for God's acts in Christ. The meal is a sacred rite, reserved for the baptized (*Did.* 9.5). It appears to have central focus within the worship gathering. The fact that the cup was taken before the bread (in contrast to later universal practice) suggests diversity in how the Eucharist was celebrated or that these aspects of worship were not particularly fixed (*Did.* 9:2-3).[22]

The fourteenth chapter of the *Didache* revisits certain aspects of early Christian worship and highlights the habitual gathering on the "Day of the Lord" and the practice of the Eucharistic meal at that time. *Didache* 14.1-2 read as follows:

> 14.1 On the day which is the Day of the Lord gather together for the breaking of the loaf and giving thanks. However, you should first confess your sins so that your sacrifice may be a pure one;

(Philadelphia: Westminster Press, 1953) for a mid-second-century document that makes this point. Also, Robert Webber's overview of early patterns in sacramental participation by the church in *Worship Old and New: A Biblical, Historical, and Practical Introduction*, rev. ed. (Grand Rapids: Zondervan, 1994) is a brief but helpful source for a basic history of liturgical practices.

[21]Justin Martyr in *Early Christian Fathers*, p. 286.

[22]Guy, *Introducing Early Christianity*, p. 33.

14.2 and do not let anyone who is having a dispute with a neighbor join until they are reconciled so that your sacrifice may not be impure.[23]

The apostle Paul in 1 Corinthians 11 is likewise particularly concerned about the integrity of the worshiping community. Frank Senn comments on this concern, also seen in the *Didache*:

> On the whole, the thrust of chapter 14 concerns less the Eucharist than the discipline of the community that is related to the integrity of the Eucharistic fellowship. If any distinction is to be made at all between chapters 10 and 14, it concerns the fencing of the table. The ones in need of repentance in 10:6 are probably the unbaptized; the ones in need of confessing their sins in 14:1 are probably the faithful.[24]

CONCLUSION

Attending to canonical texts and the earliest documents of faith and practice can also help contemporary Christians know how the church has learned to worship carefully and freely, in spirit and in truth. The early church worked hard to clarify the Christian faith in its community, uniquely authoritative documents and liturgical practice. This clarification was necessary as the church increasingly identified itself as distinct from its Jewish roots yet affirmed its foundation on the Jews who were the first apostolic witnesses. It is this biblical faith, its pattern of worship and its variety of practices that the Reformers sought to recover when Christian liturgy had become encrusted with the barnacles of historical battles as sacramental signs were separated from God's story of his saving grace.

WORKSHOP FOR CHAPTER EIGHT

1. Take time to read all the episodes in the book of Acts concerning water baptism (see the summary list on page 153).

2. Consider how baptism is practiced in your congregation.

   • What is emphasized through the visual symbols used for this part of the service of worship?

---

[23]O'Loughlin, *The Didache,* p. 170.
[24]Senn, *Christian Liturgy,* p. 67.

- When does the baptismal service usually come in the sequence of the service? Why?

- How is the inclusion of water (immersion, pouring, sprinkling) coordinated with the invocation of the triune name of God during the service?

3. How are "mandatory patterns and flexible practices" discussed in chapter eight evident in the baptismal traditions of your congregation?

    - Brainstorm ways that both these important considerations might be enhanced in the sacramental practices of the congregation.

    - Consider the importance of worship practices that "keep sign and story together." What congregational traditions like signs, symbols, words, music and the use of sacred space help or hinder keeping sign and story together?

4. Read through the accounts of the Lord's Supper in each of the Synoptic Gospels. Note similarities and distinctions between the three accounts. Read Paul's account in 1 Corinthians 11:17-33 and consider how Paul's concerns for holiness, regulation and practice might help shape the practice and patterns for the Supper in your congregational liturgy.

5. Consider how the Lord's Supper is practiced in your congregation.

    - What is emphasized through the visual symbols used for this part of the service of worship?

    - When does the Lord's Supper usually come in the sequence of the service? Why?

    - How is the inclusion of the Communion elements coordinated with the prayer of thanksgiving and the words of institution from the New Testament texts?

6. How are "mandatory patterns and flexible practices" discussed in chapter eight evident in the liturgy of the Lord's Supper used in your congregation?

    - Brainstorm ways that both these important considerations might be enhanced in the sacramental practices of the congregation.

    - Consider the importance of worship practices that "keep sign and story together." What congregational traditions like signs, symbols, words, music and the use of sacred space help or hinder keeping sign and story together?

7. Sit down with the pastor and/or worship leaders of your congregation and discuss what you have learned from Scripture and the *Didache* about sacramental practices and services of worship on the Lord's Day.

EXCURSUS: THE *DIDACHE*

The *Didache* has sixteen short chapters that deal with three distinct topics. The first of these topics is a moral code that echoes Jesus' teaching in the Sermon on the Mount. If O'Loughlin is correct in dating the *Didache* prior to A.D. 70, one must recognize that the *Didache* possibly provides the earliest partial account for this central teaching of Jesus.[25] The *Didache* actually begins with the same idea with which Jesus begins his conclusion of the Sermon on the Mount, a contrast of two ways: one that leads to life and one that leads to death. Matthew 7:13-14 states, "Enter through the narrow gate; for the gate is wide and the road is easy that leads to destruction, and there are many who take it. For the gate is narrow and the road is hard that leads to life, and there are few who find it." The *Didache* simply begins, "There are two ways: one is the Way of Life, the other is the Way of Death; and there is a mighty difference between these two ways."[26] The *Didache* immediately follows with Jesus' two great commandments to love God and to love one's neighbor, the Golden Rule and the admonition on how to love one's enemies. This latter emphasis in *Didache* 1.3 actually echoes the teachings of Jesus found in Matthew 5:46-47 and Luke 6:27-28, 31 to pray for one's enemies and bless one's persecutors and asks a question similar to that in Matthew 5:46-47 and Luke 6:32-33: "What benefit is it if you love those who love you? Do not even the Gentiles do that?"

The *Didache* 1.4 reads very much like part of the Sermon on the Mount in Matthew 5:39-41, 48 and Luke's rendition of the Sermon in chapter 6:29-30.

---

[25]Matthew's Gospel, if written shortly after the fall of Jerusalem in A.D. 70, contains the most unified account of Jesus' teaching concerning the kingdom of heaven. This dating for Matthew is very helpful in appreciating the evangelist's redactive strategy to help Jews recenter their faith around the Messiah of Israel, the person of Jesus. Having lost the geographical center of the faith as well as its sacrificial system, this was vitally important.

[26]O'Loughlin, *The Didache*, pp. 161-71.

Abstain from carnal desires. If someone strikes your left cheek, then turn the right cheek towards him also, and you will be perfect. If someone makes you go one mile, then go the extra mile with him. If someone takes your coat, then let him have your jacket. If someone takes your property, then you are not allowed to ask for it back.

The first five sections of the *Didache* focus on the moral conduct expected of those who are followers of Jesus, people of "the Way."[27] Three main categories comprise the moral code section of the *Didache*: the way to love, the necessity for sexual purity and the importance of avoiding all vestiges of idolatry. Not only does this section on moral conduct sound like Jesus, but the focus on abstaining from fornication and idolatry echoes the concern of the early church leaders for the inclusion of Gentiles in what had been essentially Jewish communities (Acts 15:19-21). One cannot forget that the Christian faith was planted deeply in the soil of Judaism and that rabbi Jesus came to fulfill the law, not abolish it (Matthew 5:17; Romans 3:31). In *Introducing Early Christianity: A Topical Survey of Its Life, Beliefs & Practices*, Laurie Guy comments on the moral code of the *Didache*, "The Jewishness of the moral code highlights the marked extent of early Christian dependence on Judaism on matters of morality. On many matters, Christian morality was simply Jewish morality."[28]

---

[27]The early church is often designated as "the Way" in the book of Acts. See Acts 9:2; 16:17; 24:14, 22.
[28]Guy, *Introducing Early Christianity*, p. 32.

REFORMATION PATTERNS
FOR CHRISTIAN WORSHIP

RECOVERING THE FAITH

Some one sent to know whether it was
permissible to use warm water in baptism?
The Doctor replied: "Tell the blockhead that water,
warm or cold, is water."

MARTIN LUTHER IN *TABLE TALK* (1566)[1]

The Reformation of the sixteenth century was, in significant measure, a recovery of scriptural teaching and simpler traditions that marked the early centuries of the Christian faith. It would be a misrepresentation of the early Reformers to say they dismissed all the teaching and practices of the late medieval church in the west. The pithy quote from Luther above is a good representation of much of the work done by the Reformation leaders to challenge the medieval church to recover, not reinvent, biblically shaped doctrine and practice. The Reformers didn't throw out the bathwater, let alone the baby!

Two significant movements marked the foundational goals of the Reformation: confirmation and correction. First, the central tenants of the Christian faith were clearly affirmed by all the Reformation leaders who led

---

[1]Martin Luther, *The Table Talk of Martin Luther,* trans. William Hazlitt (Fearn, U.K.: Christian Focus Publications, 1994), p. 253.

distinctive Protestant communities of faith. German Lutherans, French Reformed and Swiss Anabaptists all affirmed the historical doctrines of the Christian faith, such as those concerning the three persons of the Trinity, the two natures of Christ, creation *ex nihilo*, the fall of humanity, the virgin birth, the physical resurrection of Christ Jesus and the expectation of the parousia at the culmination of history. The Reformers sought, in a variety of ways, to treat central things as central and to challenge the medieval church to return to its early roots and major on the majors. In this effort, the Reformation leaders Luther, Calvin and Zwingli reached back through the centuries and joined hands with the bishops and leaders of the earliest church councils, like Athanasius of Nicaea and the Cappadocians of Chalcedon. When the Reformers disputed over differences (and some of these disputes led to significant consequences and prolonged violence between their followers) it was not over doctrines central to the faith but over things like the understanding and formulation of sacramental practice, the relationship between the church and the world, the use or prohibition of symbols, art and images for sacred space, or what kind of music was appropriate for Christian worship. That the sacraments of the church were important, that Christians were in tension with the world, that worship was important for God's relationship with his people—these things were not questioned. Luther affirmed the sacrament of water baptism but he tried to remind the church that only in the person and work of Christ Jesus was the efficacy of the rite to be found. To recenter the community of faith on the reality and meaning of the Christian's identity with Jesus' baptism, he refused to place any importance on trivial issues, such as whether the water was warm or cold.

Second, the Reformers sought to clarify and correct teaching in the medieval church that was not clearly based in Scripture and affirmed by the councils of the first five centuries of the Christian faith. Medieval church practices had marginalized the laity in the basics of Christian discipleship like understanding and participating in worship, engaging in even rudimentary Christian education, and in the reading and study of Scripture. Even Luther, who first went to school in Erfurt to become a lawyer, instead became an Augustinian monk without any significant study of the New Testament texts. People listened to the medieval Mass in Latin, a tongue they did not understand. Worship had become a performance of the priests for an audience who settled for the momentary emotional reassurance it offered. The real assurance of salvation was seen as the province of religious orders and knowledgeable clergy.

MEDIEVAL WORSHIP: PLACE AND POWER

To be fair, the noblest intention of stained-glass windows, magnificent cathedrals, the images of saints, and all the "smells and bells" of the medieval Mass was to help laypeople grasp the significance of worship and teach them a bit about the God they worshiped and the story of Scripture. But, for the most part, laypeople were relegated to the status of silent observers, not active participants. In the book *Orthodoxy*, G. K. Chesterton comments on the connection between the marginalization and silencing of medieval laity and the medieval sacred space built for worship with significant insight:

> Christ prophesied the whole of Gothic architecture in that hour when nervous and respectable people . . . objected to the gutter snipes of Jerusalem. He said, "If these were silent, the very stones would cry out." Under the impulses of His spirit arose like a clamorous chorus the façades of the medieval cathedrals, thronged with shouting faces and open mouths. The prophecy has fulfilled itself; the very stones cry out.[2]

William Dyrness, who has written quite a bit on the connection of theology, art and sacred space, comments, "We do know that medieval worshipers inhabited a unified universe that was symbolized in both the church structure and the activities that went on inside."[3] Gothic architecture in some ways reflects the story of salvation itself. One enters at the back of a long dark nave where a font of water is meant to remind those who come to worship that they enter by God's grace through the water of their baptism. The length of the nave is meant to resemble a pilgrimage, to feel like a journey. The pilgrim enters in the darkness at the back of the nave and walks into the sanctuary toward the light that illuminates the apse. The apse is the area at the far end of the nave with a large elevated platform, called the dais, at the center of which is the high altar. The elaborately decorated

---

[2] G. K. Chesterton, *Orthodoxy: The Romance of Faith* (New York: Image Doubleday, 1959), p. 102.
[3] William A. Dyrness, *A Primer on Christian Worship: Where We've Been, Where We Are, Where We Can Go* (Grand Rapids: Eerdmans, 2009), p. 18.

altar is the focal point of medieval sacred space, just as the cross of Christ is literally the "crux" of salvation. It is not unusual for the central stained-glass window behind the high altar to depict the risen Christ victorious in his eternal reign, the end point, the *telos*, of a believer's journey.

Medieval laypersons, of course, were not allowed direct access to the apse, the dais or the altar. This was the sacred space for elaborately dressed priests to conduct the Mass in a language foreign to all but themselves. The medieval worshiper would simply listen for the one catch phrase that mattered: "*Hoc est corpus meum*" ("this is my body"). Medieval worshipers believed that at the moment the priest uttered these words the elements of bread and wine were changed in substance to the body and blood of the Lord Jesus.[4] The tinkling of bells and the aroma of incense also helped center the attention of the worshiper on this sacred moment of transformation. Then the priest silently lifted the wafer of bread (and later the cup) high enough for all in the nave to see. This moment of power belonged to the priests alone who functioned under the authority of the ecclesial magisterium of Rome.

In his book *Christ, Baptism and the Lord's Supper*, Leonard Vander Zee summarizes the central importance of this moment when he writes,

> That this change takes place in the liturgy points to a very important factor in the medieval understanding and practice of the sacrament. The church, through its priests, had the "power" to make this change take place. Instead of receiving the gifts of Christ from God through the promise of his Word, the grace of Christ's presence and sacrifice were given through the consecrating power of the church as the dispenser of grace through the sacraments.[5]

The clergy leadership of the medieval church was viewed as authoritative gatekeepers of God's grace. The laity's dependence upon clergy often engendered in the laity a sense of hopelessness and insecurity. The magisterium of the medieval Roman church functioned much like a sacramental factory. The church dispensed what people sought and needed. It was in many ways "good business," and this led the church to offer more things to "sell." The

---

[4]This belief was known as *transubstantiation*, a term applied by Thomas Aquinas in the thirteenth century.
[5]Leonard J. Vander Zee, *Christ, Baptism and the Lord's Supper: Recovering the Sacraments for Evangelical Worship* (Downers Grove, Ill.: InterVarsity Press, 2004), p. 171.

Roman magisterium began to elevate other ministries in the church to the level of sacraments. This strategy took a long period of time, and much was originally well-intended; but it further empowered the clergy and continued to elevate their status in the eyes of common, mostly illiterate, people.[6] However, of all the rites of the church conducted by the clergy, none was considered more powerful or significant to the laity than that moment in the Mass when bread and wine became the body and blood of the Lord Jesus.

The Roman Catholic doctrine of transubstantiation found its fullest expression in the thirteenth century in *Summa Theologica II, quaestiones 75-77* written by Thomas Aquinas (1225/27–1274). Thomas Aquinas rethought the Christian faith in Aristotelian categories and used the philosophical language of Aristotle. This system of theology came to be known as Aristotelian Thomism. However, the theological roots of this doctrine are much older. The history of the doctrine of transubstantiation is difficult to summarize, especially if one wants to avoid a caricature of the doctrine. Vander Zee does a very credible job of outlining the historical development of the doctrine of transubstantiation and how it functioned to empower the magisterium of the medieval church even as it was used to create a nearly magical understanding of that moment in the Mass for both priests and laity.[7] This dynamic, according to Vander Zee,

> involved ecclesiastical power, money and politics. The whole edifice of Rome's power and influence was tied to its control of the Mass's spigot of grace in the lives of the people, high and low. The church, through the priesthood, controlled the words that made Christ's saving body and blood available to the people.[8]

It must also be noted that "the Mass's spigot of grace" only provided one element of the Lord's Supper, the bread, to the laity. For many centuries before the Reformation, only the priests received the wine of the Eucha-

---

[6]The Council of Trent in the sixteenth century officially ratified seven sacraments for the Roman church. The ministry of these sacraments were rites that spanned the whole of human life, from baptism to last rites for the dying. To this day, the Roman Catholic Church has seven sacraments recognized by the church: baptism, penance, Eucharist, confirmation, marriage, ordination and extreme unction (last rites).

[7]Vander Zee, *Christ, Baptism*, pp. 162-72.

[8]Ibid., p. 172.

ristic feast. When the practice of denying laity a share of the Lord's cup began is difficult to identify with any satisfying precision. The twelfth-century doctrine of concomitance (belief that the blood of Christ is part of the body of Christ, so only one element of the Eucharist is necessary for the whole) was formulated to validate a long-established practice.[9] Thomas Aquinas supported the practice in the thirteenth century, and the sixteenth-century Counter-Reformation Council of Trent reaffirmed the practice and embellished its theological underpinnings by using the christology of the hypostatic union,[10] which had been well defined at the Council of Chalcedon in the fifth century.

The leaders of the Reformation clearly supported the Chalcedonian definition of the two natures of Christ (fully human and fully divine) and the Council's apophatic[11] summary of how the two natures related in the incarnation (without division, separation, confusion or mingling). However, the Reformers clearly saw how withholding the cup had become more about heightening the power of the clergy than offering the sacramental meal of grace to all those baptized into the body of Christ.

Luther's dispute with the Roman Catholic doctrine of transubstantiation centered on the need to refocus believers on the mediation of salvation by Christ Jesus himself. Most importantly, it was medieval liturgical *practices*, not necessarily its sacramental theology, that had positioned the church to be the mediator of divine grace. "How" Christ was present in the sacramental elements was important to all the Reformers, but their overriding concern was to recognize the saving work of Jesus in the cross itself, not the ritual of the church centered on the person, acts and words of the priest during the Mass. Luther, Calvin and Zwingli, who led the three major branches of the Protestant Reformation, had significantly distinct under-

---

[9]Catholic Encyclopedia, www.newadvent.org/cathen/04175a.htm.

[10]The term "hypostatic union" summarizes the theology of the church that affirms that the two natures (fully God and fully man) of God's Son in the incarnation existed in relation to each other "without confusion, without change, without division, without separation." The excerpt in this footnote of the Chalcedonian Definition of Faith is widely used. The source used here is from the work by Justo L. González, *A History of Christian Thought*, vol. 1 (Nashville: Abingdon Press, 1970), pp. 390-91.

[11]The manner of describing something by means of what it is not. The "four fences" of Chalcedon are apophatic as they describe the relationship of the two natures of Christ Jesus as "without."

standings of how Christ is present in the Eucharistic elements, but they were more concerned about the christocentrism necessary for the life, mission and liturgy of the church under the headship of Christ Jesus alone.

Rethinking sacramental doctrine was a task that the Protestant Reformers engaged carefully and with great fervor. Sacramental doctrine and praxis were the central forces that empowered and greatly unified the Western church. It also became the source of schismatic sectarianism that greatly differentiated and divided the major denominational faith communities that emerged from the Protestant Reformation. However, one thing all the Reformers held in agreement was the idea that the body of Christ, the church, was intended to be a "priesthood of all believers." One way to reestablish this reality in worship was to offer both elements of the Eucharistic celebration to the laity.

THE GIFTS OF GOD FOR THE PEOPLE OF GOD

Martin Luther (1483–1546) wrote and published a treatise on the sacraments of the church called *The Babylonian Captivity of the Church*[12] in 1520, just a year before his formal defense and refusal to recant most of his writings at the Diet of Worms (1521). In this treatise Luther argues from Scripture to make a case for including the cup as part of the sacramental participation of the laity. (Luther also asks in the *Babylonian Captivity* [2.73], "Why may mass be said in Greek and Latin and Hebrew, and not also in German or in any other language?" but the reformer largely leaves that battle for a later time.) Luther's argument from Scripture is nicely summarized here:

> For here the word and example of Christ stand firm, when He says, not by way of permission but of command, "All of you, drink from it."
>
> For if all are to drink, and the words cannot be understood as addressed to the priests alone, then it is certainly an impious act to withhold the cup from laymen who desire it.[13]

---

[12]Martin Luther's *Babylonian Captivity of the Church* deals with all seven of the medieval sacraments of the Roman Church and the issue of indulgences. It is a masterful work and a passionate defense of Scripture as the basis of faith and practice. The Project Wittenberg website is public domain and makes this insightful and key Reformation text readily available: www.lutherdansk.dk/Web-Babylonian%20Captivitate/Martin%20Luther.htm.

[13]Ibid, 2.7.

The priesthood of all believers was a central teaching for the leaders of the Reformation. The engagement of laity in active worship was the intention of the reformers to help educate medieval Christians in the faith they embraced but did not understand. Remembrance through reenactment involving those called to worship was once again made central to the faith and practice of all God's people.

In addition to including all baptized believers to receive both sacramental elements of the Lord's Supper, Luther explained the presence of Christ in relation to the bread and wine of the sacrament differently. Luther rejected the basic categories of Aristotelian Thomism and maintained that the real presence of Christ could be joined with these elements without a change in the actual (substance) elements themselves.

Medieval Aristotelians, like Thomas Aquinas, affirmed the idea that all physical objects have two dynamic realities, *substance* that is a "core identity"[14] and *accidents,* which are observable characteristics of a particular physical object. So the *substance* of a tree is "treeness" and its *accidents* are manifest as an eight-foot maple tree with autumn-colored foliage. The Roman Catholic doctrine of transubstantiation articulated by Aquinas partially rested on the relationship between a symbol and what it symbolizes and its meaning in that relationship. So how Christ was present in the sacramental elements was particularly important to medieval Thomists. For Aquinas, the *substance* of a thing is within the *accidents*; the ideal perfection was truly present and was wedded to the particular manifestation in time and space. Vander Zee indicates the importance of this belief for the doctrine of transubstantiation when he summarizes, "For [Aristotelians] substance inhered in the thing itself, not in some heavenly ideal. . . . If the bread of the sacrament is to be the body of Christ, the actual substance adhering to the object itself has to change."

Medieval Thomists had more to explain than earlier neo-Platonists, like

---

[14]Vander Zee, *Christ, Baptism,* pp. 170-72. Vander Zee summarizes the difference between Augustinian Platonism and Thomistic Aristotelian categories using the illustration of a tree that may be helpful for addressing the key aspects of fairly complex philosophical ideas used to understand how Christ is present in the sacramental elements. My summary above relies in good measure on Vander Zee's helpful illustration. I have indicated Vander Zee's unique terms by the use of quotation marks. I have indicated common Platonic and Aristotelian terms by the use of italics.

Augustine, who maintained that "treeness" existed as an ideal (in God's mind) and could be considered apart from its manifestation in the world as a particular tree. Because Platonists held that "treeness" as an ideal reality could be distinguished apart from the particularity of "a tree," it was easier for Augustinian Platonists to distinguish the *substance* of what is really signified (Christ Jesus) from the *accidents* of the sign (bread and wine) itself. This is the basis for Luther's doctrine of consubstantiation. The prefix *con* ("with") + "substantiation" conveys the idea that the risen Lord (who was sacrificed once and for all) is joined with the sacramental elements, but there is no need to explain why the elements do not appear to change.

The doctrine of consubstantiation vigorously defended the real presence of Christ in the sacramental meal while, with equal vigor, dismissing the idea of a sacrifice in the Mass itself. The idea of Jesus' continued suffering and repetitive sacrifice for sin was a natural understanding embedded in the doctrine of transubstantiation, which emphasized the physical presence of Christ Jesus. It is important to note that Luther vigorously defended the true presence of Christ in the Eucharistic elements, but he objected to the doctrine of transubstantiation because this real presence was dependent on the work of the priest in the words of institution, not in the grace of God through the words of Christ himself inviting believers to his table. For Luther, the words of institution were Christ's words of grace and invitation, not the words a priestly gatekeeper uttered to empower himself and transfix those who depended upon him to provide access to the presence of Christ in the Eucharistic meal.

Luther's proposal of consubstantiation takes shape in *The Babylonian Captivity of the Church* (2.23–2.36), and it is clear that his concern is not so much how Christ is present but that the means of grace in the sacrament be grounded in Scripture, not in the Aristotelian philosophical categories of Thomas Aquinas. Luther argues,

> when He said, "This cup is the new testament in my blood," does it not seem as though He desired to keep us in a simple faith, so that we might be believe His blood to be in the cup? For my part, if I cannot fathom how the bread is the body of Christ, I will take my reason captive to the obedience of Christ, and clinging simply to His word, firmly believe not only that the body of Christ is in the bread, but that the bread is the body of Christ. . . . What does

it matter if philosophy cannot fathom this? The Holy Spirit is greater than Aristotle. . . . The authority of God's Word is greater than the grasp of our intellect. Even so, in order that the real body and the real blood of Christ may be present in the sacrament, it is not necessary that the bread and wine be transubstantiated and Christ be contained under their accidents. But both remain there together, and it is truly said, "This bread is my body, this wine is my blood," and vice versa. Thus I will for now understand it, for the honor of the holy words of God, which I will not allow any petty human argument to override.[15]

Just nine year later, in 1529, many of the early leaders of the Reformation met at Marburg and agreed on "Fifteen Articles" of church doctrine. However, the doctrine of how Christ was present in the sacraments was the immovable point of dissent between the German Lutherans and the Swiss Anabaptists, lead by Ulrich Zwingli. For Zwingli, the only change that happened took place not on the table but in the mind and heart of the believer. For Zwingli, grace was not mediated at all through the sacraments. Water, bread and wine were pure symbols of God's activity in the past, and they simply helped recall a point within a story; they did not reenact an ongoing reality of God's story.

On first consideration, this understanding of the sacraments as pure symbol seems simple and rather straightforward. Many post-Protestant believers who hold lightly to the historical shape of the faith after the New Testament have never thought about the importance of what Jesus meant when he said "This is" regarding the relationship of the loaf to the body of Christ broken or the cup of wine to Christ's blood poured out. Why did Jesus command the meal as an act of both remembrance and anticipation? Is there more to reenactment than remembrance? If nothing actually happens between the table and the believer, why reenact at all and not just recall or bring to mind? Is there any grace external to the believer's mindset or sincerity of heart? It is this last question that reflects Luther's central concern with Zwingli's understanding of the sacrament. Luther saw the interior nature of Zwingli's pure symbol theology as the flip-side of Rome's exterior notion of transubstantiation through the words of the priest. Both

---

[15]Martin Luther, *The Babylonian Captivity of the Church 1520* (2.35–2.36), www.lutherdansk .dk/Web-Babylonian%20Captivitate/Martin%20Luther.htm.

had to do with what worshipers did for God and both tended to place the burden of faith on the believer and not on the unmerited grace of God given to the believer.

John Calvin, whose work did not begin until after Marburg and the initial round of rethinking the faith by the Reformation's first leaders, strode into the middle of the dispute and created a different place to stand when considering the efficacious nature of the sacrament. Calvin agreed with Luther that the sacrament is endued with the reality of God's grace and rejected Zwingli's idea of pure symbol. However, Calvin saw Luther's thoughts and writing as still captive to medieval scholastic ideas, categories and practices even though he affirmed the central tenants of Luther's soteriological argument that salvation is by faith alone through grace alone understood by Scripture alone.[16] Calvin stood between Luther and Zwingli during their ongoing debate concerning the presence of Christ in the sacrament of the Lord's Supper. Calvin realized, on one hand, that if Luther had not stepped far enough away from Rome and its ecclesial language and understanding, on the other hand, Zwingli had nearly run off to a far country and was on the brink of forgetting his native tongue. When it came time for Calvin to enter the debate, it became clear that the French Reformer thought both Luther and Zwingli were answering what was essentially the wrong question.

For over a thousand years the question had been how Christ descended to be present in sacramental bread and wine. Calvin's doctrine of Christ's sacramental presence made the point that it's not how Christ comes *down* into bread and wine, but how believers are *lifted up* to God in a special way through participation in the Lord's Supper. In 1540 Calvin published a *Short Treatise on the Holy Supper of Our Lord Jesus Christ* as his answer to what he considered a better question: how does the sacrament of the Lord's Supper mediate God's grace to the believer? Calvin makes it clear that the Lord's Supper does not so much add something missing in the believer's faith but is a means of nourishment for the believer's faith, which is a gift of God's grace through the Holy Spirit and active in God's Word, the Scriptures:

---

[16]This affirmation is known as the tri-sola summary of the Reformation. *Sola fide, sola gratia, sola scriptura*: only faith, only grace, only scripture. Although the stark simplicity of this summary highlights the central argument for much of the Reformation, the framework for understanding the relationship of faith, grace and Scripture to the sacraments and the church were more complex.

But as the life into which [God] has begotten us again is spiritual, so must the food, in order to preserve and strengthen us, be spiritual also. For we should understand, that not only has [God] called us one day to possess his heavenly inheritance, but that by hope he has already in some measure installed us in possession; that not only has [God] promised us life, but already transported us into it, delivering us from death, when by adopting us as his children, he begot us again by immortal seed, namely, his word imprinted on our hearts by the Holy Spirit.[17]

In 1559 the definitive edition of Calvin's *Institutes of the Christian Religion* would be the culmination of the French Reformer's mature theological rethinking of the Christian faith. Nearly all of Calvin's writings, like the excerpt above, include references to the Gospels (particularly John), Ephesians (particularly the first two chapters) and Hebrews (with a particular emphasis on the doctrine of the ascension). Unlike Luther, Calvin did see merit in connecting sacramental theology to Jesus' teaching in John 6, and the connection between "word and Spirit" is never far from Calvin's theology. In book four of the *Institutes*, one can clearly see Calvin's emphasis on the upward direction of God's work of grace in the Lord's Supper:

For seeing this mystery is heavenly, there is no necessity to bring Christ on the earth that he may be connected with us. Now, should any one ask me as to the mode, I will not be ashamed to confess that it is too high a mystery either for my mind to comprehend or my words to express. . . . It is enough for us that Christ, out of the substance of his flesh, breathes life into our souls, nay, diffuses his own life into us.[18]

Calvin's emphasis on the necessity of the Spirit in the presence of the Word of God to elevate and nourish the believer through the sacrament is a central tenant of what came to be known as Reformed theology in distinction from Lutheran and Anabaptist formulations of the faith.[19]

---

[17]John Calvin, *Short Treatise on the Holy Supper of Our Lord Jesus Christ*, 1540, section 3 in *Tracts Containing Treatises on the Sacraments, Catechism of the Church of Geneva, Forms of Prayer, and Confessions of Faith*, volume 2, trans. Henry Beveridge (Edinburgh: Calvin Translation Society, 1849), p. 165.

[18]John Calvin, *Institutes of the Christian Religion*, book IV, chapter 17, 31-32 (Grand Rapids: Eerdmans, 1989), p. 587.

[19]Some scholars consider the early third-century Eucharistic prayer of Hippolytus that includes the idea of the participants in the meal being "lifted up" as one early source for Calvin's theology.

Regarding baptism, both Calvin and Luther opposed the idea of re-baptism as a way to emphasize that water baptism in the triune name initiated one into the body of Christ, not a particular community of the faith. Again, Anabaptists (the word simply means "rebaptizer," or those who baptize a second time) seemed to distance themselves from the historic roots of the Christian faith.

THE PLACE OF SACRAMENTS IN CHRISTIAN WORSHIP TODAY

How congregations recognize the centrality of Christ in his mediation of God's grace through baptism and the Lord's Supper is as important today as it was in the early church and in the sixteenth century. "Who" always needs to be more important than "how." And knowing the "who" means keeping the story connected to its reenactment. And this story is an "old, old story of Jesus and his love," as the hymnwriter reminds us.[20]

Sacramental practice as a part of Christian worship is an extension of biblical worship patterns that began with Israel's practice in the tabernacle, the temple and the development of nonsacrificial worship in the synagogue. Accounts in the New Testament make it clear that Jesus not only encouraged his disciples to engage in practices of reenactment but identified with Israel and his own disciples by being baptized himself, commissioning the apostles to baptize in the triune name, redefining his own inaugural Passover feast[21] to help his followers remember and, in some way, reenact his work of salvation and anticipate the final victory to be fully realized in the kingdom of God.

Water baptism in the triune name should be witnessed by the community as participation in God's grace in Christ Jesus. One is baptized into the body of Christ for nurture in the faith that, by God's ongoing grace, one will confess as their own. Or one is baptized into the body of Christ for accountability and nurture as a recognition of a person's con-

---

[20]A. Katherine Hankey, "I Love to Tell the Story," 1866.

[21]The distinction between the timing of this meal in the Synoptic Gospels and the fourth Gospel is beyond the subject of this work. However, it is helpful to appreciate how Jesus redefined and refocused the supper on the night he was betrayed in the light of his own impending sacrifice. That Jesus clearly expressed the importance of both remembrance and anticipation in the institution of this supper is clear and should be reflected in Christian sacramental practices.

fession of faith. Whether sprinkled, poured, dipped or dunked in water warm, cold, running or still, one can affirm with Luther that "water is water"; but it is the Spirit who is poured out and sanctifies all who belong to God in the body of Christ. In his role as high priest, Christ Jesus is the only mediator of God's grace, not the church, not bishop, clergy, elder or pope. It is the faithfulness of Jesus and his exaltation by the Father that results in the procession of and presence of the Holy Spirit as the agent of divine grace.

Regardless of how a believer understands the particularities of Christ's presence in the Lord's Supper, there are important ideas to verbalize and demonstrate to help contemporary Christians remember and anticipate within the integrity of biblical church history. First, the Lord's Supper is a gift of grace to the body of Christ. Both sacramental elements are served to one another as a priesthood of all believers. The New Testament, especially Jesus' inauguration in the upper room and Paul's guidance in 1 Corinthians, the *Didache* and the guidance of the early church fathers reflect the practice that the table of the Lord welcomes all believers to come and eat and drink. Thus the invitation to the sacred meal is both generous and guarded. The practice is accountable and careful.

The words of Jesus recorded in the Gospels or by Paul in 1 Corinthians should be used to amplify the connection between Jesus' sacrifice on Calvary and the loaf broken and the cup of the new covenant poured out. Visual reenactment of breaking bread and the pouring of "the fruit of the vine" (whether wine or grape juice) can be very helpful. The elements should be served, not taken by one's own initiative, to underscore the importance of the unmerited and freely given grace reflected in the meal. There should be a time for confession of sin, of course, prior to the reenactment of the Lord's Supper for the community. In most historical liturgies, the Lord's Supper is the central way a congregation participates in hearing the Word, so the sacrament would naturally come well after the time given for the confession of sin and the declaration of forgiveness.

I'd like to close this chapter by quoting a thoughtful email exchange between two brothers regarding their experience of the Lord's Supper on a Sunday. The elder brother, an artist living in Chicago, emailed his sibling who is a pastor living on the Mississippi Gulf Coast.[22]

The artist's contribution to theological discourse. I think a lot about the *aesthetic* dimensions of the sacraments. It's where the artist is most at home in worship. I've been writing some meditations on these things. It's imperative that we wrestle with them as aesthetic, because they are.

One of my more recent (last four or five months) thoughts has been on communion as a meal. In thinking of it as a meal, and of it as a visceral (literally viscera-filling), and as such, aesthetic, act, I began to long for better bread. Something I could really sink my teeth into, as opposed to something that slips between my teeth like our little wafers. Not being one to sigh and sit on his hands, I have been thinking of volunteering to come early and chop up bread for the congregation. But the week before Ash Wednesday, a sermon brought me around to a different perspective that has really enriched my understanding and experience of communion.

I wish I remember exactly what the sermon was on, probably the temptation of Christ. I'll go listen to it again, but the thing that hit me, whether it was explicit, or implicit (the Still Small Voice), was that it is the unlikely things, the insignificant things, that really satisfy. As we were about to celebrate the sacrament, I knew that there, at Christ's table, is an act, a meal, embodying that deep satisfaction—security and contentment that lays bare the subordinate nature of all others—and that's when it hit me.

The meal that I held in my hands, of all the meals that I eat, day in and day out, month to month, year to year, is *the* smallest, the least significant, the most humble. The meal that I could hardly sink my teeth into if I tried, was the one that represented a satisfaction that no lavish feast could match. We are no strangers to gut-filling meals. We Americans thrive on full bellies, "super sized" meals, and at least two or three real feasts a year. The most forgettable lunch leaves me tired as my body works to try to process all the food.

But Jesus always dealt in the unexpected, and I think it is *appropriate*, that in the United States at least, Jesus' meal has become lighter than the snacks we serve in the nursery. It reflects his character. It reflects his nature. You don't need a primer on Romans 1 or Philippians 2, but that's where it's at. He

---

[22]This correspondence from fall 2009 is included with the permission of these two brothers with minimal editing for space and clarity. These two brothers are, in fact, my two adult sons, the artist, Robert Dayton Castleman, and the pastor, Scott Breckinridge Castleman. This exchange reminded me of our "table talk" during evening meals. Conversations like this were so important that both sons insisted that the women they eventually married experience the Castleman table-talk dinner before they were engaged.

has chosen, in his providence, the smallest meal to shame the feast.

So I love it. I have been savoring my little rice cracker and my sip of wine. I have been relishing the culinary foolishness of our communal meal, knowing that in its material insignificance, is its aesthetic, spiritual, and somatic power, and there can be no more profoundly subtle image, as we wait for the wedding feast, of what it means to dine at the table of the Servant King.

The artist's brother responded from his perspective as a pastor. The incarnation of the gospel never runs out of new facets and I am always humbled by that as a pastor. I had a new member in the congregation share with me almost the exact opposite realization you shared. One Sunday he got surprised by the piece of flesh he tore from the body. It was too big, he thought. In his mind it was an "oops." It should have been smaller, less significant. But he had to deal with it. He couldn't just eat part of it. He couldn't put some back. He was stuck with more than he could handle. So he stuck it in his mouth and began to chew and chew.

For him, the aesthetic reality that he wrestled with when it came to the sacrament was not in the gospel-laden irony of a light wafer and small sip that conveyed and transferred the reality of our eternal immortal God who became a servant. As he chewed and chewed, this man was confronted in the gospel of that moment, what it meant to him that Jesus was indeed the "true bread which has come down from heaven." The incarnate act of communion appeals to your need for seeing the insignificance and humility of Christ. For this guy, at this time, it is a confrontation with that thick and meaty and jaw-tiring fullness with which Jesus longs to abide in us.

The incarnation is always a less and more reality. There is gospel in both. And while that still small voice says to one, "I have become as nothing for you," he says to another, "I am more than you ever thought." Only in that meal where words go away, where the aesthetic proclaims the gospel, can both the less and more of it be heard loud and clear. But don't be surprised when one day you accidentally tear off a piece that was bigger than you had intended and you find a lavish feast where you weren't looking for it. That's incarnation for you.

It does not surprise me that in your desire to bring meaning to the table, that the table brought meaning to you instead. As a minister of Word and sacrament I plan the meal. I calculate the word people hear as it is given and the means by which they will take it. Sadly, my mind is so often filled with the administration of it I am too busy to be spoken to in those moments by wafers or crust, plastic cups of juice or goblets of wine. I would hate to think that for my days as a pastor I will be forever administering, making me like Martha, busy about the house while Mary sits at his feet and takes him in.

Thinking through the sacraments in the presence of the Spirit and in the light of God's Word should be an internal conversation as the baptized family of faith gathers around the table of the Lord to celebrate, reenact and embody the story of salvation. God is blessed when his children come home for his supper and join Luther's tradition of "tabletalk."

WORKSHOP FOR CHAPTER NINE

1. "Confirmation and correction" were the two significant goals of the early Reformers. Think about the service of worship in your congregation in the light of its history.

   • How might the service of worship—its style(s), its liturgical structure, its music, the value of preaching, the inclusion or exclusion of creeds or prayers, etc.—be a reflection of some sort of "confirmation and/or correction" in the history of the congregation?

   • How might the denominational identification or the independence of the denomination influence how "confirmation and correction" are viewed in the congregation, by worship leaders or pastors?

2. How do secondary issues not central to the gospel (like the understanding and formulation of sacramental practice, the relationship between the church and the world, the use or prohibition of symbols, art and images for sacred space, or what kind of music was appropriate for Christian worship) continue to be the source of much congregational infighting, denominational identification and schism today?

3. Visit at least four different congregational sanctuaries or worship centers that represent a variety of denominational affiliations, congregational sizes and histories.

   • When the space set aside for corporate worship is not in use, study each congregation's sacred space, its furniture, sacred symbols, windows, lighting, where the Scripture is read, where teaching or preaching takes place, etc. If both are present, which is bigger: pulpit or table/altar?

- What does this sacred place tell you about certain priorities within this congregation? What clues are given about the liturgy used for worship from this observation of sacred space?

- Are there visual clues about the inclusion of children in worship?

4. Identify liturgical moments when "all the people" present are involved at one time in the service of worship that you attend most often. Does this seem adequate to you? Why or why not? Are children encouraged to participate at those "all the people" times?

5. Make time to discuss sacramental traditions, practice and theology with the pastor(s) and worship leaders of two or three congregations besides your own. Compare and contrast what you learn about these practices. Do you consider some traditions, practices and the theological support given for them more "biblical" than others? Why or why not?

6. Write out an explanation of baptism that you would use to summarize "what this means" to an unchurched person or a nonbeliever.

- Write out a similar explanation for the Lord's Supper.

- Ask a mentor, pastor, teacher or other knowledgeable friend to read through each summary and discuss for clarity of practice, meaning and biblical doctrine.

7. If you could design the sacramental practice of your congregation with a robustly conscious effort to connect "the" story with its reenactment, how would it look?

- What elements would you use and how?

- How might you do this within the congregation's history and its theological understanding of baptism and the Lord's Supper?

CONTEMPORARY PATTERNS FOR CHRISTIAN WORSHIP

Keeping the Faith

Worship is for our benefit, not gods [sic]—to help us feel closer to him, not meet some religious requirement.

COMMENT ON FACEBOOK

It is rather ironic that the evangelicalism that claims to be the heir of the opponents of Protestant liberalism in the nineteenth century should find itself unwillingly concurring with the father of liberalism, Friedrich Schleiermacher, who understood the source of religion to be found precisely in human subjectivity.

SIMON CHAN, *LITURGICAL THEOLOGY*

Today a service of worship that is designed to help the congregation participate in the reenactment of God's great story of salvation is one way of keeping the faith handed down to us (Jude 3). Story-shaped worship is mediated by God's Spirit to bring glory to God as it reflects God's own faithfulness to us through the Son. This is an offering which God regards, like that of Abel, as worthy of himself. Story-shaped worship can help keep God's great story at the center of Christian identity, mission and witness. This chapter will consider how difficult it is today to recognize the centrality of God's story in the life of the Christian and the church. This difficulty comes from the personalizing and privatizing of individual experience, the inroads made by marketing models for congregational programming, and supremacy of the idea of the "right" to preferential choice in the relative autonomy of life in the twenty-first century. Part of keeping God's story central is recognizing how easily we elevate the importance of our own experience at the cost of community, kingdom and even the cross of Christ.

To carefully consider the realities of corporate worship for Christian congregations today is no small task. Even limiting the focus to North America, the numbers and complexities of services of worship represented is staggering. Congregations linked to historical denominations as well as independent congregations with histories only as old as the founding pastor can reflect a variety of liturgical content and styles. One way to begin to discern biblical patterns within this myriad of liturgical options is to trace the historical roots of this rather entrepreneurial and highly personalized "salad bar" (pick and choose what you want) of worship options.

Christian historian Mark Noll states that the adaptation of the Reformation message by John and Charles Wesley in eighteenth-century England was the "most important single factor in transforming the religion of the Reformation into modern Protestant evangelicalism."[1] In terms of intention, if not direct historical links, the Wesleys shouldered the same burden for the Church of England that German Pietist Jakob Spener (1635–1705) carried for the post-Reformation scholasticism of Lutheran orthodoxy. Jakob Spener and John and Charles Wesley wanted the faith to make a practical and real difference in the everyday lives of all believers. Spener's program for small group study of Scripture sought to return the study of God's Word to the laity to develop shared understanding within the community apart from the theological disputes and fine-point wrangling of professional academics and scholastic clerics. The Wesleys and their contemporary, the eloquent George Whitefield, took the good news to the laity through "field preaching" services held outside the sanctuaries of church

---

[1]Mark A. Noll, *Turning Points: Decisive Moments in the History of Christianity* (Grand Rapids: Baker Books, 1997), pp. 223-24. Noll does include the innovative preaching and mission style of the Wesleys' contemporary George Whitefield as part of the dynamic "single factor" influencing the development of Protestant evangelicalism.

buildings and through singing new hymns to common tunes that rehearsed in memorable meter the wonder of salvation and the essential truths of the Christian faith. However, there was a tendency in both Spener's small groups and Wesleyan revivals not only to marginalize the authority and professional education of clerics, but to centralize one's experience of God in the individual apart from the church as the body of Christ. One can anticipate how this needed corrective development carried within it other dynamics that could prove regrettable.

Of course the ongoing seventeenth and eighteenth-century erosion of clerical authority followed easily from the attempts of the sixteenth-century protestors who tried to reform, if not dismantle, the absolute authority of the Roman magisterium. The rise of European nationalism went hand in hand with the success of the Reformation. In great measure Luther survived, as the fourteenth-century Johann Hus did not, because Luther found favor with a protector, a prince of Saxony, Frederick the Wise. The unfettering of the faith from a powerful ecclesial hierarchy sowed the seeds for both the "wheat" of biblical faith and the "tares" of attractive substitutes.[2]

The manifestation of both wheat and tares is parallel to another dynamic that emerged from the failure of the church to function as a unified family of faith under the headship of Christ Jesus. This, in turn, unfettered the faith from the accountability and oversight of the corrupt Roman magisterium. This parallel dynamic is often termed the "sacred-secular split" that began to privatize (and personalize) faith and to elevate reason alone to reign in all public spheres of influence. The ascendency of personal autonomy in both these parallel dynamics is discernible in a myriad of ways in both "sacred" and "secular" spheres of life.[3]

---

[2] A profoundly insightful book that works to connect religious dynamics with the currents of Western history and particularly the twentieth-century social, political and economic realities that anticipate issues of postmodernity is Peter Berger's *The Sacred Canopy: Elements of a Sociological Theory of Religion* (Garden City, N.Y.: Doubleday, 1967). Berger contends that as the "sacred canopy" of Western religious norms shrinks, partly through radicalizing individualism, the gulf between what is considered the "sacred" and the "secular" will widen. In this Berger anticipates the rise of twenty-first-century global religious fundamentalism that seeks to narrow this gulf through political coercion, sectarian violence and the increase of tribalism, not nationalism, as key to one's identity.

[3] I have placed "sacred" and "secular" in quotes to emphasize that the dichotomy is a false one. Biblical faith affirms the sovereignty of God over all aspects of creation. There is no real

Autonomy considers itself accountable only to its own desires and, not surprisingly, blows in all directions. The results of this can be seen in both the elevation of humanity in the Renaissance and the commodification of humanity in the Industrial Revolution. The wheat and tares of radical individualism in both the "sacred" and "secular" spheres of life has led to the defense and recognition of human rights as well as to the atrocities of the Third Reich. The elevation of individual desire has led to both the enactment of child labor laws to protect children as well as legalized abortion, which allows the biologically mature to make children disposable. The unfettering of the faith from a powerful ecclesial hierarchy helped change the direction of historical winds that shaped the last five hundred years of politics, science, society, economics, ethics, religion and countless other areas. From the relatively harmless results of autonomy, like the invention of the salad bar and the pledge of Burger King to let its customers "have it your way," to the more questionable outcomes of autonomy, like the parental challenges of "over choice" in raising children and church-hopping over issues of style, the self is the definitive and deciding vote.

In the church one upshot of the ascendency of individualism is the perceived "right" to have a liturgy that suits one's taste in focus, music, preaching style, comfort zone and the way personal needs are met. Our story, like our very selves, takes center stage at the expense of God's great story. What happens when individual Christians no longer primarily identify the reality of their faith within the body of Christ? The headship of Christ Jesus can also go unrecognized and unacknowledged as the vital life source of the church. Worship, no longer dependent on the mediation of the Son by the Spirit, becomes a great program or presentation designed for the preferences of the worshiper.

THE EROSION OF ECCLESIOLOGY

It not uncommon to recall that near the end of his life Martin Luther lamented that when the Reformation effort began there was "one pope on the

---

sacred-secular split, no actual dichotomy between private and public life, and no disconnection between faith and reason. *Lex orandi, lex credendi* still holds—what one prays (doing) still reveals what one truly believes (the orientation of the private self). St. James summarized the idea as "Faith without works is dead" (James 2:26).

seven hills of Rome," but within a few decades there were "seven popes on every dung hill in Germany."[4] Luther's debate with Zwingli in Augsburg concerning sacramental theology was an impassioned preamble to his end-of-life lament. Luther's longing for the reformation of the Roman Catholic Church never denied a need for structures that helped provide accountability for biblical faith and practice. The Roman Catholic Counter-Reformation movement began in earnest with the Council of Trent (1545–1563), which began to correct many issues of faith and practice in the medieval church, especially clergy life and the practice of simony.[5] The council was significantly influenced by a religious order, the Society of Jesus. This religious order, commonly referred to as the Jesuits, was founded in 1540 by Ignatius Loyola (1491–1556) as an expression of his own spiritual reformation. The order quickly became a wellspring of spiritual vigor for the Counter-Reformation movement.[6] When one considers the significance of Luther's longing for a united church reflected in his lament over its unfettered splintering as well as the willingness of the Roman Church to address its need for reform, one can readily see how complicated it can be to discern whether the results of these unfettered winds of autonomy are the wheat of biblical

---

[4]A definitive source for this popular "quote" by Luther is hard to find; however I did not discover a scholar in my research who thought it completely apocryphal. It just sounds like something Luther would say and it certainly reflects his regret that the church splintered in ways he did not imagine, whether for good or for ill.

[5]The Council of Trent met for several months-long sessions from December 13, 1545, and closed there on December 4, 1563. Trent was a city in Northern Italy. The main purpose for the council was to formally respond to what the Roman See considered the heresies of the Protestant Reformers, but the council also wanted to execute a thorough reform of the interior conduct of institutional life and eliminate the numerous abuses readily evident in church leadership. Between 1545 and 1563 there were five popes (Paul III, Julius III, Marcellus II, Paul IV and Pius IV), but none attended the council. It was the emperor Charles V who initially convened the council. Charles V was only twenty-one years old when he heard Luther's defense and the Reformer's refusal to recant at the Diet of Worms in 1521. Fredrick the Wise of Saxony, Luther's protector, was an uncle of the young emperor. For further information on Trent or other interests, the Catholic Encyclopedia provides a well-documented resource for Roman Catholic history: www.newadvent.org/cathen/15030c.htm.

[6]It is remarkable to note that Ignatius Loyola and John Calvin studied at the University of Paris during the same period of time (the early 1520s). However, Calvin began his studies when only fourteen years old, and Loyola was in his early thirties, eighteen years his senior. However, it was during Loyola's time at the University of Paris that he led a small group of friends through a series of "spiritual exercises" that centered on extended periods of meditation on the life of Jesus. That small group would become the Society of Jesus, and Loyola's *Spiritual Exercises* continue to contribute to the spiritual formation of Catholic and non-Catholic Christians today.

faith or the tares of attractive substitutes. Are these results always either-or? Can they ever be both/and?

However, if one is to keep the faith that is firmly attached to a story older than one's own history, it is good to note how unfettered autonomy influences the best intentions of many people who, in their own day, were just trying to be faithful. The ascendency of the self over accountability to any history but one's own is the bedrock of the secularized soteriologies of eighteenth-century Protestant liberals. Self-interest accounts for much of the reactionary and protective Roman Catholic conservatism reflected in the First Vatican Council late in the nineteenth century. And this same dynamic is functional in much of early twentieth-century Protestant fundamentalism. The distancing of God by deists, the fiery revivalism of Finney, the eighteenth-century Great Awakenings in Calvinist New England and Wesleyan frontier America are all influenced in different ways and to different degrees by the unfettering of the self from a more corporately conscious history, a story bigger than oneself. The winds of an increasing ahistorical individual autonomy are discernible in the latter half of the twentieth century in some aspects of the Jesus Movement, the emergence of some nondenominational "big box" congregations, and the proliferation of congregations started in someone's garage or living room in an attempt to more easily control "how things ought to be done."

The heightened sense of autonomy in congregational and worship development is also discernible in how many think about the Christian faith. Individualism has even influenced the way many people think about and articulate their understanding of salvation itself. It is not unusual today to hear Christians identify the central focus of salvation as the time they began to understand the work of Christ or a particular event that marked their decision to follow Jesus. If someone were to ask, "When were you saved?" it would not be uncommon to hear responses like, "When I was six years old," or, "When I was in high school, at a Youth for Christ conference" or, "I'm not sure when exactly, but being raised in a Christian home, I slowly but surely came to know Christ." Now, responses like these are heartfelt expressions of one's own story, but they are subtly unfettered from a longer, older and far richer story of salvation. The only deeply biblical answer to the question "When were you saved?" is one that reflects the finished work of

Jesus Christ on the cross of Calvary. That's the literal crux of the story that is the focal point of salvation for every child of God.

A Christian's personal entrance into the reality of that ongoing story is priceless, but it is good to remember that the story does not begin with that entrance. Christians belong to an old story, God's story of salvation, that is older than an individual's part of the journey, richer than anyone's personal relationship with the Savior, and wiser than anyone's understanding of what it means to belong to Christ Jesus by the Spirit.

ONE LORD, ONE FAITH, ONE BODY

In all of this, Christians belong to each other in the body of Christ, the "fullness of him who fills all in all" (Ephesians 1:23). Unity in Christ by the Spirit is not optional for biblical faith, and this unity is not idealized or theoretical in the New Testament. The church as the body of Christ is localized specifically in communities of believers who care for one another and come together for prayer, Scripture reading, fellowship around table and the Eucharistic meal, the initiation of new covenant people through baptism, and the edification of the whole through the spiritual gifts of its members. This locality of expression in the New Testament also recognized a belonging to the whole of God's people beyond its particular congregational community. This is clearly seen in Paul's efforts to collect money from Greek and Macedonian congregations for the relief of the Jerusalem congregations during a time of need. All of these localized congregational communities are the church proper.

The global church that spans the centuries must have, as it always has had, concrete manifestation in local congregational communities. It is in the long-term community life of these congregations that Christians recognize the "great cloud of witnesses" (Hebrews 12:1) of those saints whose stories are a part of Scripture's great story (Hebrews 11) and those saints who are a part of the history of that particular congregation who have died and await the resurrection of the body. Christians belong to one another for the duration of the journey, to have and to hold, for better, for worse, for richer, for poorer, in sickness and health. Even in death, they are not parted, but are unified in Christ, the head of the body, by the Spirit. On this journey, believers are not individual hikers out on a trail for the purpose of personal fitness. We are the church, the body of Christ, *together* cross-laden and following the head of the church, the Lord Jesus.

Christians need to learn to love the church like Jesus loves his bride. God's love for the church as the body of Christ is the ultimate identity of the local congregation. And, as Jesus said, by how we love one another, others identify believers as belonging to Christ (John 13:35). Someday faith communities will be without spot or wrinkle, but today, in everyday clothes covered with dirt from the journey, with skinned knees and aching muscles, the church is still God's beloved. Everything that makes God's people dependent on Christ as their head and the members of Christ's body interdependent on and accountable to each other protests against the unfettered autonomy of individualism that is championed in Western culture.

The seeds of individualism borne by such winds certainly have broadly influenced how Christians today think about church membership, denominational identity and ecclesiology in general. Roger Olson, in his book *The Mosaic of Christian Belief*, summarizes this well when he writes,

> We find ourselves now in a situation where in many places Christians seem to believe that the church is nothing more than an optional support group for Christians who need it or a tool of evangelism to win people to Christ. Many Christians regard their own "personal relationship with God" their "church." . . . [Biblical and historically based] Christianity, at least until recently, has included belief in the unity of the church and even the necessity of the church for authentic Christian living if not for salvation itself.[7]

More narrowly considered, it is no surprise that unfettered autonomy has certainly had its influence in the worship practices of contemporary congregations.

Remembering the Incarnational Shape of God's Story

There is no question that the historically anemic ecclesiology of the evangelical community has often resulted in Sunday morning programs that are focused on the experience of the individual rather than true worship that is focused on and mediated by the person of the triune God. The necessity of worship as a service mediated by the Spirit, through the Son and for the

---

[7]Roger E. Olson, *The Mosaic of Christian Belief: Twenty Centuries of Christian Unity and Diversity* (Downers Grove, Ill.: InterVarsity Press, 2002), pp. 287-88.

Father is often lost in the pragmatism of the commodified liturgies of many evangelical congregations. Dependence on the Spirit by worship leaders often seeks to control or mimic the divine encounter (the addition of cool smoke machines or special effects that God doesn't seem to provide enough of any more).

Simon Chan's comment at the beginning of the chapter about evangelicals affirming the importance of human subjectivity of classic Protestant liberalism is a startling challenge to many believers who champion the orthodoxy of biblical faith. Chan's comment, as juxtaposed to the Facebook comment that "worship is for our benefit," highlights a tendency to view worship like many other congregational programs. Chan's insight exposes how easy it is to allow God's story of salvation to be eclipsed by an individual's experience of it. This tail-wagging-the-dog scenario is a short step away from the subjective substitution of a biblically shaped liturgy for a more therapeutic, self-centered and often highly satisfying experience which, in fact, neglects worship as a reenactment of and engagement with God's great story. This, in turn, has the rather frequent tendency to place the initiative and effectiveness of a service of worship on the efforts of worship leaders. Now, worship planners and church leaders might verbalize a dependence on God's Spirit to lead, guide, move and bless the congregation in a service of worship. But if a believer's experience or congregational need shapes the service, the actual walk doesn't give evidence for such talk.

It is not unusual in discussions about worship that pleases God to ask questions about God's sufficiency. Why would God desire to be blessed by the worship of his people if God is in no need of blessing? This, of course, strikes at the mystery of creation itself and the very being of God. Because God is love, essentially and perfectly, God is triune in persons, the perfection of love. God as love created out of nothing a cosmos he did not need not for his own perfection of love, but in order to reveal himself as triune, as Father, Son, Spirit. The triune God is love for that which is "wholly other." This is the tri-personal God of love who calls those who bear his image and reflect his likeness to share in that love, to worship and to reflect divine love in relationship to him. Human parents experience the blessing of their children when those children desire what a parent desires, do what a parent would do, and choose what a parent would choose. A parent doesn't "need" what that child practices for the parent's own sake, but delights in and is blessed by the life of a child that reflects the identity and character of the parent.

There is another challenge in keeping the faith today in worship. Besides the burden of an unmediated work responsibility placed on worship leaders, there is a tendency to overspiritualize the experience with God that actually distances worshipers from a real encounter with the God whose story was and is revealed in real time and space. The denial that Jesus was really and fully the incarnation of God as a human being was a fairly early challenge, particularly for the second generation of believers. The Johannine writings in the New Testament in particular offer a clear denunciation of this errant belief known as Docetism, from the Greek verb meaning "to seem." This belief was subtle and was applied to the idea that denied the real incarnation of Jesus as fully human and affirmed that Jesus only *seemed* to be human. The opening of 1 John is particularly clear in its rebuttal:

> We declare to you what was from the beginning, what we have heard, what we have seen *with our eyes*, what we have looked at and touched *with our hands*, concerning the word of life. . . . We declare to you what we have seen and heard so that you also may have fellowship with us. (1 John 1:1, 3; emphasis mine)

John's first audience consisted primarily of people who were born after most of the eyewitnesses of Jesus' earthy life had died. To them the birth, life, teachings, suffering, crucifixion, resurrection and ascension of Jesus were unobserved stories recounted by vicarious witnesses and written documents. As second-generation people heard about Jesus, a natural first question would be, "Was Jesus *really* human?" They had no doubt, given the triumph of the story, that Jesus was truly God. In fact, John declares that the "antichrist" is anyone who denies the full incarnation of the Son (1 John 4:2-3; 2 John 7).[8]

---

[8]These are the only two books in the New Testament where the word *antichrist* (*antichristos*) is found (1 and 2 John). Both are focused on the denial of the incarnation of the Son and the relationship of the Father and the Son in the incarnation. This is important to note for purposes of highlighting the significance of reenactment and embodiment in Christian worship, but it is also good to keep in mind for issues that often emerge in eschatological discussions. See 1 John 2:18, 22; 4:3; 2 John 7. The word doesn't occur at all in the book of the Revelation!

In terms of sacramental theology, many evangelicals, in fact, are well-entrenched in a new kind of "functional Docetism" that fails to value the actual physical reenactment of the life and death of Jesus in sacramental practice. When the sacraments of the church are reduced to mere rites of personal memory and practiced out of some sort of fuzzy historical obligation, the "real presence" of God's encounter with his people in both Word and Sacrament is unexpected and unrecognized. However, the neglect of story-shaped worship through reenactment does erode the Christ-centered and historically grounded reality of God's salvation in time and space. This erosion, for example, can manifest itself in music lyrics that are as vague about the particularities of God's revelation as those of deists in the Enlightenment. The triune God of grace has loved his people through creation and covenant, supremely revealed in the incarnation of the Son and dynamically reincarnate by the Spirit in the body of Christ. The lyrics and liturgy of Christian worship should express and embody what God has done and what the people of God truly believe.

Today, as with the disciples from Emmaus, the hearts of believers must burn again as the Word is taught; worshipers must recognize the glorified and ascended presence of the Lord by the Spirit in the breaking of bread (Luke 24:13-35). Worship as the reenactment of God's great story helps ground the experience of the believer in the incarnation of Jesus and in the real presence of the Holy Spirit as the new Immanuel, God with us.

REENACTMENT AND EMBODIMENT: REHEARSING THE STORY

It has already been clearly demonstrated throughout this book how Christian worship, like Christian faith, has deep roots in the worship practices and faith of Judaism. Reenactment that rehearses the history of God's salvation is explicitly evident in God's design of sacred space and the rhythmic cycle of feasts, festivals, weekly sabbath meals, the yearly Passover Seder and the specific sequence of sacrificial offerings in the Mosaic law. Israel's worship involved the whole person, not just spirit, mind and emotion, but body posture and sacred space, gifts-in-hand as well as singing songs, reciting sacred texts and hearing Torah read aloud. Both the familial and congregational aspects of Israel's worship involved reenactment as remembrance; God's people reentered God's story spiritually, mindfully, emotionally and spatially to recall and reembody together the reality of God's work of salvation. This was the shape and intention of worship inherited by the early church and regulated by the apostolic writings of the New Testament. Throughout church history, fidelity to this rhythm, shape and intention has been corrupted as well as corrected.

A contemporary challenge for Christian worship in many congregations is to thoughtfully and intentionally consider how to correct the quest for an experience in worship that tends to overspiritualize and disembody the reenactment of God's great story of salvation. The subjectivism that clings to a disembodied spirituality is very often manifest in services of worship whose primary objective is the uplifting, satisfying experience of the worshipers, or what I term "soul massage."[9] This, of course, is a natural outgrowth of faith centered on one's experience of salvation and not on the objective story of salvation centered on the suffering, death, resurrection and ascension of Christ Jesus.

Worship practices that neglect the reenactment of God's great story of creation and redemption are in need of correction. Corrective efforts to recenter worship on God and God's work of redemption in the incarnation of the Son and the bodily resurrection and ascension of the Lord are also effective for resisting the encroachment of "soul massage" tendencies in worship practice. These corrective efforts can include the reconfiguring of sacred space and the incorporation of sacred symbols that visually help worshipers to engage in practices of reenactment and remembrance. The cross, the Communion table, and the baptismal font or pool should be more visible than drum sets, pipe organs or sound speakers. Hymn and song lyrics should be thoughtfully examined for objective content that recalls and celebrates God's great story. More than a few hymn and song lyrics could be affirmed by first-century Docetists, fourth-century Gnostics or nineteenth-century Protestant liberals. The latter neglected or denied the particularity of the incarnation, and such spirit-only faith is notable in many hymns written during the Enlightenment.

---

[9]As emphasized earlier in the text, God does bless those who honor and worship him because the God who is worshiped is the triune God of grace. However, the primary focal objective of worship is to "bless the Lord, O my soul, and all that is within me bless his holy name"! (Psalm 103:1).

Evangelicals often sing contemporary songs and choruses that celebrate the love of God but without reference to how God has shown this love in time and space. Subjective sentimental lyrics that reflect a generic affection toward a loving divine being are inappropriate for Christian worship. Hymns and songs that are purely subjective reflections of an undefined, disembodied divine affection unattached from the historical reality of the faith should be eliminated or at least minimized and given context in some way.

Services of worship designed to recognize a particular event, such as funerals and weddings, should also take on the shape and focus of God's greater story, which encompasses the stories of his people. A funeral or memorial service isn't just a service that celebrates the resurrection, but appropriately includes the reality of the incarnation of Jesus, who also grieved and suffered and hurt. It is Christ Jesus who has defeated the "last enemy" of death (1 Corinthians 15:26) through his costly self-emptying obedience (Philippians 2:5-8). And it is in Christ Jesus that believers who have died await the "redemption of our bodies" (Romans 8:23). Christian funerals are not pep rallies for the dearly departed; they are an opportunity for God to be glorified as the congregation and the grieving express faith in the God whose steadfast love endures forever.

Christian weddings reenact God's best design for humankind revealed in one of the first stories of origin. Genesis 2 is a major part of God's story that shapes a Christian wedding. Calling, coming, naming, covenantal joining through hearing God's Word, expressions of promise and identity, commissioning and blessing for a uniquely shared life are all part of how the story of a new love is enveloped by the story of God's great love as it was intended "from the beginning."[10]

In all services of Christian worship, those present, as they are physically able, should be given opportunities to express adoration, repentance, commitment and received grace through a variety of postures that help them gain a sense of reenactment and engagement with the story framed by the liturgy. And, of course, the liturgy of every service of worship should reflect the shape of the story itself: *Called* by God to respond to the divine en-

---

[10]It is interesting to note how Jesus appeals to texts of origins in his defense of the indissolubility of marriage. See Matthew 19:1-8.

counter with love and *praise*, yet unworthy of such calling, worshipers *confess* that they are sinful people who fall short of divine glory. However, God has taken the initiative to accomplish *salvation* in the death and resurrection of Jesus, the Son, and through the efficacy of the Spirit, so that his people might *hear God's Word* and *respond* to God's grace by *participation* in the present and coming kingdom of saints, dine at his table, offers gifts of sacrifice, thanksgiving and praise, and receive God's *blessing* for mission. That's the story. That's good news. That's liturgy. That's the Christian life. That is worship.

CONGREGATIONAL ENGAGEMENT WITH GOD'S GREAT STORY

Any worship leader or team of worship leaders can create story-shaped liturgies focused on the blessing of God. The spiritual gifts of members of the community of faith should be incorporated into the sevenfold shape of the story to enhance the service of worship as an offering to God by the priesthood of *all* believers.

The inclusion of all worshipers must also be intentionally considered by worship planners and church leaders. A couple of key areas are particularly challenging for congregational worship today. The first concerns the intergenerational nature of faith communities and the importance for all God's people to be engaged in the blessing of God. The elderly, younger married couples, children, youth, parents, grandparents and single adults worshiping together in a single place reflect the community of believers God has called to worship. It is also one way congregations can resist the tendency to model the church after the niche marketing structures of contemporary culture that advertise and sell to age-segregated consumers. This marketing model has been adopted by many congregations, and one unintended result is young people who have been segregated into specialty groups all their lives and never feel a part of the congregation but identify only with their "group." This tends to produce young adults who try to reproduce their youth group as adults, and so the age segregation and niche marketing continues, or they give up and wander away from the family of faith.

Including all generations in congregational worship blesses God. Intergenerational dynamics and the inclusion of children in congregational gatherings and services of worship are well reflected in the Scripture.[11] In Psalm 145:4, David addresses God and states, "One generation shall laud your works to another, and shall declare your mighty acts." Children are present in the gathering of Israel for worship to hear Torah read and to participate in community prayers in both the Old and New Testaments.[12] There are certainly many ways in a congregation that believers of different generations can share their stories of faith's sojourn with each other, but a service of worship is often the one time the whole congregation is gathered as an intergenerational community. Telling our stories of faith in the context of worship shaped by God's great story is particularly appropriate and can be included in a variety of ways and at different times in many services.[13]

Another key area that bears consideration for the inclusion of all worshipers is congregational singing. It is very easy for pipe organs and electronic sound systems to overwhelm congregational voices. Amplification technology has the capacity not only to make it hard to hear the people singing near you but can also make it hard to hear one's own voice. Instrumentation in worship is certainly within biblical parameters, so piano, organ and praise band offerings to bless God can be appropriate in worship. But when supporting congregational singing, the volume should never drown out the instruments of the many, the human voice.

Another area to consider for promoting the priesthood of all believers in

---

[11]For instance, either no generational distinction is made, as when God addressed "all the people" at Sinai, or specific mention is made for an intergenerational gathering, as in 2 Chronicles 20:13. The reading of the law in Ezra 8 is a good example of a variety of events that included whole families, as well as times "in the presence of the men and women and those who could understand." This last comment may indicate language challenges, not necessarily age segregation.

[12]See Holly Catterton Allen and Christine Lawton Ross, *Intergenerational Christian Formation: Bringing the Whole Church Together in Ministry, Community and Worship* (Downers Grove, Ill.: InterVarsity Press, 2012) for a thorough survey of the intergenerational practices notable in biblical texts.

[13]It is beyond the scope of the present work to fully elaborate on the development of intergenerational dynamics for congregations, but recently there have been exceptional contributions by scholars whose field of study and ministry focuses on this great need. The following authors are exceptionally helpful for further reading: Holly Catterton Allen, Scottie May, Catherine Stonehouse and Robert Keeley. For helping pastors, congregations and parents deal with the challenges of children in the sanctuary for worship, I recommend Robbie Castleman, *Parenting in the Pew: Guiding Your Children into the Joy of Worship*, revised and updated ed. (Downers Grove, Ill.: InterVarsity Press, 2013).

worship can include the collection and presentation of the offering of gifts to the Lord. The idea of a corporate collection equalizes the gift of the wealthy with the widow's mite and the children's tiny tithe. What is given to God for the work of ministry and mission is a congregational gift, not just an individual's contribution. Thinking through the liturgical elements of a particular congregation and being intentional about how all worshipers can be appropriately included to offer their gifts and attention is invaluable in the design of a service of worship that blesses God.

Another way for a congregation to rehearse, reenact and indwell God's great story as a community is through attending to the story through the yearly calendar. The rhythm of the liturgical year, beginning with the four Sundays before Christmas (Advent), has long been one way to walk through the story of Jesus as a part of congregational life.

Table 2 is a summary of how many congregations go about the work of worship and rehearsing the rhythm of the Christian story and faith throughout the year. Congregations may go about the liturgical year in a variety of ways, but in doing so year after year, the faith community can appreciate how rehearsing this rhythm of God's great salvation is able to shape and nurture the Christian. At the same time, the congregation truly engages in worship that honors and pleases the God who saves. Worship celebrates God's story through remembrance and reenactment.

There are variations of this basic calendar between the Orthodox communities in the East and Roman Catholic communities which have been carefully developed and revised by ecclesial councils.[14] Non-Eastern Orthodox and Roman Catholic congregations may adapt this basic calendar to include (through various combinations of prayers, readings, music and commemoration) recognition of an event or person significant to that community.

It is not uncommon in Orthodox and Roman Catholic communities of faith to add liturgical dates to highlight a particular aspect of the tradition or accent a particular time or dynamic in the church's witness in the world. For instance, the feast of Corpus Christi (the Body of Christ) focuses on the gift of the Eucharistic meal in the life of the Roman Catholic Church and is

---

[14]"Christmas" is actually a period of twelve days and Easter season is a period of fifty days that culminates at Pentecost.

Table 2

Season or Day	Time Frame	Focus on Christian Faith and Jesus' Life	Liturgical Color
The Lord's Day	Every Sunday	Christ Jesus rose on the first day of the week; marks the centrality of the resurrection for Christian faith throughout the year	Varies (see below)
Advent	Starts 4 Sundays before Christmas	The Christian year begins with a focus on the anticipation of God's promise of Immanuel, God with us	Dark Blue
Christmas Day	December 25	Celebrates the Incarnation of God the Son, Jesus Christ	White or Gold
Epiphany	January 6, twelve days after Christmas	Commemorates the visitation of the Magi, the revelation of God's salvation through Christ Jesus for the whole world	White or Gold
Lent	Begins the 7th Wednesday before Easter (Ash Wednesday) and continues through Holy Saturday; encompasses the 40 days, not counting Sundays, before Easter	Recalls the 40 days of Jesus' temptation in the wilderness and is a time to consider the need for confession and repentance and the seriousness of sin in the remembrance of the sinless life and suffering of Christ Jesus	Purple
Palm Sunday (or Passion Sunday)	Sunday before Easter, the last Sunday in Lent	Commemorates the triumphal entry into Jerusalem of Jesus Christ and anticipates the passion of Christ Jesus	Purple (and the use of palm branches)
Triduum	The "Three Days" before Easter: Holy Thursday, Good Friday and Holy Saturday	Commemorates the Last Supper, Jesus' arrest and trial, crucifixion, and death	Purple and Black
Easter Day	The 1st Sunday after the first full moon on or after the Spring Equinox	Celebrates the resurrection of Christ Jesus	White or Gold
Ascension Day and Ascension Sunday	Ascension Day: the 6th Thursday after Easter, which is 40 days after Easter; Ascension Sunday is the Sunday after the 6th Thursday	Celebrates the ascension of the Son, Christ Jesus, to the right hand of God the Father, and the promised coming of the Holy Spirit upon the church	White or Gold
Pentecost	10 days after Ascension Thursday, the 50th day after Easter	Commemorates the "birthday of the church" in the outpouring of the Holy Spirit in Acts 2	Red
Trinity Sunday	The Sunday after Pentecost	Celebrates the full revelation of God as Father, Son and Holy Spirit	Red
Ordinary (Ordinal) Time	All dates not included in the above	"Ordinary" Time is based on the numbering (ordinals) of Sundays after seasonal liturgical events, e.g., "the 3rd Sunday after Pentecost," etc.	Green

celebrated on the Thursday after Trinity Sunday. This tradition began sometime during the thirteenth century when sacramental theology shaped the whole of medieval Christian life and faith. This was a time when the laity of the church was illiterate for the most part, and the Corpus Christi festival and parade invited all to join in and participate in visual and kinetic learning. The Eucharistic bread (often known as the "sacred host") was held aloft by a priest who walked under a canopy, and paraded through the streets of the village or neighborhood parish. Certain prayers were prayed along the way during certain stops in the mini-pilgrimage. This tradition is still kept in many areas where Roman Catholic expressions of the Christian faith are prominent.

The use of colors, symbols, pageantry and a variety of artistic expressions will vary with the gifts, traditions and historical background of congregations. The point is enabling the congregation to embody the story in order to give God thanks for his story of salvation. In doing so, God as Father, Son and Spirit is blessed by the shape of a liturgy that celebrates all that God has done to redeem a people called to worship.

CONCLUSION

The supremacy of God's story to shape Christian liturgies is vital for congregations who want to bless the Lord through their service of worship. The grace of God's story that envelops the stories of his people is the foundational assurance that such worship is "holy and acceptable," indeed a blessing to God. God's great story is also the foundational assurance of salvation itself.

Like the apostle Paul, "I am convinced that neither death, nor life, nor angels, nor rulers, nor things present, nor things to come, nor powers, nor height, nor depth, nor anything else in all creation, will be able to separate us from the love of God in Christ Jesus our Lord" (Romans 8:38-39).

Keeping God's story central in worship is no small challenge in a culture that invites and encourages individuals to post, tweet, blog, IM and constantly update even the most mundane episodes of our daily stories. Biblically shaped worship is a powerful way to remind ourselves that although we are beloved by God, we're not really the star of our own story. Only in union with Christ by the Spirit are we the children of God and brothers and sisters in the community of faith. And, like our spiritual ancestors in the desert of Sinai, we find a signpost of our identity in God who has called us to worship.

Worship shaped by God's great story is a rhythm of promise on a journey of faith. Over and over as believers rehearse and relive God's story through story-shaped liturgy, God's people are reminded that God's story continues on life's journey through the Spirit's real presence in Word and Sacrament. Such worship also reminds worshipers that they are not alone on life's journey but travel in the unity of Christ's body in a particular community of faith to see the story's end, the kingdom of God's glory, grace, a place where "righteousness is at home" (2 Peter 3:13).

Worship designed to bless God is meant to demonstrate the one desire that should be central for all those called to a life mediated by divine love. In the words of David,

> One thing I asked of the LORD,
>   that will I seek after:
> to live in the house of the LORD
>   all the days of my life,
> to behold the beauty of the LORD,
>   and to inquire in his temple. (Psalm 27:4)

WORKSHOP FOR CHAPTER TEN

1. Ask about the authority structures for your congregation.

   - What is the history behind these structures?

   - Have these structures gone through changes? If so, what was the reason given for changes?

   - How is power held or shared in the congregation?

   - How are leaders, teachers, pastors, elders, deacons and worship leaders chosen?

2. How is the corporate unity of the congregation reflected (or not reflected) in the practice of liturgical elements in worship?

   - For instance, is there a time for praying in unison?

- How are tithes and offerings collected?
- How are people involved in the music of liturgy?
- Does the congregation allow for the private administration of the sacraments? If so, for whom? If not, why not? (Taking the Lord's Supper to the ill or shut-ins is a common practice that dates to the early church; but is Communion allowed for only the bride and groom at a wedding? Etc.)

3. How would you respond to a friend who said, "I am a Christian, but I have no need for the church"?

4. Think through the importance of "reenactment and embodiment" in services of worship.

   - How can these be enhanced in the liturgical practices of your congregation? Include all aspects of the liturgy, sacred space, seating, visual symbols and the like in your answer.

5. Write your own psalm of praise for use by the congregation in a service of worship.

   - Write new lyrics to a hymn tune you like and the congregation knows well for use in a service of worship.

   - Put together an antiphonal (alternating back and forth) call to worship using several passages of Scripture.

6. Look through a variety of books and resources that outline liturgies for weddings and funerals. (See the bibliography in the back of the book for some resources.)

   - Create a liturgy for a funeral that you think would be appropriate for the liturgical style and history of your congregation but also shaped by God's greater story.

   - Create a liturgy for a wedding that you think would be appropriate for the liturgical style and history of your congregation but also shaped by God's greater story.

   - Create a responsive reading for the congregation using several passages of Scripture.

7. Write a one-sentence definition of worship.

   - Locate the one-sentence definition of worship you wrote down when you began this study.

   - Compare and contrast the two statements. What is similar? What has changed? Why?

GLOSSARY

Ablution. Ceremonial washing.

Advent. Season in the liturgical year beginning the fourth Sunday before Christmas; in the Eastern Church Advent beings on November 15.

Alleluia (hallelujah). Hebrew for "praise the LORD."

Altar. A particular place where religious sacrifices are made. In the Old Testament there were a limited number of sites for sacrifice prior to the unification of worship practice in Jerusalem during the monarchy of David. From the time of Solomon until the destruction of Jerusalem in A.D. 70, the altar of sacrifice was associated with the temple cult. Most Protestant churches have replaced a symbolic altar with a table for the Lord's Supper, making the point that Christ Jesus was crucified once and for all and there is no longer a place needed for sacrifice.

Amen. A Hebrew term for "Truly, so be it," said at the end of prayers.

Anamnesis. From the Greek word for "remembrance"; part of the Eucharistic prayer in which the suffering, death and resurrection of Jesus and the expectation of his return is brought to the present experience and proclaimed.

Aniconic. Worship without physical representation of a diety.

Anaphora. From the Greek for "to offer up"; refers to part of the Eucharistic prayer that expresses the offering of the sacramental elements to the Lord from the congregation.

Antiphonal. To recite or sing lines of Scripture (often the psalms) in a responsive way between worship leader and congregation or between distinct parts of the congregation (such as men saying a verse followed by women saying the next verse).

Apse. From Latin for "arch"; the half-rounded far end of a sanctuary. The area is often the place where the baptismal font and altar or Communion table is located.

Baptism. From Greek "to immerse"; Christian rite of initiation into the body of Christ using water and the invocation of the triune name.

Benediction. From Latin "to bless"; the blessing of God given by the pastor or priest at the end of a service of worship.

Catechism. From the Greek "to instruct"; a teaching method that usually employs a question-and-answer format for the instruction of children, newcomers and seekers for learning the major tenets of faith and discipleship. A **catechumenate** is a person learning a catechism to prepare for baptism or confirmation.

Ḥazzān. Synagogue official who was charged with the upkeep of the synagogue and its furnishings and scrolls.

Collect. A prayer offered for a specific occasion or need that takes a particular shape of address and petition.

Consubstantiation. The Lutheran doctrine of Christ's real presence in the Eucharistic elements of bread and wine without a change in the elements themselves. The term means "to join with."

Creed. From Latin for "I believe"; a summary statement of Christian belief that includes trinitarian affirmation as well as major tenets of the faith.

Cultus. The ritualistic practices of religious communities; often used in reference to the offering of sacrifice or initiation rites.

Didache. From the Greek for "teaching"; an ancient document (mid-first century) that served as a how-to manual for the early church. The document appears to be a compilation of decontextualized teachings and sayings of Jesus and carried an association in its full title with "the twelve apostles."

Docetism. From the Greek "to seem"; a heresy that denies the full humanity of Christ Jesus in the incarnation.

Doxology. From the Greek word meaning "glory"; used for hymns of praise. There are several hymns and prayers of praise in the Old Testament and New Testament.

Ecclesiology. A branch of theology focused on the study of the church.

Epiclesis. Greek term for the part of prayer that addresses God and asks for divine presence. It is the part of the Eucharistic prayer that addresses the Holy Spirit to be present and the effective means of grace in the sacrament.

Eucharist. From the Greek for "Thanksgiving"; often used as a term for the Lord's Supper, the rite of Communion. It is derived from the New Testament accounts of Jesus giving thanks for the bread and wine in the inauguration of the Lord's Supper on the night he was betrayed.

Exposition. A particular pattern of biblical study and homiletics (preaching) that is based on the wording and structure of the biblical text. This manner of teaching and preaching is distinct from that which is thematic in content.

Font. A part of sacred furniture designed to hold the water used for baptism. They are often symbolically shaped, many with eight sides indicating the resurrection of Jesus "on the first day of the week" or the eighth day. In the presence of the living and ascended Lord by the Spirit, the church finds her identity and hope. Baptism is the rite of initiation into the body of Christ.

Homiletics. The study and practice of preaching. The word "homily" is from the Greek for "instruction" and is often used to indicate a short sermon focused on a single point or passage exposition. Preaching itself is sometimes considered distinct from teaching by the inclusion of a proclamation of the gospel and a particular call to faithful action and response. This proclamation is termed the *kerygma*.

Host. From the Latin for "sacrificial victim." This is the term used in Roman Catholicism for the bread set apart (consecrated) in transubstantiation as the body of Christ.

Icon. From the Greek for "image"; used in Genesis to indicate the image of God unique to human beings. People in right relationship to God were to be "icons" of the Creator, those who indicate by being and behavior the God who made them. Therefore icons or images were forbidden for use in the worship of Israel. Israel itself was to be the icon of its God. The inclusion and use of icons or images of Jesus or saintly martyrs has been controversial. Those traditions that include icons and images see their use not as idols but as a helpful means in worship and prayer to focus attention and "see through" them the faithfulness and character of the divine presence.

Kaddish. A Jewish prayer of praise that addresses God and extols God's attributes directly. The Lord's Prayer is shaped very much like a *kaddish*.

Kerygma. A proclamation of the New Testament message of salvation in Christ Jesus, the content of the gospel.

Lent. The period of time in the church calendar that goes from Ash Wednesday through Holy Week, the week ending on Easter Sunday. It is a period of forty days, not counting the six Sundays during that time. Traditionally it is a time for sober reflection on the suffering of Christ and the need for salvation from sin and death. The forty days are meant to parallel the period of temptation in the wilderness by Jesus, the Son of God.

Lex orandi, lex credendi. A Latin phrase attributed to Prosper of Aquitaine in the fifth century, which means "the law of prayer is the law of belief." The expression is often expanded helpfully by the addition of *lex vivendi*, "the law of life." What one prays reflects what one really believes, which influences how one lives.

Liturgy. From the Greek *leitourgia*, or "the work of the people" in a religious service. It is used to indicate the sequence of practices in a service of worship. All congregations have a liturgy, as the term is not a reference to style but a pattern or sequence of worship elements for practice by the congregation.

Lord's Day. A term used by the early church to indicate Sunday, the first day of the week, as the day Christians gathered for corporate worship; see Acts 20:7; 1 Corinthians 16:2; John 20:19; Revelation 1:10.

Mass. From the Latin "to send." Used mainly by Roman Catholics to indicate a service of worship centered on the "sacrifice of the Mass," an idea reflected in the doctrine of transubstantiation, the use of the term reflects the idea that the Son was sent to die for the redemption of the world, so the church is sent through association with the crucified and risen Lord to be witnesses of Christ's redemption.

Midrash. A Jewish pattern of biblical hermeneutics (interpretation of texts) that studies Scripture and considers its meaning in the light and context of a contemporary event. The New Testament book of Hebrews contains a lot of midrash as it looks at many Old Testament passages in the light of Jesus' life, suffering, death, resurrection and ascension.

Missio Dei. Latin for "the mission of God."

Mystagogy. Post-baptismal instruction used for the discipleship of new believers. The term indicates the explanation of the "mystery" of the faith which the newly baptized have entered.

Narthex. The congregation's entrance into the larger area (the nave) for a service of worship.

Nave. The area in a sanctuary for the congregation's participation in a service of worship.

Offering. The gathering of the gifts of God's people in a service of worship.

Offertory. The presentation of the gifts of God's people in a service of worship.

Ordinance. A term used for the practice of baptism and the Lord's Supper by certain Protestant or independent Christian traditions that maintain that divine grace is not mediated through the sacraments, but that rituals are purely symbolic in nature.

Pastor. From Latin for "to feed like a shepherd"; often used to designate senior clergy in a congregation.

Pelagianism. The fourth-century heresy of Pelagius, a British monk who denied the doctrine of original sin and believed that human effort could be sufficient for salvation; Augustine was his most robust critic and led the effort to defeat the teaching as heretical.

Pericope. From the Greek meaning "section"; a passage of Scripture that can be read and studied as a unit.

Priest. Clergy in the Roman Catholic, Anglican and Lutheran denominations. The term indicates a person ordained to officiate in the Eucharistic rite in traditions that understand the presence of Christ in the elements as transubstantiational or consubstantiational.

Real Presence. A term often used mainly in the Reformed tradition to indicate the presence of Christ in the elements of the Lord's Supper and the reality of grace mediated through the sacrament by the Holy Spirit. It is a term that marks a distinction from the Roman Catholic doctrine of transubstantiation, which indicates a change of the elements themselves through the presence of Christ, and the Lutheran doctrine of consubstantiation, in which Christ is joined with the elements but the elements themselves are not changed.

Rite. A religious ceremonial ritual or the form of a particular part of a liturgy, like the rite of baptism. The term is also associated with the particularizing of rituals within a denomination, such as "Roman Catholic Rite of Initiation" or "Coptic Sacramental Rites."

Sabbath. From the Hebrew for "to cease" or "rest"; Jewish sabbath observance begins at sundown on Friday and ends at sundown on Saturday. The seventh day was designated by God as holy, and Jesus taught that its observance was a divine gift of goodness from God, which meant that good could be done on the sabbath.

Sacrament. From the Latin for "sacred reality." A parallel idea is found in the Greek word for mystery. An ancient idiom summarizes the definition as "a visible sign of an invisible grace." The early church and the Protestant Reformers only recognized two sacraments due to their institution by Christ Jesus: baptism and the Lord's Supper. At the council of Trent, Roman Catholicism affirmed five more sacraments that covered the span of human and religious life: confirmation, penance, anointing of the sick, ordination and marriage.

Sanctuary. From the Latin "to set apart"; parallel to Greek term for "holy." For Roman Catholic and Orthodox congregations this space is the area in the apse where the altar is located. In Protestant and independent congregations the term refers to the entire area used for corporate worship, including the nave where the congregation participates.

Second Temple period. The period between the post-exilic reconstruction of the Jewish temple in the sixth century B.C. until its destruction by the Romans in A.D. 70.

Selah. A Hebrew word generally thought to indicate a pause to reflect on a particular reading; used most notably in the Psalms.

Simony. The medieval practice in which the Roman Catholic Church appointed men to church offices in exchange for payment. The origin of the word is related to Simon Magus (Acts 8:9-24), because he asked if he could buy the Holy Spirit. The post-Reformation Council of Trent eliminated the practice as one way of correcting the corruption of clergy.

Sola fide, sola gratia, sola scriptura. Latin axiom "only faith, only grace, only Scripture"; this is commonly rendered "faith alone, grace alone, Scripture alone." The expression summarizes the three major foci of the Protestant Reformation: that salvation comes only by faith, only by God's grace, and this is known only through the Scriptures.

Soli Deo gloria. Latin expression meaning "Only for God's glory."

Synagogue. From the Greek word "to assemble or bring together." The term indicates a place for Jews to gather together for community events and religious instruction during the displacement of the exile and where Jews lived outside Israel, the diaspora. By the time of the New Testament, synagogues had become very popular in Israel as places of prayer, the reading of Torah, community events and religious instruction. Only after the destruction of the temple in A.D. 70 did the synagogue become a place of formal worship for the Jewish community of faith.

Tabernacle. In the Old Testament, the "tent" where the Ark of the Covenant was placed; a "tent of meeting" between God and his people. First constructed under the leadership of Moses, the tabernacle was portable and could travel with the people. After the construction of Solomon's temple, the tabernacle was housed within the inner-most area of the temple.

Tithe. From a Semitic word meaning "a tenth"; used to indicate the giving of one tenth of one's earnings for use within the community of God's people to sustain and advance the mission of God. Offerings are gifts given above that of the tithe.

Transubstantiation. The Roman Catholic doctrine concerning the presence of Christ in the elements of bread and wine used for the Eucharist. It is believed that the Eucharistic elements become substantially the body and blood of Jesus during the prayer of consecration by the officiating priest. Thomas Aquinas used Aristotelian terms to explain why the bread and wine still taste like bread and wine even though they have become substantially the body and blood of the Savior.

Words of Institution. In the Eucharistic prayer, the recitation of the words of Jesus quoted from a Gospel account of the Last Supper. In the Roman Catholic doctrine of transubstantiation, this is the moment when the substantial change occurs in the elements because Jesus said, "This is my body . . ."

Worship. From the older English meaning worthy of reverence for a deity.

FOR FURTHER READING

Alexander, T. D. *From Paradise to the Promised Land: An Introduction to the Pentateuch.* Grand Rapids: Baker Academic, 2002.

Allen, Holly Catterton, and Christine Lawton Ross. *Intergenerational Christian Formation: Bringing the Whole Church Together in Ministry, Community and Worship.* Downers Grove, Ill.: IVP Academic, 2012.

Bateman, Herbert W. *Authentic Worship: Hearing Scripture's Voice, Applying Its Truth.* Grand Rapids: Kregel, 2002.

Beale, G. K. *We Become What We Worship: A Biblical Theology of Idolatry.* Downers Grove, Ill.: IVP Academic, 2008.

Bechtel, Carol M., ed. *Touching the Altar: The Old Testament for Christian Worship.* Grand Rapids: Eerdmans, 2008.

Best, Harold M. *Unceasing Worship: Biblical Perspectives on Worship and the Arts.* Downers Grove, Ill.: InterVarsity Press, 2003.

Bradshaw, Paul F. *Early Christian Worship: A Basic Introduction to Ideas and Practice.* Collegeville, Minn.: Liturgical Press, 1996.

———. *The Search of the Origins of Christian Worship: Sources and Methods for the Study of Early Liturgy.* 2nd ed. New York: Oxford University Press, 2002.

Brueggemann, Walter. *Worship in Ancient Israel: An Essential Guide.* Nashville: Abingdon, 2005.

Carson, D. A., ed. *Worship by the Book.* Grand Rapids: Zondervan, 2002.

Castleman, Robbie. *Parenting in the Pew: Guiding Your Children into the Joy of Worship.* Revised and updated ed. Downers Grove, Ill.: InterVarsity Press, 2013.

Chan, Simon. *Liturgical Theology: The Church as Worshiping Community.* Downers Grove, Ill.: IVP Academic, 2006.

Chapell, Bryan. *Christ-Centered Worship: Letting the Gospel Shape Our Practice.* Grand Rapids: Baker Academic, 2009.

Chapman, Kathleen. *Teaching Kids Authentic Worship: How to Keep Them Close to God for Life.* Grand Rapids: Baker Books, 2003.

Cherry, Constance M. *The Worship Architect: A Blueprint for Designing Culturally Relevant and Biblically Faithful Services.* Grand Rapids: Baker Academic, 2010.

Chesterton, G. K. *Orthodoxy: The Romance of Faith.* Garden City, N.Y.: Doubleday, 1959.

Cocksworth, Christopher. *Holy, Holy, Holy: Worshipping the Trinitarian God.* London: Darton, Longman, & Todd, 1997.

Daniélou, Jean. *The Bible and the Liturgy.* Notre Dame: University of Notre Dame Press, 2005.

Davis, Thomas J. *This Is My Body: The Presence of Christ in Reformation Thought.* Grand Rapids: Baker Academic, 2008.

Dawn, Marva J. *Reaching Out Without Dumbing Down: A Theology of Worship for the Turn-of-the-Century Culture.* Grand Rapids: Eerdmans, 1995.

———. *A Royal "Waste" of Time: The Splendor of Worshiping God and Being Church for the World.* Grand Rapids: Eerdmans, 1999.

deSilva, David A. *Sacramental Life: Spiritual Formation Through the Book of Common Prayer.* Downers Grove, Ill.: IVP Books, 2008.

Duck, Ruth C., and Patricia Wilson-Kastner. *Praising God: The Trinity in Christian Worship.* Louisville, Ky.: Westminster John Knox Press, 1999.

Dyrness, William A. *A Primer on Christian Worship: Where We've Been, Where We Are, Where We Can Go.* Grand Rapids: Eerdmans, 2009.

Farley, Michael. "What Is 'Biblical Worship'? Biblical Hermeneutics and Evangelical Theologies of Worship." *Journal of the Evangelical Theological Society* 51, no. 3 (September 2008): 591-613.

Ferguson, Everett. *Baptism in the Early Church: History, Theology & Liturgy in the First Five Centuries.* Grand Rapids: Eerdmans, 2009.

Firth, David G. *1 & 2 Samuel.* Apollos Old Testament Commentary 8. Downers Grove, Ill.: InterVarsity Press, 2009.

Galli, Mark. *Beyond Smells & Bells: The Wonder and Power of Christian Liturgy.* Brewster, Mass.: Paraclete Press, 2008.

Goplin, Vicky, et al., eds. *Across the Generations: Incorporating All Ages in Ministry: The Why and How.* Minneapolis: Augsburg Fortress, 2001.

Gordon, T. David. *Why Johnny Can't Sing Hymns: How Pop Culture Rewrote the Hymnal.* Phillipsburg, N.J.: P&R Publishing, 2010.

Gross, Bobby. *Living the Christian Year: Time to Inhabit the Story of God.* Downers Grove, Ill.: IVP Books, 2009.

Guy, Laurie. *Introducing Early Christianity: A Topical Survey of Its Life, Beliefs & Practices.* Downers Grove, Ill.: InterVarsity Press, 2004.

Hall, Christopher A. *Worshiping with the Church Fathers.* Downers Grove, Ill.: IVP Academic, 2009.

Hevelone-Harper, Jennifer Lee. *Disciples of the Desert: Monks, Laity and Spiritual Authority in Sixth-Century Gaza.* Baltimore: Johns Hopkins University Press, 2005.

Horton, Michael. *A Better Way: Rediscovering the Drama of God-Centered Worship.* Grand Rapids: Baker, 2002.

Humphrey, Edith McEwan. *Grand Entrance: Worship on Earth as in Heaven.* Grand Rapids: Brazos Press, 2011.

Hunsinger, George. *The Eucharist and Ecumenism: Let Us Keep the Feast*. New York: Cambridge University Press, 2008.

Jones, Cheslyn, et al. *The Study of Liturgy*. Revised ed. London: SPCK, 1992.

Kauflin, Bob. *Worship Matters: Leading Others to Encounter the Greatness of God*. Wheaton, Ill.: Crossway Books, 2008.

Kavanaugh, Patrick. *Worship: A Way of Life*. Grand Rapids: Chosen Books, 2001.

Keener, Craig S. *A Commentary on the Gospel of Matthew*. Grand Rapids: Eerdmans, 1999.

Labberton, Mark. *The Dangerous Act of Worship: Living God's Call to Justice*. Downers Grove, Ill.: IVP Books, 2007.

Leithart, Peter. *A House for My Name: A Survey of the Old Testament*. Moscow, Idaho: Canon Press, 2000.

Levine, Lee I. "The Nature and Origin of the Palestinian Synagogue Reconsidered." *Journal of Biblical Literature* 115, no. 3 (Autumn 1996): 425-48.

Long, Thomas G. *Beyond the Worship Wars: Building Vital and Faithful Worship*. Bethesda, Md.: Alban Institute, 2001.

Manahan, Roland E. "The Worshiper's Approach to God: An Exposition of Psalm 15," pp. 55-78. In *Authentic Worship: Hearing Scripture's Voice, Applying Its Truth*. Edited by Herbert W. Bateman IV. Grand Rapids: Kregel, 2002.

McConville, J. G. *Deuteronomy*. Apollos Old Testament Commentary Series. Downers Grove, Ill.: InterVarsity Press, 2002.

Meyers, Jeffrey J. *The Lord's Service: The Grace of Covenant Renewal Worship*. Moscow, Idaho: Canon, 2003.

Miller, Patrick D. *The Religion of Ancient Israel*. Louisville, Ky.: Westminster John Knox Press, 2000.

Motyer, J. A. *The Message of Exodus: The Days of Our Pilgrimage*. Downers Grove, Ill.: InterVarsity Press, 2005.

Old, Hughes Oliphant. *Themes and Variations for a Christian Doxology*. Grand Rapids: Eerdmans, 1992.

O'Loughlin, Thomas. *The Didache: A Window on the Earliest Christians*. Grand Rapids: Baker Academic, 2010.

Patton, Jeff. *God at the Crossroads: The Four Movements of Transformational Worship*. Nashville: Abingdon, 2005.

Peterson, David. *Engaging with God: A Biblical Theology of Worship*. Downers Grove, Ill.: InterVarsity Press, 1992.

Rainey, A. F. "Order of Sacrifices in Old Testament Ritual Texts." *Biblica* 51, no. 4 (1970): 485-98.

Ramshaw, Gail. *Christian Worship: 100,000 Sundays of Symbols and Rituals*. Minneapolis: Fortress, 2009.

Ratzinger, Joseph Cardinal [Pope Benedict XVI]. *The Spirit of the Liturgy*. San Francisco: Ignatius Press, 2000.

Rayburn, Robert G. *O Come, Let Us Worship: Corporate Worship in the Evangelical Church*. Grand Rapids: Baker, 1980.

Robertson, C. K. *Religion as Entertainment*. New York: Peter Lang, 2002.

Rice, Howard L., and James C. Huffstutler. *Reformed Worship*. Louisville, Ky.: Geneva Press, 2001.

Rienstra, Debra, and Ron Rienstra. *Worship Words: Discipling Language for Faithful Ministry*. Grand Rapids: Baker Academic, 2009.

Ross, Allen P. *Recalling the Hope of Glory: Biblical Worship from the Garden to the New Creation*. Grand Rapids: Kregel, 2006.

Saliers, Don E. *Worship as Theology: Foretaste of Glory Divine*. Nashville: Abingdon, 1994.

Sample, Tex. *Powerful Persuasion: Multimedia Witness in Christian Worship*. Nashville: Abingdon, 2005.

Schmemann, Alexander. *Introduction to Liturgical Theology*. Crestwood, N.Y.: St. Vladimir's Seminary Press, 1996.

Schreiner, Thomas R., and Shawn D. Wright. *Believer's Baptism: Sign of the New Covenant in Christ*. Nashville: B&H Academic, 2006.

Stapert, Calvin. *A New Song for An Old World: Musical Thought in the Early Church*. Calvin Institute of Christian Worship Liturgical Studies Series. Grand Rapids: Eerdmans, 2007.

Stein, Robert H. *Studying the Synoptic Gospels: Origin and Interpretation*. Grand Rapids: Baker Academic, 2001.

Tomasino, Anthony. *Judaism Before Jesus: The Events and Ideas That Shaped the New Testament World*. Downers Grove, Ill.: InterVarsity Press, 2003.

Torrance, James B. *Worship, Community and the Triune God of Grace*. Downers Grove, Ill.: InterVarsity Press, 1996.

Vanderwell, Howard, ed. *The Church of All Ages: Generations Worshiping Together*. Vital Worship, Healthy Congregations Series. Herdon, Va.: Alban Institute, 2008.

Vander Zee, Leonard J. *Christ, Baptism and the Lord's Supper: Recovering the Sacraments for Evangelical Worship*. Downers Grove, Ill.: InterVarsity Press, 2004.

Van Dyk, Leanne, ed. *A More Profound Alleluia: Theology and Worship in Harmony*. Calvin Institute of Christian Worship Liturgical Studies Series. Grand Rapids: Eerdmans, 2005.

Walton, John, Victor Harold Matthews and Mark W. Chavalas, eds. *The IVP Bible Background Commentary: Old Testament*. Downers Grove, Ill.: InterVarsity Press, 2000.

Webber, Robert E. *Ancient-Future Worship: Proclaiming and Enacting God's Narrative*. Grand Rapids: Baker Books, 2008.

———. *Worship Old & New: A Biblical, Historical, and Practical Introduction*.

Revised edition. Grand Rapids: Zondervan, 1994.

Westminster Shorter Catachism. Last modified December 5, 2010. www.reformed
.org/documents/wsc/index.html.

White, James F. *Introduction to Christian Worship*. 3rd edition. Nashville:
Abingdon, 2000.

———. *A Brief History of Christian Worship*. Nashville: Abingdon, 1993.

White, Susan J. *Foundations of Christian Worship*. Louisville, Ky.: Westminster John
Knox Press, 2006.

Witvliet, John D. *The Biblical Psalms in Christian Worship, A Brief Introduction and
Guide to Resources*. Grand Rapids: Eerdmans, 2007.

———. *Worship Seeking Understanding: Windows into Christian Practice*. Grand
Rapids: Baker Academic, 2003.

Witherington, Ben. *We Have Seen His Glory: A Vision of Kingdom Worship*. Grand
Rapids: Eerdmans, 2010.

Wren, Ryan. *Praying Twice: The Music and Words of Congregational Song*. Louisville, Ky.: Westminster John Knox Press, 2000.

Wright, N. T. *For All God's Worth: True Worship and the Calling of the Church*.
Grand Rapids: Eerdmans, 1997.

Subject Index

ʿābad, 36, 40, 43, 63, 75
Advent, 202
  See also liturgical year
altars, 67, 71
  building of by patriarchs,
    36-38, 45, 67
  golden calf, 71-72
  medieval, 170-71
anabaptist, 169, 177, 180
antiphonal pattern, 82, 88, 90
ark of the covenant, 96-99, 101-3
atonement, 30, 80
  day of, 46, 61
baptism, 58
  in Acts, 153
  in contemporary practice,
    155-56
  in Didache, 152-54
  meaning of, 157-58, 180
  paedobaptism, 158
  rebaptism, 180
  See also sacred space
benediction, 80, 87
blessing
  the Lord, 79-80, 82-83,
    194-95
  receiving, 125
body of Christ, 15n1, 136-37,
  188-89, 203-4
  baptism into, 156-58
  in Eucharist. See Eucharist
  unity of, 85-87, 132, 192-93
  See also church
call to worship, 37, 81-82
Calvin, John, 178-80, n190
children, inclusion of, 73, 199
church, 15, 134, 136-37
  See also body of Christ
clergy
  medieval priesthood, 171-72
  See also worship leaders
confession
  in service of worship, 67, 73,
    83, 90
  of sin, Israel, 46, 50
congregational style, 34-35,
  72-73, 78-79
  See also Lord's Supper
creeds, 155
Didache, 57, 151-64
doxology, 84, 160
Easter. See liturgical year
ecclesiology, 138, 193
  evangelical erosion of,
    189-92
Eucharist. See Lord's Supper

evangelical, 119-20, 187, 194,
  196
fundamentalism, 188
Gentiles, 55-56
  in Didache, 160, 166-67
  inclusion of, 129, 136-37
God
  as focus of worship, 79-80
  glory of, 90, 98-99, 107,
    112-16
    in Christ Jesus, 70
  presence of in worship, 38,
    73, 81
Holy Spirit, 153, 178, 181
  as mediator in worship, 38,
    87, 122, 196
hymns, 21, 155, 197-98
  See also music
idolatry, 49, 70-71, 99, 114
  prohibition of, 44-45, 63
intergenerational dynamics, 13,
  199-200
Jesus Christ
  baptism of, 157-58
  as High Priest, 65-66, 69,
    124, 137, 139
  mediation of worship, 81,
    113-14
justice as it relates to worship,
  117-19, 121-22, 131
kingdom of God, 161-62, 204
  anticipation in Lord's
    Supper, 180
Lent. See liturgical year
Levitical leadership, 67, 101-2
liturgical studies, methodology
  of, 16-21
liturgical year, 35-36, 202
  Israel's, 46-48
    Passover, feast of un-
      leavened bread, 46, 61
  in the New Testament, 58,
    132-33, 180
liturgy, 77-87
  contemporary issues in,
    193-201
  definition of, 34
  early church development
    of, 133, 149
  praxis of in Didache,
    152-54, 158-61
  Roman Catholic, 171-72
  story-shaped, 77-87
  synagogue, 141-42
Lord's Day, 55-57
  relation to Pentecost, 134

sabbath in Old Testament,
  44-45, 48-55
Lord's Supper, 87, 132-33, 135,
  148, 163, 181-84
  consubstantiation in, 176-77
  Corpus Christi festival of,
    203
  in the Didache, 158-64
  in the early church, 148-49
  Mass, Roman Catholic
    medieval, 171-73, 175
    transubstantiation in,
      172-73, 175-77
  real presence in, Reformed
    doctrine of, 178-79
  transubstantiation, 171-73,
    175-77
Luther, 173-75, 176-77, 180
Mosaic law, 42-48, 61, 66-69, 84
  See also worship, patterns in
    Pentateuch
music, 197-98
Nicaea, council of, 155
offerings
  of Cain and Abel, 28-30
  contemporary
    congregational, 86-87,
      199-201
  in the early church, 56, 107,
    132
  sacrificial, Israel's, 46-47,
    61, 69, 80-81
  tithes, 85, 131
  See also sacrifices
Paul, apostle, 56, 65, 113, 137,
  148-49, 181
Pentecost, 61, 90, 134, 202
  See also liturgical year
Pharisees and sabbath law,
  53-54
praise, 82-83, 90
prayer, 36, 55-56, 83
  confessional, 83
  in the early church, 55-56,
    128, 131, 133, 159-60
  Kaddish, 131-32
  Lord's prayer, 83, 131-32
  in the synagogue, 141-42
priesthood
  of all believers, 73, 175, 181,
    199-200
  in Israel, 46-47, 67-68
  medieval, Roman Catholic,
    170-73
Protestant liberalism, 121, 191,
  194

rabbinical leadership in the New
Testament, 54-55, 128-29
reenactment, patterns in
worship, 30, 43, 58-59, 147-49,
196-98
in liturgical year, 201-2
Reformation, 73-74, 168-70,
173-75, 177-80, 189-90
tri-sola confession, 119-20,
178
sabbath. *See* Lord's Day
sacraments, 160, 196
contemporary issues,
180-84, 195-96
Sixteenth-century concerns,
170-80
See also baptism, Lord's
Supper
sacred space, 32, 50, 62-66,
69-70, 149-50, 170-71, 197
art in, 32

contemporary issues, 72-74
See also tabernacle,
synagogue, sanctuary
sacrifices, 30, 80-81
in Mosaic cult, 46-47
See also sacred space
sanctuary, 31-32, 65-66, 68, 73,
122-24
sermon, 84-85
service of worship
funerals, 198
story-shaped, 81-87, 90-91
weddings, 198
See also ʿābad,
liturgy
Sunday. *See* Lord's Day
synagogue, 43, 128-30, 140-43,
149-50
tabernacle, 66-70, 104
See also ark of the covenant
tithes. *See* offerings

worship, 81
called to, 37, 81-82
early church, 15, 18, 55-57,
133-36
in first-century Judaism,
130-34, 149-51, 196-97
hypocrisy in, 114-15, 131-32
integrity in, 114-20, 124, 132
medieval, 170-74
Patriarchal period, 36-38
patterns in Pentateuch,
45-47
worship leaders, 13, 22, 72, 91,
108, 194-95, 199
worship wars, 15-16, 27-28,
78-79
Zwingli, Ulrich, 177-78, 180
See also anabaptist

Scripture Index

OLD TESTAMENT

Genesis
1–4, *22*
1:5, *48*
1:8, *48*
1:13, *48*
1:19, *48*
1:23, *48*
1:26, *114*
1:29-30, *28*
2, *48, 198*
2:1-3, *48*
2:15, *28*
2:24, *112*
3:9, *30*
3:21, *30*
4, *28, 39*
4:1-16, *30, 39*
4:4, *27*
4:4-5, *28, 115*
4:6-7, *30*
4:9, *30*
4:13-14, *29*
4:26, *36*
6–9, *50*
8:20, *36*
12:7-8, *36*
13:4, *36*
13:18, *36*
22, *37*
22:9, *36*
26:25, *36*
33:18-20, *36*
35:1, *36*
35:3, *36*
35:7, *36*

Exodus
3:1-15, *44*
3:3, *63*
3:5, *44, 63*
3:11, *43*
3:12, *42, 43, 44, 80, 136*
3:14, *43*
12:1-14, *61*
12:15-20, *61*
13:3-10, *61*
19–24, *80*
19:1–24:8, *67*
19:6, *44*
20, *49*
20:1-7, *44*
20:2-3, *44*
20:7, *44*
20:8-11, *45*

20:8-17, *44*
20:9-10, *60*
20:12-17, *46*
23:10-11, *49*
23:12-13, *49*
23:14-19, *45*
23:15, *61*
23:16, *61*
24:1-8, *67*
24:9-11, *67*
25–40, *69*
25:1–31:11, *67*
25:10-20, *102*
25:10-22, *98*
29:14, *47*
29:18, *47*
29:28, *47*
32:2, *71*
32:2-18, *70*
32:4, *71*
32:5, *71*
32:6, *71*
32:7-8, *71*
32:8, *71*
32:11-14, *71*
32:19, *71*
32:20-35, *71*
34, *71*
34:18, *61*
34:22, *61*
35:4–39:43, *71*

Leviticus
1:3, *47*
3:1, *47*
3:3, *46*
4:3, *47*
4:8-10, *46*
5:14–6:7, *47*
6:9, *47*
6:24, *47*
7:3-5, *46*
7:11, *47*
9, *80*
9:8, *47*
9:11, *47*
9:18, *47*
14:5-6, *154*
14:50-51, *154*
15:13, *154*
16, *61*
16:30-34, *46*
17:11, *47*
23, *45, 61*
23:5, *61*
23:6-8, *61*

23:15-21, *61*
23:23-25, *61*
23:26-32, *61*
23:33-36, *61*
23:39-43, *61*
25, *49*
25:1-7, *49*

Numbers
9, *61*
19:17, *154*
28:16, *61*
28:26-31, *61*
29:1-6, *61*
29:7-11, *61*

Deuteronomy
4:2, *112*
6:4, *84*
6:5, *132*
12:2-5, *63*
12:13-14, *64*
12:18, *64*
12:21, *64*
12:26, *64*
12:29-30, *62*

Joshua
5:13-15, *63*
6, *97*
21:16, *97*
24:14-26, *75*
24:15, *63*

Judges
21:25, *96*

1 Samuel
2:12-17, *108*
4, *97, 100*
4:1-2, *97*
4:3, *98*
4:4, *101*
4:5-9, *98*
4:10, *101*
4:10-11, *98*
4:12-22, *98*
5, *99*
5:11, *99*
6:1, *99*
6:7-8, *101*
6:13-21, *97*
7:2, *97*
9–31, *99*
13:14, *99, 107*
14:18, *97*

16, *100*

2 Samuel
2:11, *97*
5, *100*
6, *97, 100, 104, 105*
6:1, *101*
6:2, *101*
6:3, *101*
6:5, *102*
6:8, *102*
6:9, *95, 101, 102*
6:11, *102*
6:12-13, *103*
6:13, *102, 103*
6:14-15, *102*
6:16, *104, 105*
6:17, *104*
6:20, *104, 105*
6:21, *105*
6:23, *105*
7:5-11, *64*
7:11-13, *64*
7:16, *64*
7:25-29, *64*

1 Kings
1:1–2:12, *100*

1 Chronicles
15:2-15, *102*

2 Chronicles
20:13, *200*
20:21, *106*
26:1-15, *89*
26:16, *90*
26:16-21, *89*

Ezra
8, *200*

Psalms
16:5-11, *112*
19:7-11, *112*
86:9, *112*
144:15, *112*

Proverbs
1:7, *102*
3:12, *121*

Isaiah
1:12-17, *118*
5:8, *117*
5:20-21, *117*

6, *88, 89, 91, 117*
6:1, *89, 90*
6:2-3, *90*
6:3, *77*
6:4-5, *90*
6:6-7, *90*
6:8-13, *91*
6:13, *91*
11:1, *91*
12:2, *112*
18:20, *112*
58:13-14, *51*
58:14, *52*
60:21, *112*

Hosea
1:9-10, *125*
2:11, *50*

Amos
5:21-24, *121*

New Testament

Matthew
3:15, *156*
5–7, *85, 114*
5:7, *125*
5:17, *167*
5:23-24, *132*
5:39-41, *166*
5:46-47, *166*
5:48, *166*
6:1-18, *114*
6:5-15, *131*
6:5-18, *131*
6:9-13, *83, 139*
7:13-14, *166*
7:22, *115*
7:22-23, *118*
7:23, *115, 124*
7:24-27, *85, 116*
8:23-27, *50*
10:34-36, *56*
11:28-30, *54*
12:1-8, *53*
12:9-13, *130*
12:9-14, *53*
12:10, *54*
12:13, *54*
19:1-8, *198*
19:4-5, *112*
19:4-8, *32*
19:8, *32*
21:12-17, *131*
22:37-39, *132*
26:26-28, *87*
26:26-29, *132, 162*

26:29, *161*
28:19, *157*
28:19-20, *154*

Mark
1:21, *55*
1:21-28, *53*
1:22, *53*
1:29-31, *53*
1:32, *53*
2:23-28, *53*
2:27, *53, 58*
3:1-5, *130*
3:1-6, *53*
3:2, *54*
3:5, *54*
4:35-41, *50*
6:2, *55*
10:3-9, *32*
11:15-19, *131*
12:30-31, *132*
14:22, *148*
14:22-25, *87, 132, 162*
14:25, *161*
15:42, *55*
16:1-2, *55*

Luke
1:1, *130*
1:3, *130*
1:5, *130*
2:10, *112*
2:21-38, *130*
2:41-51, *130*
4:16, *55*
4:16-17, *128, 140*
4:20, *128, 140*
4:31, *55*
4:31-37, *53*
4:32, *53*
4:38-39, *53*
4:40, *53*
6:1-5, *53*
6:6-10, *53, 130*
6:7, *54*
6:10, *54*
6:27-28, *166*
6:31, *166*
6:32-33, *166*
8:22-25, *50*
10:27, *117*
11:1-4, *139*
11:42-44, *131*
12:51-53, *56*
13:10, *55*
13:10-17, *130*
15:11-32, *84*
18:9-14, *131*

19:45-48, *131*
22:15-20, *132*
22:17, *162*
22:17-19, *162*
22:19, *148*
22:19-20, *87*
22:29-30, *161*
24:13-35, *196*
24:18, *148*
24:27, *112*
24:29, *148*
24:30, *148*
24:32, *148*
24:44, *112*

John
1:14, *70*
2:13-22, *131*
4, *143*
4:14, *136*
4:15, *136*
4:21, *125, 136*
4:23, *119, 125*
4:23-24, *136, 140*
4:24, *79*
4:42, *136*
6, *179*
6:59, *130*
7:39, *116*
9:22, *56, 143*
9:34-38, *143*
9:38, *143*
10:23, *55*
11:25, *59*
13:2-5, *149*
13:14-15, *149*
13:35, *193*
15:4, *119*
15:5, *122*
15:7, *119*
15:8-10, *120*
15:10, *119*
15:11, *112*
16:2, *55, 143*
20:30-31, *112*

Acts
1:1, *135*
1:1-4, *130*
1:8, *134*
2, *134, 202*
2:3, *90*
2:38, *153*
2:41, *153*
2:42, *133*
2:46, *161*
2:46-47, *133*
3–5, *55*

3:1, *55, 133*
3:11, *55*
4:23-26, *133*
4:24-30, *92*
5:1-11, *107, 134*
5:4, *107*
5:11, *107*
5:12, *55*
5:42, *133*
6:6, *134*
8:4-25, *134*
8:12, *153*
8:14-17, *153*
8:34-38, *153*
9:2, *56, 167*
9:17-18, *153*
9:20, *134*
9:31, *135*
10:46-48, *153*
11:15-18, *153*
11:26, *133*
12:5, *133*
12:12, *133*
13:3, *134*
13:14, *134*
14:1, *134*
14:27, *134*
15:1-35, *134*
15:7-11, *153*
15:19-21, *167*
15:21, *134*
16:11-13, *129*
16:14-15, *153*
16:17, *167*
16:32-34, *153*
17:1, *134*
17:11, *112*
17:24-25, *65*
18:4, *134*
18:5-7, *150*
18:7, *134*
18:8, *153*
18:24–19:7, *153*
19:23, *57*
20:7, *56, 134, 161*
20:7-8, *134*
20:16, *55*
20:20, *134*
21:23-26, *55*
21:27-28, *55*
22:12-16, *153*
24:5, *56*
24:14, *167*
24:22, *57, 167*

Romans
1, *182*
3:23, *83*

3:25, *135*
3:31, *167*
5:8, *84*
6:3, *158*
8:3, *135*
8:9, *137*
8:11, *137*
8:15, *158*
8:23, *198*
8:38-39, *203*
11:36, *112*
12:1, *27, 74, 79, 86*
12:2, *27*
12:5, *137*
12:16-18, *132*

1 Corinthians
1:12, *15*
2:13, *112*
6:20, *112*
10:16, *162*
10:16-17, *137*
10:31, *112*
11, *164*
11:17-21, *161*
11:17-33, *165*
11:17-34, *162*
11:22, *161*
11:23-25, *148, 162*
11:23-26, *132*
11:23-33, *87*
11:33-34, *161*
12:12-27, *137*
14:37, *112*
15:26, *198*
16:2, *56*

2 Corinthians
2:15, *135*

Galatians
2:19, *23*
2:19-20, *158*
3:26-29, *156*

Ephesians
1:3-23, *140*
1:4, *23, 158*
1:13-14, *158*
1:22-23, *137*
1:23, *24, 192*
2:4-6, *84*
2:16, *137*
3:6, *137*
4:1-16, *87*
4:4, *137*
4:5, *15*
4:12, *108, 137*
4:16, *137*
5:2, *135*
5:30, *137*

Philippians
1:6, *24*
2, *182*
2:5-8, *115, 198*
2:5-11, *155, 158*
4:4, *112*

Colossians
1:9-12, *92*
1:15, *113*
1:18, *137*
2:17-19, *137*
3:3, *23*

3:15, *137*

1 Timothy
3:16, *155*

2 Timothy
3:15-17, *112*
3:16, *151*

Hebrews
4:14-16, *81*
4:16, *74, 139*
9–10, *76*
9:11-12, *69*
9:12-14, *135*
9:22, *30*
9:23-26, *135*
10:5-22, *135*
10:23-25, *87*
10:25, *57*
11, *192*
11:1, *45*
11:1-2, *31*
11:3, *31*
11:4, *31*
12:1, *192*
12:5-6, *121*
13:15, *135*
13:16, *135*

James
1:22, *122*
1:22-27, *127*
2:26, *189*

1 Peter
1:18-21, *135*
2:5, *135, 137*

2:9, *135, 137*
2:9-10, *137*
2:9-12, *124*

2 Peter
1:20-21, *112*
3:2, *112*
3:13, *204*
3:15-16, *112*

1 John
1:1, *195*
1:3, *195*
1:4, *112*
2:2, *135*
2:7-11, *132*
2:18, *195*
2:22, *195*
3:16-17, *132*
4:2-3, *195*
4:3, *195*
4:9-11, *132*
4:19, *23, 79*

2 John
7, *195*

Jude
3, *186*

Revelation
4:8, *82*
4:11, *82, 112*
5:8, *135*
8:3-4, *135*
21:1-7, *138*
21:3-4, *112*
21:22-27, *138*